50 Hidden Gems
of Greater
Western New York

Christopher Carosa

Published by Pandamensional Solutions, Inc., Mendon, NY

Cover design by Teresa Florence Carosa

ISBN-10: 1938465016
ISBN-13: 978-1-938465-01-7

DEDICATION

This book is dedicated to my wife Betsy,
the greatest hidden gem in all of Greater Western New York.

CONTENTS

ACKNOWLEDGEMENTS

As usual, there are too many people to thank. All the many museum directors, town and county historians and local history buffs. But, especially, I want to thank all those plain regular folks who, after doing me the honor of sitting through one of the many presentation I've given in the last year or so, came up to me and asked, "Chris, did you know…" You might be surprised to discover that little item made it somewhere in this book. To the extent possible, and with their gracious permission, I've acknowledged their contributions where possible.

Specifically, I want to thank the Board of the Bullfinch Fund, who encouraged me to pursue this little hobby of mine; Joe LoMando, a Research Associate at my firm who also brought the Audrey Munson story to my attention; and, the many Rotary Clubs, Kiwanis Clubs and various Chambers of Commerce who've allowed me to speak to their members and who've promised to have me back when the book is finally out.

It's finally out.

Though this is my third book, it's the first one for which I've done a video trailer and sneak preview, and thanks goes to Ander and Jimmy for making their deadline and coming up with a real snazzy video. It's up on the book's website (50HiddenGems.com) if you haven't seen it. And speaking of website, kudos to Michael Murphy for not only doing a great job on the book's site, but also helping me revise GreaterWesternNewYork.com into the kind of interactive curated Western New York news and info site I've always imagined it could be. Special thanks also to Mark Frisk who helped edit portions of the original manuscript.

Of course the biggest thanks goes to my wife, Betsy, who put up through my book-related delays in getting the dining room ready for Thanksgiving (don't worry, I did meet that deadline – on Thursday morning – like I always do). And, well, let's just say this was almost a year without Christmas.

Finally, it's important for me to recognize the people of Greater Western New York, whose heart, spirit and drive have inspired me my whole life. I only hope my work here lives up to the task of that tradition. And, don't worry, I know there are a lot more hidden gems that I have yet to write about.

FOREWORD

I first met Chris shortly after he started his Greater Western New York mutual fund. I admit, although I had confidence in my own firm as a publicly traded company, I was a bit skeptical anyone could pull off any sort of such promotion of the Greater Western New York region. Nonetheless, rather than discourage him, I egged him on, at one point telling him to stop talking about his great ideas, and actually start fulfilling them.

And, boy, did he. I especially enjoyed how he was able to rub the success of Greater Western New York's publicly-traded companies in the face of naysayers in the major financial centers across the country. He's been able to not only get the national press to trumpet the achievements of his fund, but in the process actually get positive press for our region. That is no small feat.

What made my heart smile most, though, were our combined efforts, together with (and primarily due to the hard work of) Debbie Pawlowski, to channel one of his many creative ideas into an amazing triumph for Greater Western New York – convincing hundreds of professional securities analysts to make the journey to Western New York and kick the tires of our local publicly-traded companies. We've been doing this for ten years now. I truly believe that, without Chris' passion to promote the place of his birth, this event would never have happened.

Chris is someone who really thinks has displayed a repeated skill to thinks "outside of the box" and who knows how to convert vision into reality. This book is another example of his unique abilities!

Brian Lipke
Chairman
Gibraltar Industries, Inc.
Hamburg, New York
September 28, 2012

PREFACE

I couldn't see the city for the university when we entered New Haven that pleasant late summer day in September of 1978. From what I can remember, it immediately struck me as maybe a little bigger than Rochester but definitely smaller than Buffalo. Besides, I'd already been to a real east coast city. As part of an exchange program Gates-Chili had with a downstate high school, I had travelled to New York City a couple years before, and the size of that city didn't really move me one way or another. In fact, other than a particularly expansive cemetery in Long Island, the thing I remember most about that trip was listening on the bus ride home as the Sabres lost another game to the Flyers in the Stanley Cup Finals.

But at least back then I knew I was going home. I arrived in New Haven fully aware this was not going to be a mere weekend away, but a four-year tour of duty at a University my grandmother, it turns out, had always dreamed of visiting. Ultimately, for my graduation, she did and I unknowingly fulfilled my duty as the first grandchild, repaying her for all those times she repeatedly insisted I could do anything I wanted, become anything I dared and achieve anything I envisioned (although I'm pretty sure she didn't use that word). In exchange, she explained, all I would need to do is share the talent God gave me.

And so I have. And so I hope to continue to do.

It turns out one of those "talents" is an insatiable love for and an incurable sense of pride in my hometown and its immediate environs. It also turns out, I'm not alone in possessing this talent. Thousands if not tens of thousands of folks from across the globe share this same love for, this same pride in and this same devotion to the greater Western New York region.

I know that now. I didn't know that as a scrawny wide-eyed Yale freshman…

Chris Carosa
Mendon, New York
July 15, 2012

3

Chris Carosa

Part I

LOGOS

– Plain Thoughts –

CHAPTER 1: LITTLE RED HOUSE

Tucked away in the southern portion of Cattaraugus County on the edge of the New York-Pennsylvania border sits the town of Red House. Guess what the town is named after? A red house, right? Nope. It's named after the creek flowing through it – Red House Creek. The creek is named after a red house.

But did you know the story behind the crimson abode that gave the creek its name? Originally owned by one of the area's first settlers, it is a sorry story of family division, betrayed love and mysterious death. In the 1860's Johnny Frecks went off to fight in the Civil War, leaving his young wife behind. Poor Johnny died during the war between the states and his widow took up with and eventually married his younger brother James. Only the "took up with" part apparently started before anyone even knew Johnny had been killed. When the family discovered this infidelity, it banished the lovers. The despondent couple committed suicide and, shortly thereafter, Jonathan Frecks II, father of Johnny and James, died for reasons unknown. The surviving family members abruptly moved far away, leaving the town a pile of money and an empty red house said to be haunted by three despairing ghosts. Every so often, a skeptical buyer makes an attempt to live in the house, but quickly moves out.

Cool story, huh? Chances are pretty good you've never heard it. I never did, either, until I started researching this book. From the face of it, it certainly merits inclusion in a book about the "Hidden Gems of Greater Western New York."

Except for one tiny problem. When I undertook the usual due diligence to find out more, no one I spoke with had ever heard the story. And this includes the editor of the book on the Bicentennial of Cattaraugus County (Franklinville historian Madelynn "Maddie" Fredrickson), the author of the book's chapter on the history of Red House (Llewellyn "Hook" France) and the Cattaraugus County Historian (Sharon Fellows).

And yet, there is the story, both on Wikipedia[1] and on the official website of Cattaraugus County Tourism.[2] I didn't know who to contact at Wikipedia and they have yet to return the message I left at the 800 number provided on the Cattaraugus County Tourism website. But this highlights the challenge posed in writing a book like this. Mind you, I am not a professional historian, nor am I an amateur historian. Heck, for that matter, I can't remember the last time I even stayed at a Holiday Inn Express.

So don't get too upset when you see all these footnotes. To be honest, they really bug me whenever I read a book that has them. Too often they contain useful information that adds to the experience of the book. Rest easy, dear reader, for I can assure you these footnotes merely contain source document information. That way, if you can't believe what you read, at least you can read the original material (in many cases, freely available on the web).

The point of the Red House folklore, though, is not merely to reinforce the warning to be wary of anything you read on the Internet or to explain why this book has so many footnotes. Rather, the ghost story represents a metaphor for the two prongs of pessimism habitually associated with Greater Western New York. First, it's a pessimism that seemingly prefers to live in a past that never was. We hear a lot about past achievements in a tenor suggesting we'll never again attain those heights. Incidentally, Fellows told me she researched the name "Frecks" and couldn't find a land owner by that name. Indeed, she found the only "John Frecks" who served in the Civil War enlisted in New York City. And he deserted.

Me, I'm a glass half-full sort of guy. Some people come to a mountain, see it as an obstacle, and stop. When I come to a mountain, I see it as a curtain yet to be unveiled. Instead of stopping, I dream of discovering what's beyond the peak before me. (But that's the subject of another book I'm writing.)

There are many inspiring, interesting and invigorating people, places and events associated with Greater Western New York. This book isn't a collection of fake ghost stories. It's a collection of actual real-life reports – "Hidden Gems," if you will. For you, some might be immediately recognizable, some might fall under the category of trivia, but I can almost guarantee you there'll be more than a few times you catch yourself whispering, "I never knew that."

Take Red House, for example. The town's claim to fame is its population. Red House has very few permanent residents because the vast bulk of the town was consigned to the Allegany State Park by New York State in 1921. In 2007, Allegany State Park was named one of the top 100 "Amazing Spots" by Reserve America, a camping reservations provider operating in the 48 contiguous states.[3] Much of the rest of the town is taken up by the Allegany Indian Reservation. According to the 2010 U.S. Census, the Town of Red

House has 38 inhabitants. This makes it the smallest town (by population) in the entire state of New York. Did you know that?

And this fact brings up our second metaphorical prong of pessimism. That same U.S. Census has for decades now emphasized our ever diminishing stature. By the end of the nineteenth century, Buffalo's city rank peaked at #8 in the nation and Rochester wasn't too far behind at #24.[4] The latest census data shows Buffalo has slipped to #72 and Rochester barely hangs on to the top 100 at #100.[5] No wonder some see us as a "small" market.

Well, that's certainly one way to look at it.

Not me, though. I explain why in a later chapter.

Incidentally, regarding New York State's smallest town, you might be interested to know there really was a red house. Long before the Town of Red House was established in 1868, it offered lodging for the many lumberjacks who worked the region.[6] They'd cut their logs then float them down the Allegany River all the way to Pittsburgh. According to Hook France, the trip downstream would take three days. It took three weeks to walk back upstream. The little red house stood at the mouth of Red House Creek where it empties into the Allegany River as a way station for these itinerant raftsmen and, by 1879, the famed red house had "long since gone to decay," its original proprietor just as gone and forgotten.[7]

So, you can see, there's a perhaps less well known – but true – story within our first hidden gem.

Before we get too far into our story, though, perchance it makes sense to start at the very beginning of this journey, namely, what motivated me to take such joy in sharing these trinkets.

CHAPTER 2: WHY AM I DOING THIS?

In the very shortest of answers, I am writing this book for you. Not "you the reader" in general terms, but you. Yeah, I mean you. The one whose fingers are holding the book open to this page right now. I might not know your name, but I know you. I know you like I know myself. We share an inseparable bond, one that has broken our hearts, has made us the butt of many a joke, but, without hesitation, causes us to stand tall with a pride very few can ever claim to have. Yes, it is our shared experience that makes you know me and me know you, even though we may have never even met.

This experience, this feeling, this focal point of our essential being we call "Western New York."

OK, let's be honest. We don't all call it "Western New York." We may call it "the Niagara Frontier," "the Queen City," "the Flower City," "the Southern Tier" or even "the Western Finger Lakes." For the purposes of this book, let's agree to call it all "Greater Western New York." If at first you don't believe how I can justify grouping so many area codes under one umbrella, you might be pleasantly surprised to discover the truth of our commonality in a particular story I will tell you in a later chapter.

But for now, let's return to the original question: Why am I doing this?

I'm on a mission.

I've been on this mission all my life.

I just didn't realize it until I was eighteen. Here's the event that caused me to recognize my true calling.

Sharing a room with three other perhaps less naïve classmates on a cozy floor with two other rooms of four, the very first thing we did, as all college freshmen do, was to tell each other where we're from. Though it possessed a somewhat complicated back story, I kept my answer short and consistent:

"I'm from Buffalo by way of Rochester." (Today we might refer to this as an elevator pitch answer.) I then went on to explain how I "grew up" in the South Towns of Buffalo (Blasdell, Hamburg and Lackawanna) but moved to Rochester (actually a suburb called Chili), ultimately graduating from Gates-Chili High School.

Pretty standard fare. Everyone had similar stories, most shorter but a notably few much longer. In other words, few cared to notice the adoring twinkle in my eye as I told the tale of my origin.

But events would soon conspire to make my adulation of my hometown apparent.

With a couch and a TV, our suite fast became the social center of the floor. This meant, if you couldn't guess, every Sunday immediately after brunch our room filled with up to a dozen young men. Back then, college TVs were a rare commodity, even in the Ivy League, and word travelled fast, especially during the football season. So we partook of the same ritual every honest-to-goodness red-blooded American male does on Sunday afternoons during the fall – we gathered round the smallish TV to watch football.

Now, it being the 1970's, the Bills were in the midst of their oh-for-the-decade streak against the Dolphins. Fortunately, the room had more Patriots and Jets fans, teams the Bills would beat often enough. Yes, I was talkin' proud not just about the Bills, but about the city of Buffalo, too. I spoke proudly of the Erie County Fair. I spoke proudly of making steel, the glory of the melting pot culture and the beautiful sunsets on Lake Erie (conveniently forgetting to attribute their cause to the smoke belching from the steel mills). I voiced my fond recollections of the many people I had met and places I had been to while growing up in Western New York. Moreover, and no doubt to the annoyance of my roommates who heard these anecdotes repeated ad infinitum as each new stranger came into the room, I narrated these tales as if they could only have happened in the Greater Western New York region.

I soon became a bit of a Freshman celebrity – a "Mr. Western New York" of sorts – with my knowledge of the Queen City (and of Western New York in general). People came to pay homage with gifts of Genesee Beer (the drinking age was 18 then) as I regaled them with tales of Buffalo Wings, Beef on Weck and the smells of Woodlawn Beach. It amazed me what they said, though, and nearly all the native Western New Yorkers said this same thing. "Chris," they said, "thanks for making it OK to be from Buffalo." Back then, even if you were from Jamestown or Rochester or Dansville, you said you were from Buffalo. That was the only Western New York city most non-natives had ever heard of.

But what struck me was the fact they thanked me for "making it OK," as if others had disallowed this opportunity. At the time, I assumed everyone had the same hometown spirit I had, no matter what part of the country they came from. Don't get me wrong, I had heard some of those favorite Lake

Erie jokes from late night comedians, but those were mostly aimed at Cleveland. By 1978, Buffalo had cemented itself in the national lore as the snow capital of the world. And those same stand-up comics who thought they were making fun of Western New York really only pointed to something we've always been quite proud of – keeping the neon "Open" sign lighted despite whatever Mother Nature might effect from our lakes.

It wasn't long, though, before I fully understood the nation's tendency to make Buffalo the butt of various monologues. You see, one of my roommates was from Burlington, Ontario. For those of you not familiar, Burlington lies just outside Hamilton about halfway from Buffalo to Toronto. People from that part of Canada always had a bit of enmity for Toronto and gravitated towards the Buffalo media. That fact allowed this hockey player to reveal my one Achilles' Heel when it came to all things Buffalo.

You see, back then, the television news of Buffalo had become a constant source of local humor, especially for AM DJs like Danny Neaverth and Stan Roberts. It seemed like every lead story dealt with a fire of some sort, and many of those had the following clause attached to them: "arson suspected." Worse, the news stations must have decided reporting fire stories drove viewership. No sooner would WBEN's Chuck Healy announce on Channel 4's First Team News a four-alarm fire, than WKBW's Irv Weinstein would see his four-alarms and raise it to five-alarms on Channel 7's Eyewitness News. To my Canadian roommate, it was as if Buffalo was burning itself down.

Try as I might, I could not overcome the stigma of Buffalo burning. Just as those blazing images captivated the television audiences of Buffalo, so too they must have stuck in the imaginations of my classmates. I might have succumbed right then and there to the doom of forever wearing the Albatross of Western New York.

But, no. It was then at that very moment I made a vow – a promise, until this day when you're reading these words before you, I made only to myself. I swore to use all those talents my grandmother insisted God gave me to counter this international obsession with degrading greater Western New York.

But before I get there, did you realize…

CHAPTER 3: THE NIGHT THEY BURNED OLD BUFFALO DOWN

John Candy died of a heart attack in his sleep on March 4, 1994 while on location shooting scenes for what was to be his final film *Wagons East!*. Carolco Pictures released the 107 minute movie later that year. It flopped. Oddly enough, it wasn't the last John Candy picture released. More than a year later, *Canadian Bacon*, featuring a cavalcade of Canadian-born actors, hit the screens. It quickly left those same screens, for the farce of a Canadian invasion of Western New York seemed too outlandish for cinema goers to believe.

Of course, in real life, America did fall victim to a Canadian invasion across the Niagara Peninsula. Throughout college, my Canadian roommate would no doubt remind me of this fact at the most inopportune moment, but his claim that "Canada won" cost him his credibility (at least in terms of his knowledge of the stateside version of history) with his American classmates. Fortunately for him, he spent most of his time with the hockey team, where his countrymen (hailing from such places as Thunder Bay, Ontario and Moose Jaw, Saskatchewan) held a slight majority. That I was manager of the team only meant I had another venue – with more voices this time – to receive ribbing on all those arson fires in Buffalo the local newscasters so faithfully reported in the late 1970's.

Ironically, nearly two hundred years ago, Canadians were, in fact, the cause of such arson in the then village of Buffalo.

In the winter of '13 (as in 1813) they were no doubt hungry and barely alive. There weren't many of them as Buffalo itself was barely there. The settlement was bigger than an outpost but not quite a town much less a city. This is what it was and this is how it came to be.

After a series of fits and starts, the land we now call Western New York fell into the ownership of the Holland Land Company. We'll talk about these folks and their history a little more in a later chapter. Right now we'll stay focused on Buffalo. The good people representing the Holland Land Company immediately saw the point where the Buffalo River empties into Lake Erie as an ideal place to start a settlement. Unfortunately, a large sand bar blocked the river's mouth, barely enabling rowboats to enter its waters. Surveyors were forced to look elsewhere.

At the time, the "Black Rock Ferry" was vital to the area in that it provided transportation to and from Fort Erie, then a well-established settlement. Located across the shore from Squaw Island, Blackrock itself represented the terminus of the Batavia Stage-Road, a road linking eastern New York to western New York.[1] It also offered a better environment to dock and land sailing ships. The name "Blackrock," by the way, originated from the dark limestone rock which created the perfectly natural harbor.

Joseph Ellicott saw the potential of Blackrock as a settlement which could compete with the area his Dutch proprietors sought to establish. In May 1802, Ellicott wrote to Paul Busti, then General Agent for the Holland Land Company and living in Philadelphia, asking to act under his own authority for the best interests of the Netherlanders.[2] He saw that, should the State start selling the newly-acquired "mile-strip" near Blackrock, the opportunity of beginning a settlement at the mouth of the Buffalo River would be lost. Busti agreed with Ellicott and immediately dispatched Ellicott to survey the holdings of the Holland Land Company.

In 1803-04, Ellicott surveyed the proposed sight of the Village of "New Amsterdam" and quickly put the lots up for sale.[3] The name "New Amsterdam" demonstrated Ellicott's loyalty to his Dutch bosses. Indeed, a look at an 1805 map of "Buffalo Village" shows Ellicott also tried to preserve the names of the Dutch on the streets of the new village. The settlers, however, did not particularly agree with the need to honor the financial backers of the Holland Land Company. They rejected both of Ellicott's proposals. The street names ultimately used, for the most part, remain with us to the present-day.

I had a chance to look at the geography of that 1805 map. In it, you can easily see they located the original settlement atop a terrace far from potential flooding. These inner lots were sold for residential purposes only. Residents used the outer lots – those below the terrace – primarily for farming purposes. Being close to the shore, the land of the outer lots offered fertile soil; consequently, it was best suited for agricultural purposes. The price of the lots ranged from $25 to $250 for the inner lots and $5 to $10 an acre for outer lots.[4]

In 1805 the "District of Buffalo Creek" was established.[5] Over the next seven years, a spurt of growth occurred. The Village witnessed the erection of inns, taverns and government buildings, as well as residences. From its very beginning, Buffalo has had two squares in its heart. Even the 1805 map contained these two squares. Government houses were located on both of these squares in the convenient hub of the city.

The Reverend Timothy Dwight, while passing through the area in 1804, wrote, "The period is not far distant when the commerce of this neighborhood will become a great national object, and involve no small part of the interest and happiness of millions."[6] Given that Buffalo achieved national prominence by the end of the 19th century and became a beacon of the future heading into the 20th century, the Reverend Dwight proved to possess gifted insight. But first, the small village would fall victim to the British.

Britain, having admitted defeat to the Americans in the Revolutionary War nearly two generations earlier, apparently never fully accepted the concept of the United States as an independent country. By the end of the first decade of the 1800's the English, at war with Napoleon and the French, saw an urgent need for men to crew their ships. In a flash of brilliance, they decided, what better place to go than to America? After all, these folks already knew how to speak English (granted, it wasn't the King's English, but it was close enough). And so, with little regard for a thing called "national sovereignty," British warships soon began impressing U.S. merchant sailors by kidnapping them from their ships and forcing them to serve against their will in the Royal Navy.

Needless to say, this action did not impress the U.S. government. At the time, Peter B. Porter represented the Western New York district in Congress. He also chaired the House Committee on Foreign Affairs and, in December of 1811, he prepared a report which recommended war with the British Empire. Upon the formal declaration of War in June of the following year, Porter immediately resigned from his seat in Congress and was appointed Quarter-Master-General of the New York State Militia.[7] The War of 1812 was just starting when he arrived back at his home in Blackrock in time to see the British capture a schooner at the headwaters of the Buffalo River. He quickly arranged for the movement of much needed arms and ammunition to the Niagara Frontier.[8] (It's good to be the Quarter-Master-General.)

Being on the frontier in 1812, Buffalo figured prominently in the western front, particularly in the Battle of Lake Erie. Though there were skirmishes on the outskirts, no actual battle occurred within the Village until the final days of 1813. After the Americans had burned the settlement of Newark on the British side of the Niagara River, the British decided to return the favor.

On December 29th, at midnight, the British and their Indian allies beat through the resistance of some 2,000 volunteers and proceeded to burn the Village.[9] Only three structures survived the burning, including the jail and Reece's blacksmith shop, the latter on the north side of Seneca near

Washington.[10] Both benefited from the nature of their construction, (stone has a tendency to not burn). Amid the still smoldering black ashes and cold white snow stood a third surviving structure: the St. John house on Main Street. Mrs. St. John, a widow with two daughters, sought out a British officer and convinced him to prevent the Indians from burning her home.[11] Mrs. Lovejoy, the neighbor across the street from Mrs. St. John, tried to convince the Indians herself (as opposed to going through their British commanders) and lost her life, making her the only woman to die in the burning of Buffalo.[12]

In the middle of winter, the homeless refugees had to flee and lived elsewhere, including as far away as Batavia. By the following Spring, however, they had returned and rebuilt a more lasting settlement. Perhaps taking the story of the Three Little Pigs to heart, one of the first complexes built was a brickyard.[13] By April of 1814, some thirty or forty houses were either already built or in the process of being built.[14] In proving their resiliency, they revealed a trait which had become associated with all that is Greater Western New York.

But there's one thing about this story I haven't told you...

CHAPTER 4: MY MISSION BECOMES
MY BUSINESS

O K, here's what I didn't tell you about the last chapter. The bulk of it was written more than thirty years ago. It was a short part of the exposition of my final paper for a course I took called "Study of the City." The professor asked us to use what we had learned in class and write a "Biography" of the city we were born in, including a suggestion or two about where the city might be heading in the future. You'll probably have a greater appreciation of the hidden gems presented in this book if you had a little better picture of my own biography – at least the part that relates to this book.

I wrote the "Study of the City" paper in the spring of 1982. Per the professor's instructions, I concluded with a recommendation for the city planners and administration. My suggestion: "In the future, Buffalo should become a high-tech and service industry city." Remember, we were still a year or so away from the introduction of the IBM-PC and the personal computer revolution. The Internet wasn't on anyone's mind, (except maybe Al Gore's).

The paper represented my "I told you so" to all those Western New York naysayers I had encountered while living and learning in New Haven. All those establishment sophisticates could say anything they wanted, but they could never take away my pride – and my desire to put my words to action. What my paper made clear, and what later years would prove, was that from the dawn of Western New York in 1812 through the Super Bowl years and beyond, its people have demonstrated a trait necessary not only for survival, but for success itself. My eyes saw this growing up, my heart wanted to shout this from the highest mountain for all to hear, but, ultimately, it was my brain that connected the dots, allowing me to understand my own limitations and the best way for me to promote Greater Western New York.

You see, although I could dream like a poet, all that scientific training forced me to deal with the one thing that can quash any noble aspiration: reality. Simply put, I was a nobody. How could I, a humble native of Blasdell, the grandson of working class immigrants, educated in the shadow of the Bethlehem Steel plant, graduate of a high school that didn't receive accreditation until my sophomore or junior year, and employee of a small investment firm, even begin to think I could convince a nation that Greater Western New York not only shouldn't be the butt of some late-night comedian's joke, but actually had a lot to offer?

Well, I'll let you in on a little secret that an immersion in mathematics – the foundation of all true science – does to people. If resiliency is the mother of success, then problem-solving is the father. If math teaches you one thing, it teaches you how to connect the dots. And for me those dots connected in, of all places, a conference room of a casino hotel in the Grand Bahamas.

Each year, my firm would hold an off-site strategic planning meeting at some resort. It was during a particularly gloomy day (for the analysts) that I realized my true mission. The owner of the firm sternly disciplined the stock-pickers in front of everyone. If you recall, the market crashed in 1987 and, although our firm had done well, the owner believed (rightly) it was because he had come in and saved the day. He even remarked that he could have done better than the analysts just limiting himself to stocks that began with the letter "A." (Years later, while in business school, I confirmed the plausibility of his boast).

Frustrated, he bluntly asked if any of them knew which Dow Jones stock had performed best in 1987.

The analysts just cowered in their seats and remained silent.

The owner then turned to the rest of us and repeated the question.

Due to my love of Western New York, I knew the answer. It was the company I knew intimately; my two elementary schools in Woodlawn sat in the very heart of its complex.

"Bethlehem Steel," I answered.

The owner's jaw dropped. Then he verbally expressed his disbelief and angrily shouted at the analysts: "The operations guy?! The operations guy knew the answer and you didn't!"

This series of fortunate events smacked me on the side of the head (fortunately, although I'm sure they wanted to, none of the analysts did). It was then I concluded what I wanted to do. I might not have enough money to buy "I ♥ WNY" TV spots during prime time (or even late night for that matter), but I did know how to do one thing – build mutual funds – and I could learn another thing – how to pick stocks. So, at the age of 28, I decided to create a Western New York mutual fund. I knew, theoretically at least, there could be at least one performance period when the Western New York stocks could beat all other stocks.

Of course, it would take a few more years before I could do this. Eventually, with two years of expenses accumulated, I left my firm and started the Bullfinch Fund, a family of no-load mutual funds. One of the funds is called the "Greater Western New York Series." This Series invests only in companies with an economic presence in Greater Western New York. As I've told everyone ever since, the idea was to attract like-minded boosters of Greater Western New York and use the fund as a vehicle to promote our region.

The fund officially opened on December 30, 1997 and by the first quarter of 1998, both *Forbes* and the *New York Times* wanted to run a story on it. I spoke to a *New York Times* reporter named Carole Gould and she promised to run the article ahead of *Forbes*.

Needless to say, I was thrilled. No longer would the nation see our region as an economic backwater. In short order, I would be accomplishing my mission to promote Greater Western New York – and in the *New York Times*, Sunday Business Section no less! On Sunday, May 17, 1998, I purchased the paper, pulled out the business section and turned immediately to page 6. I read the opening paragraph. As high as I was going in, my heart sank to an equal low.

Here's how Carole Gould started the article: "Here's an idea for a fund: Find one of the most economically depressed areas of the country. Then invest most of the fund's assets there." The sarcasm only made it more painful, especially the tongue-in-cheek "Go Bills" she used to close the story.

Rather than extol the benefits of Greater Western New York, and despite the optimism of my quotes, the article merely perpetuated the myth of economic malaise.

As depressed as I was, friends and clients congratulated me on getting the fund in the *New York Times*. They noted I must have done something right as a customized illustration by Daniel Abraham accompanied the story. They saw glory in that picture. I saw a buffalo with what seemed to be a sheep's head wearing the headgear from the Bedrock Chapter of the Royal Order of Water Buffalo. The animal stood on a New York State map within the fenced-in pasture outlining Greater Western New York. Worse, it wasn't chewing grass. It was eating dollar bills. Oh, the imagery! Oh, the humanity!

In the face of this *Gray Lady* snub, we trudged on, counting on the theory that any specific portfolio – even one made up of Greater Western New York stocks – would eventually have its day in the sun. But the theory and I were wrong. The Series had more than one day in the sun. In fact, in my office I have a section of our front hallway I call the "Wall of Fame." On it are media clippings of our fund, including nearly half that came from the Wall Street Journals "Top Ten" listings. These feature both our funds, but most of them contain the Greater Western New York Series.

By far the greatest triumph occurred in early March 2004. Every month, USA Today lists the top performing funds of the nation, regardless of category. Most don't take this seriously, because you really can't compare funds of different categories. In fact, the slots are usually taken up by sector funds, not by diverse funds like ours. But on this one occasion, the top performing fund was a multi-cap value fund called "Bullfinch Fund Greater Western New York Series."

This was all too much. I gathered the nerve and called Carole Gould to ask for a follow-up story. She wasn't there so I left a message.

She never returned my call.

Despite all the great performance numbers and media accolades, my most satisfying Greatest Western New York moment occurred not in the media, but a week before Thanksgiving 2003 at the Hyatt Hotel in downtown Buffalo during the annual "Festival of Lights." There, amidst two floors of scintillatingly lighted Christmas Trees, hundreds of my biggest competitors came to see some of my greatest ideas. I bet you're wondering, "There must be a story behind that."

There is.

And here it is.

I had this idea. It started this way: Soon after the fund started, I visited Gibraltar Steel (now called Gibraltar Industries) and spoke to its then President, Brian Lipke. He was excited to hear about the creation of the Greater Western New York Series and loved the idea of promoting the region. I told him of my dream: to earn enough revenue to sponsor a regional investors conference where local publicly-traded companies could make their case to institutional investors (i.e., professional investment advisers). Most of these companies had few followers among Wall Street analysts and would welcome the attention. Brian agreed. And that's the last I would speak of it until Gibraltar's next annual meeting.

This went on for several years.

Finally, in May of 2003, Brian had had enough. He told me, "Chris, when are you going to stop talking about doing it and just do it?"

I explained what I expected the cost to be and how the fund was just too small to pay for the conference. Brian responded, "Is that all? Don't you realize you don't have to pay a dime? The companies will all chip in enough to pay for it. You just figure out the logistics and I'll help get the companies."

Only problem was, now I had a firm to run. Plus, except for my own wedding, I had no experience putting together an event of this magnitude. But, again, a scientist connects the dots, and I quickly scanned my memory for someone more suitable, more capable, than I when it comes to organizing such a happening.

That person was Debbie Pawlowski. She had been in charge of investor relations at a publicly traded company called American Precision (one of the early holdings of the fund) and had started her own firm – Kei Advisors, an investor relations consulting firm – after American Precision got bought out. She was (and continues to be) well-liked and very well-respected by the local investing community, she could benefit from the exposure of organizing a local investors conference and, most importantly, with the precision one comes to expect from a West Pointer, she's one of those people you can trust to get things done. If I've been called "can-do," she's "consider it done."

On November 20th, 2003, the Founder Members of the Western New York Investors Conference gathered at the Hyatt Hotel. We had become concerned about our venue when we found out our event conflicted with the annual "Festival of Lights." But the sparkling lights covering the Christmas trees that line the interior of the hotel gave our event added luster. Folks started dribbling in, settling our nerves. Soon we had more than two hundred people, far exceeding our goals. They listened to presentations from 22 companies and heard from the Buffalo Bills' General Manager and from (then CNBC personality) Ron Insana.

By all measures, the first ever Western New York Investors Conference was a success. We (really Debbie) have been organizing these events regularly since then. In fact, I still remember what Brian Lipke said at the very first conference. In alluding to that familiar adage, he said, "Success is 1% inspiration and 99% perspiration. If Chris and I were the 1% inspiration, then Debbie and her crew have been the other 99%."

The Western New York Investors Conference, you see, is the one accomplishment I am most proud of. It has allowed me to fulfill that part of my lifetime dream that, quite possibly, has been with me the longest. In the end, the Bullfinch Fund Greater Western New York Series, still trucking after all these years, really has helped me realize an important part of my mission: my rebuttal of Carole Gould's piece in the *New York Times*. Indeed, over the years we've had analysts from coast to coast come to the conference. We've continued to bring in many big-name speakers. And, most delightful of all, we all continue to have a great time doing it.

But, like I said, the conference represents only part of my mission. My greater mission remains to continue to spread the good news of Greater Western New York, to uplift the spirit of the community and to provide ammunition to others willing to join my campaign.

But before I go and get all serious on you, now might be a good time to have some fun and test your knowledge of some business and product trivia about Greater Western New York.

CHAPTER 5: FUN TRIVIA GAME –
GUESS THE COMPANY

I began this journey with a professional objective – to find and invest in hidden gems in the Greater Western New York region. As Chapter 4 explains, the mutual fund I created to accomplish this has been the source of fun, discovery and, of course, success. Now, various regulations prevent me from making stock recommendations in a book like this, indeed, that's not even the purpose of the book. I should add; It's probably not a good idea to buy stocks based on what you read in a book. Too many things can happen between the publication date and the time you read the book to preclude sound analysis. Still, I can't ignore all the knowledge and research that has gone into building the Bullfinch Fund Greater Western New York Series. There's some pretty interesting, entertaining and downright magnificent stories about our local companies – both the publicly traded ones that I look at every day and the private ones we all regularly visit.

So I said to myself, "How can I share this in a way that makes a fun read?" Well, the answer was obvious: Make a game out of it.

And here are the rules. Each of the numbered paragraphs describes an amazing trait of one of our local businesses, at least as of the publication date of the first edition of this book (December, 2012).

Can you guess which company it's describing?

1. The largest mailbox manufacturer in North America.
2. The company with a large stable of products, including the one with the most Facebook likes in its industry.
3. The #1 manufacturer of hoists in North America, selling more units than all its competitors combined.

4. The only manufacturer of standard size 9-volt battery designed to last 10 years when used in ionization-type smoke alarms.
5. One of the few companies whose product was featured in a classic Top 40 radio hit.
6. The ~~second~~ largest operator of short line and regional freight railroads in North America.
7. A company whose product is on nearly every jet fighter in the Western Hemisphere.
8. A grocery store on the "must see" list of nearly every visiting celebrity.
9. The company everyone turns to whenever there's a major earthquake.
10. A manufacturer that not once, but twice and separated by 50 years, rode a major technology wave to spectacular growth.

OK, I'll be nice. I'll give you a big hint. I'll list the companies that you need to match to the above list:

a. Astronics Corp.
b. Corning, Inc.
c. Eastman Kodak Co.
d. Taylor Devices, Inc.
e. Constellation Brands, Inc.
f. Gibraltar Industries, Inc.
g. Wegmans Food Markets, Inc.
h. Columbus McKinnon Corporation
i. Ultralife Corp.
j. Genesee & Wyoming, Inc.

If you can't wait, turn to Appendix I and you'll find the answers to this "Guess the Company" trivia game along with some interesting trivia about those companies. Otherwise, can you answer this question: Just what is a "hidden" gem? The next chapter explains.

CHAPTER 6: SUCH IS FAME – THE REAL ENDURING LEGACY OF NIAGARA FALLS

When crafting a list of hidden gems of Greater Western New York, it helps to define what the word "hidden" means. Certainly, if one of these not-so-hidden gems turns out to have inspired something truly outstanding, well, that would be worth writing about. Before I get to that, though, let me share with you my methodology for compiling this list, but allow me to do this by showing you, not telling you (assuming that's even possible in the format of the written word).

For example, we have plenty of gems that have received broad national attention. Indeed, several people, events and activities from, in and around the Greater Western New York region have found themselves honored with places in our history books.

What school-aged child doesn't know the name of Frederick Douglass or the underground railroads inspired by the anti-slavery movement? Likewise, who hasn't heard of Susan B. Anthony or the first Womens' Rights Convention in Seneca Falls?

Much has been written of these two events and, in fact, they are intertwined in history with actors of each movement actively supporting the other. People often ask me to write about these people, places and things, but, to be honest, I don't think I could offer anything more or better than you can find from other sources. These are certainly gems, but they fail my (admittedly subjective) "hidden" test.

So what is this "hidden" test? As I implied, anything found in a secondary school textbook probably wouldn't qualify as hidden. Most certainly, something called "The Eighth Wonder of the World" would fail to qualify as hidden. I'm referring, of course, to our own Niagara Falls, which *U.S. News and World Report* once ranked the third most outstanding natural attraction in the United States (behind The Grand Canyon and Yellowstone National Park).[1]

There's no question Niagara Falls represents our nation's first tourist attraction, although it perhaps became well-known first as an obstacle to navigation. Certainly, if we recall the significance of Western New York in the War of 1812, there's no doubt many military participants saw the Falls. With the completion of the Erie Canal and then the early railroad lines, Niagara Falls offered an enticing destination for travelers.

But, if you're going to become the first tourist attraction in the nation, then there's a good chance you're also going to become the first tourist trap in the nation. We all laugh about the obviousness of this today, but do you realize how early in American history this phenomenon first appeared?

In the extreme August heat of 1831[2], Alex de Tocqueville visited our region on his famous tour of American. DeWitt Clinton completed his ditch (a.k.a., the Erie Canal) in 1825, so by the time de Tocqueville toured Niagara Falls, it had already become a target of choice among adventurers and vacationers. Indeed by 1830, the cataract had attracted its share of "so-called sharpers and hucksters of every kind."[3] When he made his way through Niagara Falls during those hot summer days of 1831, de Tocqueville foresaw the ruin to come. He warned his friend to "hasten to see this place in its grandeur. If you delay, your Niagara will have been spoiled for you. Already the forest is being cleared."[4] He further predicted Americans would, within ten years, "establish a saw or flour mill at the base" of the Falls.[5]

As a matter of fact, that defacement was about to occur. As Joseph L. Sax, House & Hurd Endowment Professor Emeritus, at the University of California, Berkeley and former Counselor to the U.S. Secretary of the Interior, wrote in an article for *Natural History* in 1976, "Swarms of petty swindlers took up posts at every point near the falls; tourists were importuned, cajoled, lied to, harassed, and abused by hack drivers, landowners, and every sort of self-appointed guide. By the 1860's not a single point remained in the United States from which the falls could be viewed without paying a landowner an entry fee."[6]

With the coming of the California Gold Rush in 1848, Yosemite Valley, long considered too inaccessible by non-natives, suddenly became accessible. By the middle of the next decade, outsiders discovered the wonders of the valley, including Yosemite Falls – "fifteen times taller than Niagara Falls."[7] But height wasn't the only yardstick offered by Niagara, for, much like today, the Falls of Greater Western New York represented a measure of awe. As Frederick Law Olmsted said of the giant Sequoia trees located within the adjacent Mariposa Grove, "There are hundreds of such beauty and stateliness that, to one who moves among them in the reverent mood to which they so strongly incite the mind, it will not seem strange that intelligent travellers have declared that they would rather have passed by Niagara itself than have missed visiting this grove."[8]

But, unfortunately, it was that other measure of Niagara that most frightened those mid-nineteenth century environmentalists. Josiah Dwight Whitney, director of the California Geological Survey, suggested that, without proper precautions, Yosemite Valley would become, "like Niagara Falls, a gigantic institution for fleecing the public. The screws will be put on just as fast as the public can be educated into bearing the pressure."[9] On June 30, 1864, President Lincoln signed into law the Yosemite Grant, which gave the then federally-owned Yosemite Valley to the state of California, what amounted to the first time federal action created a park, albeit one run by a state, not the federal government.

With the subsequent discovery of Yellowstone, the movement to declare the nation's first national park gained momentum. Unlike Yosemite, which could be immortalized by the State of California, Yellowstone had no state (yet), for it lay in Wyoming Territory. After surveying Yellowstone in the summer of 1871, Dr. Ferdinand Vandiveer Hayden, professor of geology at the University of Pennsylvania and the director of the United States Geological and Geographical Survey of Territories, issued a formal report to the House Committee on the Public Lands.[10] In that report, Hayden decried those who wanted to claim Yellowstone as their private property. He went so far as to say they wanted "to fence in these rare wonders so as to charge visitors a fee, as is now done at Niagara Falls, for the sight of that which ought to be as free as the air and water."[11] Hayden said if Congress failed to act immediately, "decorations more beautiful than human art ever conceived" would be tarnished "beyond recovery in a single season."[12]

Hayden's reference to the unfettered despoiling of Niagara Falls worked and, on March 1, 1872, President Ulysses S. Grant signed the Yellowstone Park Act, creating America's first national park.

So, for probably reasons the good citizens of Niagara Falls do not want to hear, the early plight of Niagara Falls inspired what eventually became the national parks movement. The government preserved natural wonders throughout the nation just to prevent them from suffering the "shame of Niagara."

Well, that's one way to view it. I view it a little differently. It all starts with de Tocqueville, who, perhaps unknowingly, really describes the heart of the American spirit when he laments the state of Niagara Falls. Like many Europeans, he snobbishly looked down his nose at a new nation more interested in taming the wild than preserving it. We need look no further than Niagara Falls as proof of this American self-confidence. In a sense, we believe nature offers no obstacle a little bit of good old-fashioned American ingenuity can't overcome.

In the early years, jumpers, tight-rope walkers and bridges provided evidence of man's conquest of nature. On October 7, 1829, Sam Patch – the "Yankee Leaper" – became the first person to successfully survive a jump over Niagara Falls.[13] He did it again ten days later and survived. On November 6, 1829, he survived a jump from the Genesee River High Falls gorge in Rochester. He leaped again a week later on Friday the 13th. He didn't survive that one and was buried in Charlotte Cemetery near where his frozen body was found the following spring (on St. Patrick's Day) with the epitaph: "Sam Patch – Such is Fame."[14]

Less than a century later, we would harness the power of the Niagara itself to provide the first source of cheap electricity in the nation. The brilliant wonders of electrical power were highlighted at the 1901 Pan-American Exposition in Buffalo and that fueled an economic boom across the region. In fact, cheap power was one of the reasons a Scranton-based steel company called "Lackawanna Steel" relocated (in 1902) from Lackawanna County, Pennsylvania to the shores of Lake Erie in (what was then) the town of West Seneca. A few years later (in 1909), residents of this section of West Seneca voted to secede and form the City of Lackawanna. A few years after that (in 1922), the Bethlehem Steel Company bought the Lackawanna Steel Company. A little more than a decade later, my grandfathers met for the first time in jail after being arrested for marching in a union parade with other Bethlehem Steel workers. About twenty years later, my parents married and, a year later, I was born.

So, you see, I have a personal interest in the industrialization of Niagara Falls. Without it, there would have been no me. Maybe you, too?

But I can't leave Niagara Falls without this testament to man's dominance of nature. From June through November 1969, the U.S. Army Core of Engineers "turned off" the American Falls to clean the centuries of rock debris from its base. The damming of the American Falls occurred at the same time as America's Apollo 11 marked man's first lunar landing. To this newly nine-year old's eyes, these engineering marvels convinced me to believe we – as a nation and as a species – could do anything if we put our mind to it. That, in the end, is the true legacy of Niagara Falls.

But there is one thing that bothered me about turning off the Falls. Shortly after the water stopped flowing, engineers discovered a certain layer of rock that, as it got dryer, was becoming brittle. This endangered the rock layers above it. To solve the problem, they piped water down to keep this layer wet. What got me, though, was the name of the brittle rock. It was called "Rochester Shale." That befuddled me. Why would they call it "Rochester" shale when it should have been called "Niagara Falls" shale (or even "Buffalo" shale)?

I wouldn't discover the answer to this nagging question until some four decades later when I wrote the next chapter.

CHAPTER 7: THE ABSOLUTELY TRUE STORY BEHIND THE REAL BIRTH OF GREATER WESTERN NEW YORK

"It's a Sicilian message. It means Luca Brasi sleeps with the fishes."
– Clemenza, The Godfather (1972)

Our story starts approximately 400 million years ago. Back then, Western New York wasn't really western, it was more northern. And by northern I mean north – as opposed to west – of the east coast, which itself might have been more appropriately called the south coast. Oh, and another thing. We weren't hanging at a cool 42° North latitude. We were closer to the equator. In fact, we were just south of the equator.[1] To prevent further directional confusion, I will continue to refer to the geography in modern terms, not the way it actually was back then.

And we were totally under water: a shallow, but vast, inland sea of the pre-Pangean continent of Laurentia[1,2] (the precursor to North America). This sea stretched from the Hudson Valley to the area that would eventually hold the Rocky Mountains and from modern Ontario to Alabama.[2] In fact, this period of time – the Devonian Period within the Paleozoic Era – is called "The Age of the Fishes."[1] Within 10-20 million years – 380-390 million years ago for those counting – Laurentia collided first with Avalonia[1] and then with Baltica[1,3], squeezing the Iapetus Ocean between them out of existence and forming the new continent of EurAmerica. In its wake, though, this collision – known as the Acadian orogeny – produced a large mountain range to the immediate east of Western New York.[2]

Now, if you're a student of geology, then you're sure to know the one underlying trait of most of these early mountain ranges: you can't see them anymore. Why not? Because Nature, in her infinite wisdom, saw to it that these earthen behemoths eroded themselves into oblivion. But that's not to say they haven't left their DNA strewn across the country-side. In fact, much of the study of Devonian geology takes place right here in the Greater Western New York region. This is where those Acadian mountains left their fingerprint – in the form of the rocks beneath our feet and jutting through the various "rock cities" among us.

In the case of the Acadians, water erosion from the west side of those mountains brought down silt and small pebbles into a gigantic delta known as the "Catskill Delta."[5] This was no ordinary delta formed by a single river (like, for example, the Mississippi Delta), but a huge complex of deltas formed by many small rivers.[2] The Acadian mountains spent the remainder of the Devonian period bleeding themselves into the delta. As a result, the shoreline moved from the Hudson Valley to Western New York over this time.[2]

As the sediment was deposited, the layers above crushed the layers below into various forms of rock. According to *Nature's Blog* ("The Devonian Coast," April 29, 2007), "...Western New York harbors one of the most extensive outcrops of Devonian rocks in North America."[6] It's a tribute to the significance of Western New York geology that many types of rock from the Devonian period are named for the Western New York locales where they were first discovered. (Unfortunately, the period itself is named for the region in England where these rocks were first identified.) For example, that infamous Rochester Shale that so easily crumbled under the dry Niagara Falls represents a form of shale first discovered in the vicinity of Rochester.

The downside of all this geology, however, is the relative lack of biology. The less disturbed shallow sea in Pennsylvania found itself the graveyard of the exotic ferns and other plant life, while Western New York became a cemetery of marine life. The former meant Pennsylvania got most of the oil, although Western New York did get its fair share of natural gas. The latter meant Western New York received layers and layers of limestone, a key resource for, among other things, the processing of steel. Anyone traveling on I-90 just east of Buffalo will see two large open Limestone pits. Shallow salt-water seas also left one other deposit as they evaporated: salt. As those in the Livingston County Town of Retsof – home of what was once the largest salt mine in North America and second largest in the world – can attest, Western New York residents have mined this resource for more than a century, much to the delight of winter road travelers everywhere.

Why? Salt, if you don't already know this, lowers the freezing temperature of water, keeping winter roads slushy, but not icy. Of course, salt doesn't lower the freezing temperature of water forever. In fact, once the temperature falls to 6 below zero (Fahrenheit), the salt molecules in the solution crystalize out, allowing the now-naked water to freeze.[7] Since it would be an awful shame to see all that Mesozoic salt go to waste, it's sort of a good thing winter temperatures rarely get that low around here. Of course those pesky artic blasts from Canada occasionally do bring our temperatures towards zero (or below), thanks to the moderating influence of the Great Lakes, our average low winter temperature remains in the upper teens – that's above zero for all you wise guys.

And, speaking of wise guys, thanks to Western New York's impersonation of Luca Brasi, its sleep beneath the salty sea during "The Age of the Fishes" yielded not just the rocks all around us, but the very salt we use today to help keep our winter drivers safer.

While the ravages of time (and glaciers) have unearthed the secrets of ancient geology, there remains one relatively recent (in geological terms) Greater Western New York mystery that many might not know about.

Turn the page and allow me to enlighten you.

CHAPTER 8: THE LOST TRIBE OF GREATER WESTERN NEW YORK

By the summer of 1679, René-Robert Cavelier, Sieur de La Salle had approached his wit's end. His faithful lieutenant, the Neapolitan Henri de Tonti, had already repulsed one attempt by the Seneca Tribe to burn La Salle's soon-to-be sailing ship *Le Griffon*. A year earlier, in hopes of attaining a promise of peace, La Salle had travelled seventy-five miles east to the Seneca village of Ganondagan, located on present-day Boughton Hill, just outside of the Village of Victor, about 20 miles south of Rochester.[1] Peace was promised, but as the attempted arson proved, wasn't necessarily guaranteed. So, ahead of schedule, on August 7, 1679, La Salle gave the order to weigh anchor and commanded twelve burly sailors to grab tow-lines and walk *Le Griffon* from the shallow ten-foot waters of Squaw Island, through the rushing rapids of the Niagara River and, with the help of a much hoped for northeast breeze, into the calm waters of what his native tongue called *Lac du Chat*.[2] Embarking on La Salle's mission in search of the Northwest Passage, *Le Griffon* thus became the first large ship to grace the waters of the Great Lakes above the Niagara Falls.

But it also left several intriguing questions: How did the Lake he sailed into get its name? More interestingly, why did he need to travel to the east side of the Genesee River nearly at the other end of Western New York to speak to the Indians? Indeed, what had happened to the native (at least relative to the Europeans) Western New Yorkers?

We don't know who first settled Western New York, but we have a good idea who called our region home just before the Europeans showed up. If you think "a good idea" sounds a little tentative, you're right. In fact, it's likely the only contact with this tribe occurred in 1615 when famed French explorer Samuel de Champlain dispatched several missionaries led by Étienne Brulé to meet these people near Niagara Falls.[3,4] The Huron, in perpetual war with the

31

Iroquois, told Champlain of a non-allied tribe called the "Attiouandaronk" or "Neutral Nation" that lived between the Hurons and the then Five Nations of the Iroquois.[5] The expedition reported the previously unknown tribe occupied a vast territory extending from the Niagara gorge to the Genesee River, north to just shy of Lake Huron and south into the Allegany watershed in what is now Western Pennsylvania and Ohio.[6,7]

Who were these mysterious early inhabitants of Western New York and why have they become lost to history?

The Iroquois called them the "Long Tail," tribe. However, what Champlain reported as one tribe may actually have been two, for competing histories say the Long Tail Tribe was merely allied with the Neutral Nation.[9] We just don't know. In fact, the only contemporary written record we have on the Long Tail Tribe comes from the Jesuits. For example, the Jesuit Relation of 1653 says the region surrounding *Lac du Chat* "was at one time inhabited toward the south by certain peoples whom we call the Cat Nation; but they were forced to proceed farther inland in order to escape their enemies whom they have toward the west."[10] This helps explain why French maps during the time of La Salle refer to Buffalo's lake as *"Lac du Chat."* Although we don't know much of their history, the Jesuits did report the Long Tail Tribe was not migratory, settled in many villages and had a population of about 14,500 in the mid-seventeenth century just prior to their demise.[11]

We also know the Long Tail Tribe had an important role during the early years of European colonization. It's a role that may have also led to their eventual extinction. You might recall from your high school history class that, rather than focusing on colonization like their Spanish and British brethren, the French, Dutch and Swedes instead focused on acquiring some of the niftier natural resources our region offered – namely furs and pelts. This fur trade market impacted interior tribes like the Long Tail Tribe just as much as those having direct contact with the Europeans. Tribes like the Long Tail Tribe became harvesters, if you will, while tribes like the Huron and the Susquenhannock became the intermediaries, obtaining goods from the harvesters and trading them directly to the Europeans. Although it's not clear why, most of the history suggests these intermediary tribes astutely avoided trading firearms or metal weapons to the Long Tail Tribe in exchange for their trappings.[12] One source suggests it was the Dutch that entered into a treaty with their Iroquois trading partners to insure the Long Tail Tribe would receive no black powder muskets.[13]

The lack of gunpowder weapons may have hurt the Long Tail Tribe in their eventual showdown with the Iroquois, but it was likely their lust for beaver pelts that prompted the onset of hostilities with the Alqononquin in 1635 and the Long Tail Tribe's abandonment of their western territories.[14] Shortly thereafter, after a series of diplomatic missteps on the part of the

Long Tail Tribe, the Iroquois attacked and defeated their northern allies, including the Huron. In 1651, several thousand escaping Huron sought refuge with the Long Tail Tribe.[15] The Iroquois, however, would have none of that. Led by the Seneca Tribe – their largest tribe and the one nearest the Long Tail Tribe – the Five Nations demanded that the Long Tail Tribe turnover the refugees. Perhaps feeling threatened by both the loss of its northern ally and the eastern (Mohawk Tribe and Oneida Tribe) Iroquois' war with their southern ally the Susquehannock, the Long Tail Tribe declined to release their new-found warriors.[16]

Tension between the two sides grew. The Jesuit Relation of 1654 indicates some of the Huron refugees fanned the flames of war.[17] Things really came to a head in 1653 when, despite attempts to insure the peace, violence erupted and saw the Long Tail Tribe raiding the Seneca Tribe, killing a Seneca sachem by the name of Annencraos.[18] According to the Jesuit Relation of 1655-58 (Chapter XI), a delegation of thirty ambassadors of the "Cat Nation" (i.e., the Long Tail Tribe) went to the Seneca Capital of Sonontouan in an attempt to prevent war.[19] Unfortunately, tempers flared and "through the misfortune of accident," one of the Long Tail representatives killed a Seneca.[20] The Seneca Tribe responded "in kind" by killing twenty-five of the ambassadors.[21]

This is where the lack of firearms became significant. Although the Jesuit Relation of 1656 indicated an Long Tail palisade fell because of a munitions failure, it is commonly thought the Long Tail Tribe had no firearms.[22] As the same Relation says, the Long Tail "fight like Frenchmen, bravely sustaining the first charge of the Iroquois, who are armed without our muskets, and then falling upon them with a hailstorm of poisoned arrows."[23] How significant was this "hailstorm." Think of the movie *300*, as the good Jesuits tell us the Long Tail Tribe could fire 8-10 rounds of arrows before the Iroquois could reload their muskets.[24] The Long Tail Tribe proved they could match the combined forces of the Seneca and their allies as campaign was fought in several locations across Western New York. Iroquois tradition, admittedly much less reliable than the more objective Jesuit Relations, claim the two warring parties first met in Seneca territory at Honeoye Lake (about half-way between present-day Canandaigua and the Genesee River) with the final battle occurring near Buffalo Creek with no surviving Long Tail.[25] Ironically, it was only after two young Iroquois chiefs agreed to be baptized by the French missionary that the Long Tail Tribe met their match. These new converts donned the dress of the Frenchmen and talked their way into the now surrounded Long Tail Tribe stronghold. They told the Long Tail, "The Master of Life fights for us; you will be ruined if you resist him," and then asked the Long Tail Tribe "Who is the Master of your lives?"[26]

The Long Tail, perchance presaging a Clint Eastwood squint, coldly responded "We acknowledge none but our arms and hatchets."[27]

The Iroquois showed no mercy and wiped out the entire village and "wrought such carnage among the women and children that blood was knee-deep in certain places."[28]

By 1656 – more than a decade before the arrival of La Salle – the Long Tail Tribe was extinct, the last six hundred surrendering and anonymously assimilated into the Iroquois tribes[29], ending the long reign of the original inhabitants of Western New York. In truth, they suffered a fate worse than mere extinction, as all records of these once-proud people have been obliterated from the annals of human history. Oddly, the Seneca Tribe did not settle their newly won territory (at least until forced from their homeland while suffering losses by siding with the losing British during the Revolutionary War).[30] That is why La Salle had to travel to the original Seneca Tribe territory to negotiate his tentative peace.

It has been said some of the Long Tail Tribe escaped and, indeed, the Iroquois did track a few down in what is now southern Pennsylvania in 1680.[31] But as far as our region is concerned, they have become the Lost Tribe of Western New York. Still, for all their mystery, including the fact we never had any direct contact with them, the never really left us. For you see, the Iroquois word for "long tail" is "Erielhonan,"[8] and, being the lazy speakers we are, we've shortened the name to "Erie." Of all the tribes historically associated with Western New York, it is the name "Erie" that remains most often on our modern tongues. Between the namesake lake and county, Western New Yorkers pay respect to their region's original inhabitants on a nearly daily basis.

CHAPTER 9: WE PREEMPT WESTWARD EXPANSION FOR...

A funny thing happened on the way to researching the book *50 Hidden Gems of Greater Western New York*. For years I had been trying to explain to people just what exactly I meant by "Greater Western New York." From the Bullfinch Fund's perspective, it was easy. The Securities and Exchange Commission (SEC) requires all regional funds to specify the municipalities covered by the fund. In the case where a fund's region encompasses only a portion of a state, the fund's prospectus must list all the counties included in its unique definition of the region covered.

Beyond that, though, I had to justify why we chose those particular counties. This was especially important because we market the fund only to New York residents, specifically, Western New York residents. And the folks we consider "Western" New York residents don't necessarily consider themselves "western." Or, in the case of those in the Buffalo-Niagara metropolitan area, they don't consider anyone other than themselves to be "western" New Yorkers.

Allow me to digress for a quick moment on that issue. Remember, I was born in Buffalo and moved to Rochester when I was in fifth grade. It turns out my experience was far from unique. Many Buffalonians had moved to Rochester, and a few Rochesterians had moved to Buffalo. I believe as more people migrated from Buffalo to Rochester, the Rochester area began viewing itself less as "Upstate" New York (indeed, that was the name of its daily newspaper's Sunday supplement) and more "Western" New York. Today, it's not unusual for a Rochesterian, upon hearing his region referred to as "Upstate," to shudder and respond, "Westchester County is Upstate New York. Monroe County is 'Western' New York." But let's return to my dilemma.

If you go to any randomly picked town in Greater Western New York, there's a good chance the locals will describe themselves as something else. Besides "Western New York," you'll hear phrases like "Southern Tier," "Central New York," "Finger Lakes," and even a few scattered "Upstate New York" references. In describing the Bullfinch Fund Greater Western New York Series, I had to somehow convince this divergent citizenry they really belonged to the same community.

Here's how I did it: I pulled out a map of New York State, pointed to the locations of the cities of Rochester and Syracuse, and, just east of 77° longitude, drew an imaginary line between them from Lake Ontario to the Pennsylvania border.

As lame as that was, it seemed to work. At the very least, it got across the idea Syracuse was not part of Greater Western New York (something of which I think Syracusians would agree).

Still, it was arbitrary and, being a rational scientist by training (and, some would say, by disposition), I cowered every time I had to use this justification.

Until, that is, my research for *50 Hidden Gems of Western New York* revealed one hidden gem that surprised even me. In the course of that revelation, I discovered what all good scientists know but never admit: intuition, while not always logical, can often be correct. In fact, far from being imaginary, my line was very real, very controversial and very definitive when it came to mapping the true boundaries of Western New York. To understand the story behind this, we'll need to return to colonial America.

It should be fairly clear to any student of history that several European powers had, at one time or another, claimed Western New York as their own. We all know Christopher Columbus pronounced the entire New World for Spain (which then apparently decided it only wanted the parts with warm weather). We've already seen the French were the first to traverse our territory. Of course, who can forget the Dutch, the first settlers of what is now New York State?

But, in the end, it was the British who captured the crown jewels of Western New York, having defeated both the French and the Dutch. You'd think that would've made things easy, right?

You'd be wrong.

Thanks to the flippancy of English royalty (or perhaps their failure to attend geography classes), Western New York was given to not one, not two, not even three different colonies. In fact, it had been promised to no fewer than five different colonies.

England, unlike its European competitors, relied on private enterprise to colonize the New World. Of course, that didn't mean the King wasn't pleased by their independent efforts. In fact, these private companies ultimately were granted their land rights by the King. Sometimes, one King forgot what an earlier King had done. Sometimes, the same King forgot what he himself had done earlier. Here's a rough chronology of the bowl of land-title spaghetti created by the British monarchy (bear in mind, the Greater Western New York Region is roughly between the 42nd and just above the 43rd lines of latitude):

The first wave of English settled in the early 1600's. In 1606, James I granted "North Virginia" all lands between the 38th and 45th parallels westward to the "South Seas" (presumably the Pacific Ocean).[1] So, we're part of Virginia.

But wait! In 1628, Charles I granted the Massachusetts Bay Colony all of North Virginia's land above the 42nd parallel, again, extending to the "South Seas."[1,2] So now we're part of Massachusetts, right?

Not so fast! In 1662, Charles II decided to create the Connecticut Colony from the old Warwick Grant (between the 41st and 42nd lines of longitude) and extend that westward by 3,000 miles.[3] I'm losing track. Are we Connecticut or Massachusetts? And when does New York even enter the picture?

It enters when the same Charles II who, completely forgetting what he had done two years earlier, in 1664 grants a Royal Patent to his brother James, the Duke of York (get it?).[4] This Royal Patent gives James part of lands previously deeded to Massachusetts and Connecticut.[5] Can this get any more confusing?

Yes, it can. In 1681, the crown granted William Penn (the guy from whom we get the name "Pennsylvania"), land rights up through the 43rd parallel.[6] This parallel runs just south of Syracuse, north of Waterloo and Geneva, clips the southern half of Monroe Country, slices through Batavia and bisects Buffalo and Niagara Falls, thus sparing Mr. Penn from dealing with the vagaries of lake effect snow from Lake Ontario.

So there you go, a total of five colonies, of which at any time four of them held competing claims on Western New York. Eventually, and prior to the Revolutionary War, Connecticut and Pennsylvania withdrew any pretensions for our beloved homeland. That left New York and Massachusetts both with legitimate, albeit awkward, rights to our region.

The conflict was finally settled with the Treaty of Hartford on December 16, 1786 (a.k.a., the birthday of Greater Western New York), when New York and Massachusetts agreed to divide New York along a boundary line running from the 82nd milestone of the New York-Pennsylvania border straight north to Lake Ontario.[7] This boundary line would become known as "Pre-Emption Line" because, while New York would govern everything west of the line, Massachusetts held the pre-emptive right to buy the land from the Indians and resell it (which it did, twice, but that's another story).

As recently as 1990 the 82nd milestone could still be seen. According to one source, "The marker for Milestone 82 which is 82 miles west from the west bank of the Delaware River along the 42nd parallel, is a stone still visible alongside Wedger Hill Road about four miles northwest of Millerton, Pennsylvania."[8]

There's an interesting coda to this story (other than the one alluded to previously about how Massachusetts actually got to sell the land twice, although the two stories are related). It turns out the initial survey of the line wasn't quite as "due north" as had been hoped. In fact, despite starting at the correct point (the 82nd milestone), the original line drifts to the west. You can still see the remnants of the old line and the new line in roads named "Old Pre-Emption Road" (you guessed it, that's for the original line) and "Pre-emption Street" or "Pre-Emption Road" (which might refer to either the old or the new line) in the various towns and counties the line passes through.

The divergence, at its greatest extent, is three miles. This is where the controversy begins. That's enough to move the town of Geneva from the east side to the west side of the line. In fact, if you drive to Geneva, like I have, you can drive on Pre-Emption Road on the west side of the city (in Ontario County) and on Pre-Emption Street east of the city (actually in both Ontario and Seneca County). There was speculation the surveyor of the original line – Colonel Hugh Maxwell – may have purposely directed the line in such a way as to place Geneva to the east and firmly into New York State territory, but his notes prove otherwise.[9]

One final nugget: Remember my imaginary line just east of 77° Longitude? The Pre-Emption line lies just east of 77° longitude. So now, when asked why I define the Greater Western New York region the way I do, I simply say it includes all counties west of the Pre-Emption Line including those counties that touch it in any way.

Incidentally, when you look at those 17 counties, you may just find one of the most important hidden gems of all – one that may help create a better future for all those living in Greater Western New York. What is this hidden gem? I'll give you a hint: Look in the mirror, then turn the page.

CHAPTER 10: A WHOLE GREATER THAN THE SUM OF ITS PARTS

N ow that we've marked the boundaries of Greater Western New York, the fun really begins. We can delineate the 17 counties included in Greater Western New York. These represent all the counties west of or touching the correct Pre-Emption Line:

- Allegany County
- Chautauqua County
- Cattaraugus County
- Chemung County
- Erie County
- Genesee County
- Livingston County
- Monroe County
- Niagara County
- Ontario County
- Orleans County
- Seneca County
- Schuyler County
- Steuben County
- Wayne County
- Wyoming County
- Yates County

The Pre-Emption Line marks the western border of both Seneca County (maybe, depending on who owns Seneca Lake) and Chemung County. The Line slices through the counties of Wayne, Yates and Schuyler. As it stands, the eastern borders of Wayne, Seneca, Schuyler and Chemung form a fairly straight line from Lake Ontario to the Pennsylvania line. OK, maybe it's not quite straight enough to convince an officer you're not unduly influenced, but it's close enough.

What exactly does this constellation of the 17 western-most counties of New York State tell us? I discovered this particular hidden gem while preparing for a January 2004 presentation for the Buffalo/Niagara Chapter of the Public Relations Society of America (PRSA). On the heels of our first ever and highly successful Western New York Investors Conference, I was invited to take five minutes to provide an economic forecast for Western New York. Now, mind you, I once almost got hired to be the weekend weather forecaster for Channel 13 in Rochester. I was comfortable giving weather forecasts. There's at least a little bit of science behind that. The economy? That's a totally different matter. By that time I'd been in the investment business long enough to realize most economic forecasts were useless and, well, philosophically, I just couldn't condone wasting people's time by doing anything useless.

So, as I often do in my presentations, I took a different track. (For example, upon being inducted in the Gates-Chili High School Hall of Fame, while all the other inductees spoke eloquently of their business experience and stick-to-it-ativeness – you know, the usual Chamber of Commerce fodder – my speech to the senior class told, in a humorous and self-deprecating fashion, the true story of how math saved my life.) As I considered the options, I focused on the most important driver to success in our region (or, for that matter, any other region).

When it comes to gauging economic accomplishment, we often point to things like housing starts, unemployment and taxes, just to name a few. But the real measuring rod for success isn't financial, it's people, as in "population." Initially, my thought was to focus on invigorating public policy that concentrates almost exclusively on attracting more citizens to our region. I thought that would be the ultimate secret to our success. But then I looked at the actual numbers.

Boy was I surprised.

The secret of our future success isn't so much bringing more people in – although that would be the end result – but to take a hard look at how we define our footprint. The process of consulting the U.S. Census numbers led me to discover Greater Western New York's greatest hidden gem, one that, if properly used, can not only sustain us in the immediate term but provide a launching point for even greater future success.

According to the 2010 census, the 17 counties in our region contain 2,822, 996 people.[1] That number is more than two times bigger than usually quoted.

Wow. That's not something we can or should dismiss. Why?

Let's take a moment to analyze how the U.S. Census organizes its data. According to OMB Bulletin No. 10-02, "Metropolitan Statistical Areas have at least one urbanized area of 50,000 or more population, plus adjacent territory that has a high degree of social and economic integration with the core as measured by commuting ties. Micropolitan Statistical Areas – a new set of statistical areas – have at least one urban cluster of at least 10,000 but less than 50,000 population, plus adjacent territory that has a high degree of social and economic integration with the core as measured by commuting ties... If specified criteria are met, adjacent Metropolitan and Micropolitan

Statistical Areas, in various combinations, may become the components of a new set of complementary areas called Combined Statistical Areas."[2]

In our case, the U.S. Census has been kind enough to divide Greater Western New York into two different Metropolitan Statistical Areas, one with Buffalo as its core and the other with Rochester as its core. Furthermore, both of these have been combined with adjacent Micropolitan Statistical Areas to create two separate Combined Statistical Areas. The Buffalo-based Metro area includes Erie and Niagara Counties with a population of 1,135,509 and its Combined Statistical Area adds Cattaraugus County for a total population of 1,215,826. The Rochester-based Metro area includes Livingston, Monroe, Ontario, Orleans and Wayne Counties with a total population of 1,054,323 and its Combined Statistical Area adds Genesee and Seneca Counties for a total population of 1,149,653.

Believe me, it's a lot easier to digest these numbers in my presentations. I use lots of pictures. And no math.

Here's another way of looking at it. What if we redefined the U.S. Census definitions and called the entire 17 county Greater Western New York Region a Combined Statistical Area? It would then compare to North Carolina's fabled Research Triangle (which consists of 23 counties and a similarly-sized population).

But wait! There's more!

What if we just called the entire region a Metropolitan Statistical Area? At just under three million inhabitants, that would place us in the top twenty of all Metropolitan Statistical Areas in the country. Currently (again as of the 2010 Census), the Buffalo Metro Area sits at number 47 with the Rochester Metro Area not far behind at 51. A combined Greater Western New York Metro Area would rise to #18, just ahead of the 16 county St. Louis Metro Area as well as the tri-city area of Tampa Bay-St. Petersburg-Clearwater and a tad behind San Diego.

The news gets even more amazing. Greater Western New York has a larger population than 17 other states and would rank #34 among states in terms of the number of people living within its boundaries.[3] In fact, its population exceeds the combined populations of the four least populous states – Alaska, North Dakota, Vermont and Wyoming.[4]

Greater Western New York a separate state? It's not as far-fetched as you might think. After all, Vermonters got their own piece of sovereignty from the New York territory during the Revolutionary War in 1777.[5] Heck, they even operated as their own country until they decided to join the newly independent United States in 1791. Who knows, what if the Treaty of Hartford in 1786 had gone differently? Rather than creating an Ontario County from all New York State land west of Pre-Emption Line, the negotiators might have instead agreed to create the nation's first new state. Perhaps we would have had a fourteenth original colony called "Ontario."

(Imagine how that would even further confuse folks wondering if the Niagara Falls you're talking about is the one in Ontario, Canada or the one in Ontario, United States!)

The good news is we don't have to become a separate state to take advantage of the huge critical mass our combined population affords us. Truth be told, smart marketers are already utilizing this hidden gem. Regional marketers, most notably the Buffalo Bills and the Buffalo Sabres/Rochester Americans, have seen how their apparently "small market" teams really aren't small market at all.

By the way, the term "small market" refers to our media markets. As long as we continue to divide Greater Western New York into a "Buffalo" and a "Rochester" media market, we'll continue to be viewed as a small market. Imagine the potential gold mine if some media entrepreneur understood the power of population (I believe Adelphia Cable, before its demise, was headed in this direction).

When I concluded my presentation to the Buffalo/Niagara chapter of the PRSA, I told them I'd given them less of a forecast than a call to arms. You see, that's the way I use forecasts. While most people, somewhat understandably, view forecasting as watching things happen, I see it as a way to make things happen.

Before we leave this chapter, some of you might be interested to know national marketers have long recognized the usefulness of our population. Rochester has always been among the top locations chosen by test marketers. In 2004, a study listed the city as the #2 test market in the nation.[6] A combination of factors make this area attractive for test marketers, including a demographic make-up that has historically approximated the U.S. population. Yet, we cannot isolate this "national trend-setting" persona to Rochester alone. You might get a lump in your throat to learn our next hidden gem, one with equal national ramifications, hails from the Buffalo area.

CHAPTER 11: IT'S NOT WHAT YOU SAY, IT'S HOW YOU SAY IT.

Winters in New Haven, Connecticut aren't nearly as severe as those in the Greater Western New York region. As you've already read, I had proudly proclaimed my home town pride ever since the moment of that sun-drenched day in September of 1978 I first stepped onto campus. When the winds of winter arrived, as a native of Buffalo, I felt obliged to walk the talk. That meant, on a regular basis, when temperatures "dipped" into the low thirties, I would trudge out of my dorm in nothing but gym shorts and walk to the post office to get my mail. (Before you get too impressed, the post office was located in the basement of my hall. There was no interior access, so I had to walk outside into the raised courtyard, down the steps to ground level, turn a quick right before descending another set of stairs before entering the mail center.)

I remember one of those treks quite vividly. There I was, sauntering (after all, walking hastily would make it seem as though I feared the "frigid" temperature) through the courtyard without a shirt one coolish evening. Establishing a different form of cool, I stopped to talk to some friends. (I remember one saying to the other, "It's cold, why isn't he wearing a shirt?" The other responded, "He's from Buffalo." The first person said "Oh" with a knowing nod.)

So I was in this courtyard with nary a goosebump talking to some classmates when another friend strolls by. She's not just from Tennessee, she sounds like she's from Tennessee. She had one of the most pronounced dialects among all my college friends. Well, maybe except the two guys from Oklahoma. Anyway, along she comes and says in her too familiar drawl, "How y'all doin'?" Then she turns to me and asks, "Chris, can you be my project for linguistics class?"

That's not a question you get asked every day.

Ever the friendly guy, I agreed, but asked, "Why me?"

Her response knocked me off my feet. She said, "'cuz y'all have the most interestin' accent I've ever heard!"

Accent? I've got an accent? She was the kettle calling the pot black.

I smiled a quick come-back: "You realize that Walter Cronkite said the Buffalo-Cleveland accent represents the true American accent, one that every aspiring anchorman needs to emulate."

She wasn't impressed.

But the advice of America's Anchor guided me, as did the tones of Irv Weinstein and Danny Neaverth, when I embarked on a three-and-a-half year radio career. Whether DJing against the General Manager's play list (I had this thing about insisting I play listener requests) to blurting play-by-play for the football and hockey broadcasts, I kept my "accent" All-American. It came out cool, clear and crisp. Except, that is, when I channeled my inner Van Miller or Rick Jeanneret, depending on the venue.

Now, I can't find any record of Walter Cronkite saying that, but I do remember him referencing the primacy of the Buffalo-Cleveland accent, perhaps on a visit to Buffalo in the 1970s. I even recall him saying Erie was not a "halfway" point as it had a totally different dialect. At the time, I thought the comment a bit strange. Incidentally, my brother tells me that, during World War II, the army preferred to use people from our region as air traffic controllers because our accent was easiest to understand. I couldn't find any evidence of that claim, either, but here's what I did find out about our "accent."

Whatever Walter Cronkite may have been referring to was long gone by the time he referred to it, or so say the academic researchers. But, I did discover what he meant about Erie.

In an interview published in *The New Yorker*, famed linguist William Labov said our region's "Inland North" dialect was the "standard American dialect" – the "model for standard American pronunciation" – at least until it fell victim to the "Northern Cities Shift."[1] Apparently this shift, which Labov says started around 1950, has something to do with how the vowels are pronounced.[2] For example, the word "pot" sounds like how we used to say the word "pat," which we now pronounce as "pee-at," or something like that (or is it "thee-at"?).[3] Labov says the Northern Cities Shift is making our accent stronger.[4] I really can't explain it, other than to say I don't seem to have noticed this shift. Thankfully, it appears I haven't fallen victim to the Northern Cities Shift.

How do I know? I took this "What American accent do you really have?"[5] test on the Internet. I have no sense for its veracity, but it claims my accent is "Northern" and this accent "used to be the media standard in the '50's and

'60's." This at least seems to be consistent with what Labov says, and also what I remember Walter Cronkite saying four decades ago.

Back then I considered Buffalo to have the "pure" dialect (i.e., un-accent) with Rochester possessing a "nasal A" whose natives pronounced their city "Ratchester." But, if we are to believe Labov, Buffalo now shares this same accent.

It seems Labov isn't the only one who views our accent as unique. A recent skit on *Saturday Night Live* tried to spoof a Buffalo news broadcast.[6] To me, the actors sound like they're making fun of Chicago. I don't recall Irv Weinstein ever sounding like that. Do you?

Oh, and about Erie not being the average of the Buffalo-Cleveland accent? It turns out, while both Cleveland and Buffalo possess this Inland North linguistic flavor, Erie has instead opted for the tonality of Pittsburgh. Who knows. Maybe it's a Pennsylvania thing.

More important to me, though, is this whole "pop" vs. "soda" thing. Growing up, there was a clear line of distinction somewhere between Rochester and Syracuse (was it Pre-Emption Line?) that divided those who drank pop (to the west) and those who drank soda (to the east). But, it appears "soda" has infected at least the eastern fringe of Greater Western New York. Despite my protestations that the term applies only to a malted fountain drink favored by rambunctious teenagers in the 1950's, my oldest daughter can't seem to stop calling carbonated beverages "soda."

I don't know. Maybe I should send her to Tennessee for some voice lessons.

In either case, this pop/soda dichotomy isn't the first to split Greater Western New York. No, the first split occurred shortly after the region's birth in a new America. We'll explore that next.

CHAPTER 12: GREATER WESTERN NEW YORK'S SPLIT PERSONALITY EXPLAINED

To the uninitiated, Batavia might seem like a mere crossroads on the map, but the hustle and bustle of Route 5 (a.k.a. Main Street) tells a much different story. Any visitor will immediately see a testament to a thriving community. Without the telltale skyscrapers of a modern city, the heart of Genesee County clearly doesn't come across as a quaint nineteenth century town. No, there's a hint of modernity in its traffic, its business and even in the complexity of its inner city layout.

Yet within this bastion of modest progress lies a jewel with a much deeper backstory than meets the eye of the casual passerby. But before we get there, perhaps it makes sense to first return to pick up the Pre-Emption Line story where we left it off in Chapter 9.

If you recall, the 1786 Treaty of Hartford settled the dispute regarding the ownership of Western New York by creating the Pre-Emption Line – a straight line from the 82nd milestone west of the Delaware River on the Pennsylvania border due north to Lake Ontario. According to this agreement, Massachusetts held title to the land but New York State held political jurisdiction over it. The Pre-Emption rights gave Massachusetts the "pre-emptive" or first right to buy the land from the Indians.

Massachusetts sold their pre-emptive rights to Oliver Phelps and Nathaniel Gorham on April 1, 1788 for $1,000,000 – the Phelps and Gorham Purchase.[1] That same year, the two negotiated what turned out to be a controversial treaty with the Seneca to formally acquire roughly a third of the six million acres they had rights to. Phelps paid £2,100 in New York currency for these nearly 2 ½ million acres that included lands primarily east of the Genesee River and a portion on the west side of the Genesee River known as the "Mill Yard Tract," located on the river's northern end.[2] Phelps agreed to pay the Seneca in two equal annual installments, but, when he came to make the second payment in the summer of 1789, the Indians were surprised to find he had only $5,000, not the $10,000 they expected.[3] Apparently, the Indians were unaware of currency exchange rates and had been used to dealing in terms of the Canadian dollar which was valued at a rate of only half that of New York currency.[4] The deal went through anyway. Phelps and Gorham then set up the first land office in America in Canandaigua, not in their originally intended location of Geneva because the then well-established trading post fell on the New York State side of the mistakenly surveyed original Pre-Emption Line.[5]

This would not be the last time continental currency issues would impact this story. When Phelps and Gorham purchased the preemptive rights from Massachusetts, they promised to make their three annual payments in Massachusetts securities, then valued at 20 cents on the dollar.[6] Unfortunately, before the third payment came due, the Continental Congress guaranteed the Massachusetts securities at full face value.[7] Phelps and Gorham thus defaulted and gave all the unsold land back to the state of Massachusetts in 1790. A year later, in 1791, Massachusetts again sold its preemptive rights, this time to Robert Morris, Revolutionary War financier and signer of the Declaration of Independence. Morris immediately sold that portion of unsold land east of the Genesee River known as the "Genesee Tract" to Sir William Pulteney in 1792.[8]

But our story here focuses on Morris's purchase on the west side of the Genesee River. This consisted of five tracts of land. He kept the eastern most tract for himself. Called the "Morris Reserve," this tract includes a protrusion once called "Allens Hill," then "Richmond Hill" which today we call "Mount Morris." Bonus points for those readers who can correctly guess which Revolutionary War financier and signer of the Declaration of Independence the Town and Village of Mount Morris are named after.

Morris sold the four westernmost properties (tracts 2-5) to a group of six Amsterdam bankers in 1791-1792, although this sale didn't become final until the Treaty at Big Tree, just outside the current village of Geneseo, on September 15, 1797.[9] On November 20, 1795, the "Club of Six" merged their holdings into a single company called the "Holland Land Company."[10] But our hero enters the picture in 1792. That's the year Joseph Ellicott, surveyor par excellence, was hired to resurvey the original Pre-Emption Line (and discover the error that placed Geneva on the wrong side of the line).[11] In the summer of 1797, the agent of the Holland Land Company hired Ellicott, who had previously surveyed the Company's western Pennsylvania properties, to survey their Western New York properties.[12] After spending nearly four years in the wilds of Western New York, Ellicott travelled to Philadelphia on November 1, 1800 and signed a contract to become the Resident-Agent for the Holland Land Company.[13]

Fast forward two centuries and a bit more. Unless you grew up in any one of the traditional eight Western New York Counties, you're not going to believe the following statement. Joseph Ellicott is a Saint, a hero, a cultural icon of unequalled status. He was, quite literally, the creator of Buffalo and much of Western New York. And there's a shrine in his honor right in the heart of Greater Western New York. More than a shrine, it remains an artifact from his duties as Resident-Agent.

When he was initially hired, Ellicott set up a temporary office in Asa Ransom's Inn (in present day Clarence) before spotting an ideal site centrally located at the intersection of two Indian trails.[14] Although the Seneca called this traditional meeting place "Tonawanda," Ellicott chose the name "Batavia" to honor his Dutch paymasters who lived in the Republic of Batavia (but only after his immediate boss, Paul Busti, rejected Ellicott's initial suggestion to call the place "Bustiville").[15] So confident was he in his choice to build this new city, that Ellicott declared, referring to the natural harbor on the eastern shore of Lake Erie, "God made Buffalo. I will try and make Batavia."[16]

By 1810, land sales were brisk and Batavia became the *de facto* capital of Greater Western New York, even more so after, as described in Chapter 3, the British burned Buffalo to the ground in 1813.[17] Perhaps with this recent blaze still lingering, in 1815, after working out of his mansion for more than a decade, Ellicott decided to build a two-story stone building to house all land office papers.[18] It is this building that we see today as the Holland Land Office Museum on Main Street (Route 5) in downtown Batavia.

And let me tell you, this is one solid building. I have twice visited it and, rest assured, Museum Director Jeff Donahue keeps a remarkable shop. Rightfully proud of his charge, he exudes a passion for his region's rich history. He explained to me how, much like Ontario County after the formation of the Pre-Emption Line, Genesee County became the "Mother of all Western New York Counties" following the Holland Land Purchase. (Does that now make Ontario County a grandmother?)

The interior of the museum contains many wonderful displays not only from the Ellicott era but through the early twentieth century. It even houses the gallows once used by Batavia to administer capital punishment, although Donahue is quick to point out it wasn't used that often. He's also aware enough to keep the morbid relic hidden behind a curtain during the festive and joyful Christmas season.

While the contents of the interior will please many visitors, I remain struck by the exterior of the building. Its pilloried façade evokes my imagination, taking me back to the Pantheon in Rome. The cannons displayed on the porch only add more muscle to the already quite apparent strength of the museum's stone walls. No doubt the foundation of this building remains as strong as the foundation of Joseph Ellicott's ultimate handiwork: that of

Western New York itself. Well at least the half on the west side of the Genesee River. The east side half was already underway thanks to the work of several different civic architects. And that, my dear reader, is perhaps the best explanation as to when Greater Western New York first developed its split personality, an ailment that, thanks to the ongoing work of the U.S. Census, (see Chapter 10), continues to this day.

As often happens when considering this history and this issue in particular, my mind gets to wandering into the realm of "What-If." The story of the Holland Land Purchase is no exception. What if that section of New York State west of Pre-Emption Line – Greater Western New York – had become an independent territory instead of falling under the jurisdiction of New York? We've already (Chapter 9) discussed the likely name of this hypothetical territory and state it might eventually birth ("Ontario"). Would "Ontario Territory" have eventually become "Ontario State"? Given the requirements and timing of statehood qualifications at the time, Greater Western New York would have been eligible to become a state in the years on either side of the War of 1812. Because of the significance of its role in that war, it would have most certainly been invited to join the United States of America by the end of the war. And, upon entering the Union, which city would "Ontario State" have selected to be its capital.

The answer, without question, is Batavia.

And with that imaginative digression, let us move on to those hidden gems that most evoke the "playful" spirit of our region and its people.

Part II

ETHOS

– Playful Thoughts –

CHAPTER 13: BACK AT THE OLD PIZZA STAND

In the early scene of the 1962 movie version of *The Music Man*, Harold Hill, con man extraordinaire, unexpectedly bumps into his old friend and accomplice Marcellus Washburn. Marcellus has since married a "nice comfortable girl" and settled down in the idyllic Midwestern town of River City ("Gone legitimate, huh? I knew you'd come to no good," laments Hill). When he asks Harold if he's still pitching steam automobiles, Hill shakes his head "No" and says, "I'm back at the old stand" whereupon he pantomimes conducting a band.

I can't say Hamburg had the stubbornness of River City, Iowa, (after all, Hamburg is the "Town that Friendship built"), but I can attest to an idyllic feeling growing up off South Park Avenue when it had only two lanes. And like the magical concluding scene of *The Music Man*, my brother and I (and maybe even my mother and father, too) couldn't wait to gaze in awe as the marching band led the parade down South Park to signal the beginning of the Big Tree Fireman's Carnival. We'd watch from the second floor apartment above my grandfather's pizza parlor across the street from Abbott Parkway where we lived. There was something dazzling about that marching band, and something incredibly comfortable about watching it from the large picture window overlooking the Avenue. There was also something indescribably exciting about that annual parade. It was an anticipatory pleasure for me and my brother, for we knew as soon as the parade ended, we would immediately head for the carnival.

But the carnival, while fun, only signaled the coming of something even bigger: the annual Erie County Fair, or, as we (and many others) called it, the "Hamburg Fair." Funny thing about the two events, though. While the Big Tree Fireman's Carnival parade reminded me of *The Music Man*, the carnival did not. On the other hand, although the much larger Fair parade didn't evoke feelings of *The Music Man*, the fair itself oozed of River City. You might think *Meet Me In St. Louis* a better movie to compare to the Fair, and, for some, that may be true. For me, however, the sly con of Harold Hill and, much to his own surprise, his and River City's eventual transformation matched my own journey from boyhood to manhood, a journey that trekked through the Fair.

Before I get too involved in how the Fair helped shape my character, let's go back in time to the very beginnings of the Fair. Greater Western New York grew first as an agricultural region. It was (and some say it remains) colored more by the same soft brush of the Midwest farm belt rather than the spray painted tag of the urbanized East Coast. And if there's one American tradition best suited for farmers, it's the annual county fair. It seemed like every county in America's rich heartland held these yearly affairs and they became more than a social gathering of the local growers, but a showcase for the county and its people.

You might not know this, but the Erie County Fair is older than Erie County. The first Fair was held in October 1820 in the city of Buffalo on Main Street near the Terrace overlooking the waterfront.[1] In 1821, the very next year, Niagara County ceded its southern portion – including Buffalo – to create Erie County. The Fair's sponsoring organization, the Niagara County Agricultural Society, was renamed the Erie County Agricultural Society to become the oldest civic community member organization in Erie County.[2] The Society held a second Fair in 1821 but a poor economy and transportation logistics made continuing the Fair impractical.[3] The area's economy would soon change for the better as, on August 9, 1823, construction of the Buffalo end of the Erie Canal began.[4] By 1840, the Canal encouraged tens of thousands, some 40,000 in Erie County alone, to populate the westernmost section of the Holland Land Purchase.[5] In 1841, things had brightened up and, on October 5 and 6, the Erie County Fair started anew and has been held annually ever since (with the exception of 1943 as a result of World War II rationing).[6]

The success of the Fair received broad attention, and when New York State decided to hold its first State Fair in Buffalo in 1848, Robert McPherson, president of the Erie County Agricultural Society, said, "If the State of New York means to beat us in 1848, when they visit us, they must do their best."[7] In the early years, the City of Buffalo proved adequate as a location, but as the region grew, so, too, did the Fair. The Agricultural Society soon found it required a larger footprint than the City could provide, so in 1850 the Fair moved to Aurora.[8] After spending time in Lancaster, East Hamburgh (now Orchard Park) and West Seneca, it settled in Springville from 1851-1867.[9] In 1868, by a vote margin of but a single trustee, the board of the Erie County Agricultural Society approved a permanent move to its current location and, on September 23, 24 and 25, 1868, held its first County

Fair in Hamburgh.[10] (By the way, it wasn't until 1877 that the Town decided to drop the second "h" in "Hamburgh." It is unknown if Pittsburgh picked up this superfluous h on waivers or not.) With the increase in publicity in the 1880s, the Erie County Fair quickly became known as "The Hamburg Fair." For example, in 1895 the *Buffalo Courier* wrote, "…not to have seen the Hamburg Fair… is to have missed one of the institutions in the vicinity of Buffalo."[11] Indeed, such was its success, a director of the Buffalo Pan-American Exposition committee, so frustrated by early proposals for that event, complained those drafts offered "a show of the size of the Hamburg Fair or the Toronto Exhibition."[12]

I still call it "The Hamburg Fair" and I expect many who grew up in Hamburg still proudly refer to it by that name. The Fair generated a lot of pride in our community and in our family. Historically larger even than the New York State Fair, in 1970 it became the country's largest county fair.[13] It has since slipped to the third largest county fair and, in that last decade or so, the New York State Fair has finally generated more visitors than the Erie County Fair (but just barely).

That the Fair is such a part of me and such a jewel in our community, I naturally assumed everyone felt the same way. But I'm constantly surprised, even to this day, when I find someone from the north towns of Buffalo who has never benefited from partaking of the Fair. Heck, there are people in Rochester who make the annual trek to the Erie County Fair! How could these Buffalonians forsake their own county's shining star?

Oh well, here's why the Fair became so important to me. Like the glamor of *The Music Man*, the Fair was one big show, with Hollywood entertainers often headlining the acts. It possessed a circus atmosphere; it even had (and still has) a Midway that arrived by train, just like an old circus. But there was one thing that made it most special to me and my family – it was a show that, since 1957, we were in!

You remember my grandfather's pizza parlor on South Park I mentioned earlier? It turns out my grandfather, although an entrepreneur – he once owned a grocery on Ridge Road in Lackawanna – only started the pizza parlor because my young mother nagged him. "Dad," she said one day in 1954, "it's the latest thing. All the kids are going. Besides, you can't make any money in the grocery business anymore, not with those big guys like A&P coming in." My grandfather, of course, reacted like any father would when his smart-aleck teenager tries to tell him what to do. I'm not saying there was a sonic boom on Ingham Avenue that day, but you get the picture. Apparently, he refused to believe anyone would order out something they could easily make at home. Still, by 1956, my grandfather had started the area's first pizza parlor, at least according to my mother. Now, I don't know how you reconcile "all the kids are going" with my mother's claim that it was the first pizza parlor in the area, but that's her story and she's sticking to it. There must be some truth to the story because, when word got around at the Lake-Erie Italian Club that Ilio DiPaolo wanted to start a pizzeria, my grandfather gladly gave Ilio the benefit of his experience.

Well, back in the old days, the Erie County – er – Hamburg – Fair had a tent where the local restaurateurs would set up to sell their culinary creations. It was there my grandparents first brought their pizza to sell to fairgoers. Soon, that makeshift booth beneath a shared tent became a free standing wooden stand across from the original main entrance to the grand stand at the top of the Avenue of Flags. That's where I remember hanging out as a little kid when I was too tired to tour the Fair or when my parents wanted to go see one of those Hollywood headliners. It's also where we'd escape from the crowd after witnessing the ultimate in coolness (for an eight-year-old at least) – like the Hell Drivers or Joey Chitwood's Thrill Show – or the ultimate in excitement – the massive demolition derby. Our neighbors always had a car in it. We cheered for them, but they never won.

Perhaps the greatest personal impact the Fair had on me occurred during the few years I worked there for my grandparents. Oh the stories I could tell. In fact, one of these days I might be inclined to pen a book along the lines of *Everything I Learned I Learned at the Hamburg Fair*. For the purposes of this book, though (and this chapter is already running too long), suffice it to say the Fair shares that quaintly all-American feel of the *The Music Man's* River City – for all its charm, all its lost innocence and all its carnival atmosphere. Judging from an Orange County (NY) reporter's account in the 1890s, "This Fair is unique among the County Fairs of the Empire State. First, it is well attended, and therefore successful financially; and, second, it can boast of being the most remarkable gathering of fakes on this earth…,"[14] since more than a century ago, the circus-like magic of *The Music Man* rings true.

Or at least it once did. Perhaps, in briefly calling itself "America's Fair" as it did in the 2000s to broaden its appeal, the Fair began trying too hard. The success of the Hamburg Raceway's Casino hasn't helped. The soft pebble gravel – that you once walked on, that once kicked up that country dust, that once coated your country sweat on those especially hot days – has long ago been replaced by the heartless hardness of asphalt. Yes, they paved paradise and made it a parking lot.

But they can make as many changes as they want. They can get rid of the double Ferris Wheel, which we could see from Highland Avenue on a clear day. They can get rid of the Sky Way that once flew above the Midway and, from which, much to the distress of those walking below, occasionally rained little red I-Got-It! balls. They can outlaw rickety wooden vendor stands and replace them with antiseptic Jetsons-like trailers. They can even charge vendor rates so high the Boston Church can't sell enough pies to afford the rent.

They can do all that, but they can never remove the memories of River City. The memories where, for one week (or ten days) a year, I got to live the

16-hour work day life of a carny (my grandparents insured I never found out what they did the other eight hours). Or, the memories where, by working so closely with my grandparents, I received invaluable education about life, family and fun. Among these include the showing of unconditional love for their children despite yelling at them for the silliest reason, like the time my uncle showed up one afternoon with a cardboard display of cigarette lighters. Boy did my grandfather's voice explode when my uncle suggested we sell them. Still, he frightened no one as, despite his obvious expression of anger, we just couldn't get past those crazy oversized novelty sunglasses he was wearing. Finally, there are also the memories where, by seeing how my grandparents managed the pizza stand, I gained practical experience so important today in running my own business. Heck, how could I ever forget the lesson covering inventory control and open-minded flexibility, or, as we liked to say, "thinking outside the pizza box." One night we ran out of pizza just as the evening rush from the grandstand descended upon us. Desperate – in a Mr. Krabs sort of way – to satisfy those many customers all too willing to separate their dollars from their wallets, my grandfather began selling anything not nailed down in the stand. This included all those lighters in the cardboard mounted display my uncle had brought in earlier that day. My grandfather sold the first one before letting my uncle sell the rest.

As long as the Erie County Fair continues to promote local celebrities (along with the headliners), as long as they continue to feature long-time local vendors (yes, the family pizza stand – now a trailer – remains, operated by my [other] uncle and his family), as long as they continue to feature the arts, crafts and historical exhibits of local creators (alongside the traveling road show of James E. Strates Shows), then I'll be happy knowing future generations will be able to experience a county fair the way past generations have. And this I can guarantee, for, despite all these changes, my own children, who never experienced the same Fair I did growing up, nonetheless look forward to the annual visit to the Fair.

And while every time I step through Gate 2, imagining I'm going back to that old pizza stand, I'm content knowing my children are building their own "River City" memories. On a scale of one to ten, they, like I, rate the Erie County Fair "76 Trombones." But they also have experienced more than just the Hamburg Fair, for Greater Western New York was once and still is filled with these destinations of amusement. We'll explore some of the interesting history in and around these sites in our next chapter.

CHAPTER 14: THE MAGICIAN REVEALS HIS REAL TRICK

One by one the hockey heroes skate up towards the camera from the far blue line, stop with a spray of ice just missing the lens, then announce their name and team. Finally, the last professional pumps his legs forward with the smooth motion of the others and stops in the same controlled fashion. But when he announces his name, I'm shocked to discover he's no hockey player, he's just another famous Canadian.

"Bill Shatner. Loblaws," states the confident former Captain Kirk.

For those not familiar, Loblaws is a Canadian grocery chain. In the 1960's and early 1970's they had stores in Buffalo (primarily) and Rochester (maybe just one, but I lived next to it). It was an era before Wegmans went on supermarket steroids and totally dominated the market. Loblaws was Canada's pride but eventually sold out to Bells Markets.

In 1975 Loblaws was a player – at least in my neighborhood – and no more so because it offered free NHL "Action Stamps." They even provided a book to put the stamps in. My brother and I each filled a book. It was an exciting year for the hockey fans of Greater Western New York as the Sabres, led by the French Connection, were about to play themselves into the Stanley Cup Finals for the first time. It was the first NHL Championship to feature two non-"Original Six" teams. It would also signal the last time a pure Canadian roster would win the Stanley Cup. Indeed, the series featured only one American born player – Sabres defenseman Lee Fogolin, Jr., a native of Chicago, Illinois. The 1975 Stanley Cup Finals, though, might be most remembered for Game 3 in the Aud. Unseasonably warm temperatures caused the ice to fog up, but not before a bat (the mammal kind, not the baseball kind) strafed the skaters – at least until quick-wristed Sabres center Jim Lorenz slashed the flying pest with his stick. As far as we know, this was the first and only premeditated murder of an animal during an NHL game. Lorenz served no time in the box, but Rene Robert scored the winner in overtime, giving the Sabres their first Stanley Cup victory.

But before NHL Action Stamps, and when I still lived in Blasdell, Loblaws (along with other area supermarkets) gave away something of even greater value: free tickets to Fantasy Island. Each year at the end of school, we'd count our A's, since for every A we got, we received Fantasy Island tickets.

Now, for those of you not familiar with the Fantasy Island of the 1960's, and for those who think Darien Lake represents the epitome of summertime fun, every school child's dream was to get an A to get free tickets to Fantasy Island. Why? Because Fantasy Island would be the closest most of us would ever get to going to Disneyland way out in California. Remember, this was both before the creation of Disney World in Florida and before transcontinental air travel became the norm for working class families.

Ergo, Fantasy Island was a big thing.

But it wasn't (and isn't) the only thing. Jamestown (actually, Maple Springs) has Midway, Rochester (actually, Irondequoit) has Seabreeze and Canandaigua (yes, really, Canandaigua) had Roseland. As a minor, I went to all but Midway, but as an adult (as opposed to a "major"?) I did bring my kids to the Chautauqua Lake park. None of these fine places could measure up to the Erie County Fair (or even Crystal Beach), but it would be foolish to expect them to. They also can't hold a candle to Darien Lake, but, if you're like me, that's a good thing.

Of all, though, Fantasy Island deserves the "hidden gem" label. Why? Two reasons. First, many people don't know it's still operating. That's because the original park, which opened in 1961 shortly after Walt Disney opened his west coast theme part, went bankrupt in 1982. Under new ownership, it went bankrupt again in 1992. For two years the amusement facility was called "Two Flags Over Niagara Fun Park" until, after being purchased by Martin Dipietro, it regained its original name with a slight Dipietro twist. It's now called "Martin's Fantasy Island."

The second reason is, unlike like most amusement parks, Fantasy Island comes closest to mimicking Disney's magic. What I remember liking the most about the 1960's version of Fantasy Island wasn't the rides – to tell the truth, I never liked rides anywhere – it was the various adventures offered by Fantasy Island. It had a little circus show that featured a real lion tamer with a real lion. It had a steamboat that chugged around a small island. It had a train that chugged around the entire park. Most of all, it had a wild west show that, at several appointed hours each day, offered a fine outdoor melodrama that always ended with a climactic shoot-out, where the good guy would always get the bad guy.

These exact same shows were played out multiple times during the day. Since we would generally spend the bulk of the day at Fantasy Island, my brother and I would clamor to go see the show again and again. It got to the point where I started to think it was make believe because the "dead" bad guys would always reappear again – fit as a fiddle – at the very next show.

It's funny. Some kids imagined themselves the sheriff. Some kids imagined themselves one of the bad guys. Me? I imagined myself one of the stuntman. I really liked how they could pretend they'd been shot while up on the roof, die dramatically, roll down lifelessly off the eaves to the ground below, then bounce back up unharmed once the show was over. I wanted to do that, and I knew just the place to do it. Our house on Abbott Parkway had a raised patio in the rear and it presented a very easy – and safe – way to get to the garage roof. And the garage roof was just the right height where I was sure it would deposit my rolling body down without harm onto the soft grass below.

I never got the chance to try. Upon hearing of my plan, my brother immediately told my mother, who, shocked at my stupidity, immediately told my father, who, less shocked by my stupidity and probably secretly thinking it was a cool idea and why didn't he think of it, immediately told me – carefully making sure my mother could see him tell me – to "not even think about it" and, just to be sure, "never go close to that part of the patio that leads to the garage roof." He made an exception, of course, when we had to paint the siding of the house above the garage roof.

In addition to daredevil ideas, Fantasy Island left me with many spellbinding trinkets. My parents bought me my first (and only) magic trick there. So enchanted was I by the magician's disappearing/reappearing dime trick that I went up to him and insisted he tell me how it was done. I was old enough to know it wasn't real, but not smart enough to figure out the trick without some help. He showed me how it was done, then he revealed his true trick: to get me to buy the prop that would allow me to entertain any audience of my choosing. Given the honest excitement I had for the trick, my father allowed the con and bought me the prop. For several weeks, I performed the disappearing dime trick for all my friends at school until it became old hat, whereupon I stuffed it in my "special" desk drawer. To this day, it remains there, (unless, since the desk is now in his room, my son has decided to clean out its drawers).

Fantasy Island originated in an era dominated by westerns. Its theme recreated the boyish charm and innocence of white hats vs. black hats quite successfully. In a way, the "Old West" theme fit perfectly with the "frontier" motif so prevalent in our region (recall from earlier chapters, Greater Western New York truly represents America's first frontier).

But did you know you can find remnants of the real frontier of the old west only an hour or so south of Fantasy Island? To discover the story behind that, simply turn the page.

CHAPTER 15: THE WILD WEST RIDES AGAIN

In the heart of downtown Jamestown on a June night in 2002, despite the dim light of the late hour, the construction workers hired to take down the deteriorating brick façade of the ancient hotel on Pine Street thought they were seeing faces, until they came to the word "Buffalo."[1] They stopped all work. They didn't know what they had just uncovered, but their collective instinct told them it was something historic. It turns out they were right.

Beneath the decaying bricks of the old lodging house lay a wooden wall containing an entire advertisement for a May 1878 "Buffalo Bill Combination" show to be held in Jamestown's Allen Opera House. The Buffalo Bill Combination starred William Cody (a.k.a. "Buffalo Bill") and presaged his more famous "Wild West" shows. According to Laura Schell, the woman who restored the billboard to its full glory, "the billboard is one of the earliest, most rare and largest Buffalo Bill items known" and "is the oldest paper billboard of this size actually used for advertising still existing in the United States."[2] I'm not kidding. This discovery was big news. It was covered across the nation, and not just by William Cody fans[3] but even by at least one west coast newspaper.[4]

I remember learning about Buffalo Bill in third grade deep in the bowels of Woodlawn Elementary School. I remember him because I remember anything that references "Buffalo." That his nickname referred to the animal and not the city didn't bother me. As a child the fantastic life of William Cody captivated my attention, just like the Wild West shows at Fantasy Island. Little did I know, although the famed Pony Express rider and expert marksman did shoot all those buffalo, his on-stage persona was more similar to those make-believe shows at Fantasy Island. Buffalo Bill had become a star only after dime-novel author Ned Buntline wrote a series of adventure stories about

Cody to help promote his early tours. Perhaps even the one performed in May 1878 at the Allen Opera House in Jamestown, New York.

In either case, the real-life original 10'x26' paper poster, which "crumbled like potato chips" when first uncovered and had to be put together like "a huge jigsaw puzzle" when restored, remains on public display on the same site as the original opera house.[5] The site today is called the "Reg Lenna Civic Center." The Reg Lenna Civic Center is housed in the renovated Palace Theatre, which was built in 1920 on the same lot as the original Allen Opera House, which burned down a few years after Buffalo Bill performed there.[6]

Don't fret, fans of the era of Buffalo Bill, the west hasn't left Greater Western New York. Just a few miles up the road from Jamestown (Route 60, to be specific), you'll find, still in Chautauqua County, the town of Gerry (pronounced like the name "Gary" and named after Elbridge Gerry, a signer of the Declaration of Independence[7]). Travelling on that same route you'll come to a crossroads, a hamlet also known by the name of Gerry. Now, your first thought might be that this quiet rural community might have once been used as a stage lot for a Hollywood western.

As far as I know, you'd be wrong.

What it does feature is an honest-to-goodness real-life artifact of the wild west – an annual old fashioned rodeo – "the oldest running rodeo in the east."

According to the Gerry Rodeo website[8], it all started when this fella by the name of Jack Cox wandered into these here parts way back when. A lotta folks kinda wondered about ol' Jack when, in 1945, he suggested puttin' on a rodeo as a way of raisin' money for the Gerry Volunteer Fire Department. Ya see, back in them days they still had workin' cowboys – mostly out west – and, well, ol' Jack used to be one of 'em. Now the good folks in Gerry got to thinkin' and, shucks, didn't they go and turn four acres of swamp into an arena and parking lot in all of seven days. And this was jest in time, too, 'cuz right then Colonel Jim Eskew showed up with all his livestock and – wouldn't ya know it – the first Gerry Rodeo was held.

Today, the Gerry Rodeo counts itself as one of the longest running events in Chautauqua County. The seating capacity of the arena is 4,000 and there's even a modern midway for those young'uns just itchin' to leave the west behind and spin themselves dizzy. And if you thought Chiavetta's at the Erie County Fair (which usually occurs the week after the Gerry Rodeo) was finger lickin' good, then wait 'til you try the famous Gerry Rodeo home-made barbecue sauce. Just don't go there looking for beer.

Now, you might be wondering why a rough and tumble cowboy event like the Gerry Rodeo doesn't serve beer. There's a story behind that. Paul Cooley told me the story. Paul is a long-time member and unofficial historian of the Gerry Volunteer Fire Department as well as a retired teacher of English and journalism at Cassadaga Valley Central School (which I just can't help but saying in an Antonio Banderas accent every time we pass it on the way to visit my wife's parents). In 1944, a year before the Rodeo started, the Department decided to have a tractor/horse pull for a fundraiser. The vote to offer a beer tent went narrowly in favor of those wanting to serve the adult beverage. The decision, however, sparked controversy, leading several members, including at least one official, to resign.

The day of the event started well, with a veritable tent city surrounding the pulling field. The largest tent, of course, was the beer tent. But then a monumental rain and wind storm – Paul called it a mini-tornado – swept through the area, deluging the already moist grounds into a swampy quagmire and toppling several tents, including the notorious beer tent. My mother-in-law, who was there, remembers tractors and horses pulling the cars out of the axel deep mud. Since that ominous affair, the Department has never again approved serving beer.

The heyday of cowboys might have vanished with the arrival of Alan Shepard and the Mercury Seven. Sure, when it comes to excitement, more folks picture a Ford Mustang rather than a bucking bronco. The idea of a rodeo may be as old as the Pony Express, Bill Cody's first employer, but, face it, what little kid still doesn't get excited about watching – and maybe even riding – horses?

Of course, if we're talking about something old that kids would enjoy, stay tuned for the next chapter. I passed by this particular place for decades until my teenage daughter Catarina interned for a photographer. It was on that job that she, not I, discovered our next hidden gem.

CHAPTER 16: THE BEST LITTLE HOLE HOUSE IN GREATER WESTERN NEW YORK

Our family moved to the Rochester suburb of Chili during the Christmas break of my fifth grade. There are a lot of things I can tell you about that particular transition. It's amazing what I still remember. There's the "long" (because it was written on a narrow roll of paper) letter I received from the fifth grade classmates I had left behind in Woodlawn Intermediate. There's my rediscovery of the game of chess while partaking in what was promoted as "science" class. (Apparently, "mapping" the moves – not even real chess notation – had something to do with scientific thinking.) Most relevant for this tome, however, was my new classmates' anticipation of summer.

For many youngsters in and around the Rochester area, the summer not only brought the welcome end of "pencils, books and teacher's dirty looks," but it also ushered in the season of Seabreeze. I can't say Seabreeze offered the same "cash in your A's for free tickets" promotion that Fantasy Island did. I can't say that because I didn't get any A's at the end of fifth grade. In fact, nobody got A's at Florence Brasser Elementary School back then – or B's or C's or D's, for that matter. No, we got "E" as in excellent, "S" as in satisfactory, "U" as in unsatisfactory and, in the few cases where students spent the bulk of the term in sickbay, an "I" for incomplete. My friends back in Blasdell expressed shocked disbelief when I revealed my report card contained a disproportionate share of E's – at least until I told them the scoring system.

So, sans the "A gets you free tickets" incentive, we didn't get a chance to visit Seabreeze that summer. I just got to hear stories about it. Lots of stories. They told stories of the famous carousal, which probably excited my sister more than me. They told stories of its legendary roller coaster, which, admittedly, did pique my interest. What they didn't tell, however, were stories of the rich and fascinating history of Seabreeze.

Located on the west side of Irondequoit Bay on the shores of Lake Ontario, Seabreeze has long attracted attention, and not just because of its purifying waters. After a thwarted war with the area natives in 1687, the French decided to play nice with the Seneca Tribe and, in 1718, built a trading post (*Fort Des Sables*, which is French for "Fort of the Sands").[1] While this might have pleased the Seneca Tribe, the British didn't take too kindly to the idea. They built a competing fort (Fort Schuyler) in 1721 down the Bay and by 1759, had run the French out of Greater Western New York all the way through Fort Niagara,[2] signaling the beginning of the end of the French and Indian War.

Skip ahead a century. With the advent of rail expansion across America, and, in particular, the northeast, following the cessation of Civil War hostilities, iron horse entrepreneurs sought attractions which would lure passengers to use their train service. One such railway system – the Rome, Watertown & Ogdensburgh (there's that pesky superfluous "h" again) Railroad Company – had tracks running along the south shore of Lake Ontario, including through Seabreeze.[3] Though under the miserly rule of the Delaware, Lackawanna and Western Railroad at the time,[4] on August 5th, 1879[5] the Rome, Watertown & Ogdensburgh Railroad carved off a piece of its property in Seabreeze to open a picnic area.[6] The Seabreeze picnic area also marked the end of the line for the Rochester Railway, a horse-drawn trolley line until it went fully electric in 1887.[7]

I first visited Seabreeze as a teenager, anticipating the much talked about Jack Rabbit roller coaster ride. In the end, I preferred that old standby, the bumper cars. The Jack Rabbit is still there, just as it was (with the requisite maintenance upgrades of course) when it first arrived in 1920 as the then fastest roller coaster in the world.[8] While not so hidden, you might not know CBS rates this gem among the top roller coasters in North America. It labels the Jack Rabbit – the oldest continuously-operating roller coaster in America – as "Most Nostalgic."[9]

Though this fact may have been concealed from many, the real hidden gem in this story lies a few blocks away in a densely urbanized section of Irondequoit. It's a wonderful slice of sentimentality, perfect for the young and old alike. I didn't discover it. My daughter Catarina did while interning for a photographer the summer before her senior year in high school. She didn't realize just what a gem she had discovered. It was the oldest miniature golf course in the United States.

Miniature golf began as a sport for elites and its courses were actually artistically designed miniature versions (though not replicas) of regulation courses.[10] After World War I, released from its highbrow roots, miniature golf became the rage of the masses. The year 1926 marked the advent of rooftop miniature golf and the Manhattan skyline soon found itself with 150 such courses, each bringing in handsome profits to their owners.[11] You would think the stock market crash of 1929 would have quelled excitement for this leisure time activity. It didn't. In fact, 1929 saw the creation of the first miniature golf franchise, Tom Thumb Golf, and while the rest of the stock market sagged into oblivion, Tom Thumb Golf soared like an 1990's Internet stock, quickly capturing a quarter of the entire miniature golf market.[12] And so began the era tabbed by miniature golf historian John Margolies as the "1930 Gold Rush."[13] Less expensive than comparable entertainment alternatives, people often chose miniature golf over movies.[14] Alas, much like the Internet boom of the 1990's, the "get-rich-quick" era of "midget golf" came to an abrupt end in 1931.[15] It wasn't until post-World War II prosperity that a new era of miniature golf would return, albeit a quite different one, one filled with oversized structures and Rube-Goldberg-like ball paths.[16]

But we move too fast. Go back to 1930 and the height of the miniature golf gold rush. In that year, in the middle of a typical working class community, the Tall Maples Miniature Golf Course was built. Now called Whispering Pines, it, together with the adjacent Parkside Diner, is currently owned by two brothers, Jim and Greg Papas. Parkside Diner and Miniature Golf is nestled off the shores of Lake Ontario in the Seabreeze neighborhood of Irondequoit, Monroe County.

One Saturday my son Peter's high school football team played in Irondequoit. After the game I visited Whispering Pines. It really is a comfortable setting. Surrounded by trees, it's a small, shaded park amidst a modest urban neighborhood. The course itself is a throwback of sorts. Without the ostentatious glamor of modern courses, it's perfect for younger kids as the holes lack the complicated geometry of the newer layouts. Though a full 18 holes, it also has the advantage of a small footprint, meaning mom and dad can sit on a nearby bench and sip an ice cold pop without the fear they'd lose sight of their kids, who can play safely within the park's fenced-in perimeter.

I snapped a few pictures and then went in to the diner to find one of the owners. It was a busy place for a Saturday, but the waitresses were most accommodating. Jim Papas was in the back cooking for the crowd and, despite my insistence he not be disturbed, his staff went and got him. Jim told me he and his brother had owned and operated the Parkside Diner since 1990. They purchased the golf course in 1996 and, as far as they know, there have been only two prior owners of the property. "We thought the miniature golf course would be a great investment and easy to operate since we were already on the premises. At the time of purchase, we really knew nothing of the history of the course," says Papas.

In 2011, they hired Bob Horwath from Cape May, New Jersey to renovate the entire course. Papas says Horwath "spent three weeks in Rochester and brought in a nice nautical theme to the course. The feedback from our customers has been wonderful."

Being the oldest existing miniature golf course in America, Whispering Pines has received its fair share of national accolades. In 2002, it was listed on the National Register of Historic Places.[17] It's been named by the NileGuide as one of "America's Classic Miniature Golf Venues"[18] and has even been featured on ESPN.[19] "The course is a landmark the whole town can be proud of," says Papas.

One more thing about Whispering Pines: its builders dug up cobblestones from the historic Erie Canal and brought them in to create the original course in 1930. By strange coincidence, the location of our next hidden gem got its very name from that same canal.

CHAPTER 17: *LOW BRIDGE, EVERYBODY DOWN*

By the time Thomas S. Allen wrote *The Erie Canal Song* (as the song is commonly known) in 1905,[1] the famous canal had already been in operation for 80 years. Allen chose the title *Low Bridge, Everybody Down* because the canal had just ditched the mules for steam power and he wanted to pay homage to the animal so critical to canal operations.[2] That Allen celebrates the mule Sal tells us he's commemorating a then not-too-distant past. Incidentally, the title wasn't the only thing about the song that changed over the years, including, ironically, the word "years." The original lyrics were "fifteen years on the Erie Canal," referring to the length of the partnership between Sal and his owner, while the new lyrics are "fifteen miles on the Erie Canal," referring to how many miles an average real-life Sal would pull a barge before resting.[3]

Today we think of the Erie Canal as a pleasant linear recreation park we get to play in every summer. It's hardly a hidden gem given its notoriety (I mean, besides *The Erie Canal Song*, there are at least five other folk songs about it[4]). We cannot, however, understate the power of the canal. Just as Joseph Ellicott had earlier predicted, the Canal would spur both economic and population growth into and around the Greater Western New York Region. And as we'll discover in a later chapter, its early life led to a dramatic national cultural phenomenon. But you'll have to wait for that story.

This story is about one of the many canal towns that sprung up with the advent of the Canal. In fact, it's the town where the final piece of the Canal was constructed. Here's why. It involves two things we've already addressed: 1) the Mesozoic Era that created Greater Western New York's geology; and, 2) Niagara Falls, specifically, why the water falls the way it does. It's called the "Niagara Escarpment" and it stretches all the way from Watertown, New York across the Great Lakes through Wisconsin and into Illinois.[5] The

Niagara Escarpment is a geological formation known as a "cuesta" – essentially layers of rock with a slight upwards tilt.[6] At the edge of a cuesta, the different layers erode at different rates and, like the Niagara Escarpment, often form a cliff.[7]

The Niagara Escarpment is not only responsible for the Niagara Falls, but also for the Genesee Falls in Rochester. While these wonders of nature certainly merit the awe they've received, it's the man-made waterfall created by the Erie Canal in the town of Lockport that we honor in this chapter. The Niagara Escarpment presented a never-before-seen engineering challenge for Canal builders. Somehow, they needed to devise a method for moving the water up and down the sixty foot drop caused by the Escarpment.

Nathan Roberts came up with the idea of a dual set of five locks, considered by many at the time (and even today) an engineering marvel.[8] Visiting America to celebrate our country's 50th birthday in 1825, the French General Marquis de Lafayette, after seeing Niagara Falls, went out of his way to travel to Lockport's famous "Flight of Five" locks and wrote, "Lockport and Niagara County contain the greatest natural (Niagara Falls) and artificial (Lockport Locks) wonders, second only to the wonders of freedom and equal rights."[9] Within a decade after his visit, Asher Torrance, owner of a Lockport foundry, and Washington Hunt, a lawyer and future governor, had the idea of reversing Lafayette's path to direct some of the thousands of Canal passengers on a 23 mile detour to become America's first tourists[10], but we've already covered the consequences of that in our chapter on Niagara Falls.

During the construction of Roberts' locks, contractors bored the first tunnel through the Mesozoic rock, ostensibly to carry surplus canal water.[10] More than a generation later in the 1850's, Birdsill Holly, inventor of the fire hydrant, central steam heat and the rotary pump, blasted the 1,600 foot Hydraulic Tunnel through the literally rock-solid limestone.[11] The tunnel used natural gravity to create a water race that powered adjacent industries.

Back then, the tunnel was filled with water. It was last used in 1941. Today it is an empty shell – and a very cool place to visit. And by cool, I don't just mean "hip," "jazzy" or "wow-did-you-see-that!" No, I mean temperature wise. Just like any underground journey, the tunnel remains relatively cool no matter how hot the outside temperature is. And it all comes courtesy of Lockport Cave and Underground Boat Ride. Billing itself as "America's longest underground boat ride," your flat-bottomed vessel floats in two feet of water as you proceed through the latter half of the tunnel on what's been described as a "peaceful and eerie" tour.[12]

Once you emerge from the tunnel, your journey continues as the boat passes under the widest bridge (399') in the United States and then – my favorite – the legendary "upside-down" railroad bridge.[13] It's not really upside down, it just looks that way. It's really a deck truss bridge, itself a less well-used but still very viable form of the more popular truss bridge. The reason why you don't see deck truss bridges too often is because they require an awful lot of space beneath the bridge, space not usually available.

Thanks to the Niagara Escarpment, that space comes in plentiful supply. Unless, perhaps, if you're traveling by boat.

"Low Bridge, Everybody Down…"

And just as the "upside-down" bridge symbolized the railroad's eventual dominance over the canal, so do we move into this past future in the next chapter.

CHAPTER 18: POSTCARD PERFECT, IN ANY SEASON

On July 4th, 1828, nearly three years after the opening of the Erie Canal, Charles Carroll, 91 years old and the last surviving signer of the Declaration of Independence, turned over the first shovel of dirt, marking the beginning of construction of the Baltimore and Ohio Railroad, America's first railroad.[1] With this single action, the Erie Canal's death notice was signed. Even before the B&O was created, however, the Mohawk and Hudson Railroad was incorporated in New York on April 17th, 1826, less than six months after Governor Dewitt Clinton dedicated the grand opening of his "ditch."[2] Ironically, the purpose of the Mohawk and Hudson was to compete with the Erie Canal. When New York's railroad finally managed to finance itself, (delayed financing allowed the B&O to be constructed first), it could be built. Completed a year later in August, 1831,[3] it took less than an hour to travel the 17-mile rail line compared to the all-day meandering 40-mile segment of the Erie Canal it replaced.[4] The name of the steam locomotive to make this first run: none other than *The Dewitt Clinton*.

By the time Birdsill Holly made his Hydraulic Tunnel in Lockport, President Millard Fillmore and four of his cabinet members had already sat aboard the first two trains to travel across the 459 mile mainline of the New York & Erie Railroad between Dunkirk and Port Jervis, New Jersey.[5] The Erie Railroad, in catering to New York's southern tier, bypassed Lockport and the Canal altogether. On the other hand, in 1853 eight separately operating railroads, all running from Albany to Buffalo and including two through Lockport, would consolidate to become the New York Central.[6] The future in transportation had arrived, and Greater Western New York would soon find itself right in the thick of it.

I'll save that for the next chapter. Here, we pay homage to the little engines that could; all those short line railroads that once traversed Greater Western New York only to disappear into the afterthought of history.

Except not all of them disappeared. This is the story of one that didn't. Actually, it's a story of one that tried its best to disappear, but just couldn't. Here's what I mean:

In 1852, the Attica and Allegany Valley Railroad was formed but construction was halted in 1855 shortly after grading had begun. The Attica and Arcade Railroad was then organized in 1870 but was unable to raise funds to even start building. In 1880 the Tonawanda Valley Railroad was created and a year later actually had revenue runs between Attica and Arcade. Apparently so excited by this success, they incorporated the Tonawanda Valley and Cuba Railroad in 1881. But then the money problems started and finally, after a severe snowstorm (it is Greater Western New York, after all), the line to Cuba was closed in 1885. In 1886 a continuing decline in service forced the road to close south of Sandusky. Finally, in 1891 the entire railroad was sold. The Attica and Freedom Railroad was then formed, but it went into bankruptcy and was sold in 1894. That same year the Buffalo, Attica and Arcade Railroad was incorporated. This new entity rebuilt the line and service began anew by the end of 1895. In 1897, a two-mile connection was built, giving this once isolated short-line access to the main line railroads. Alas, in 1902, the Clear Creek bridge (between Arcade and Sandusky) collapsed and, without the funds to rebuild it, the line was closed between Arcade and Freedom. In 1904, the Buffalo & Susquehanna Railway absorbed the Buffalo, Attica and Arcade Railroad, but the B&S went belly-up in 1916 and on March 10, 1917, the Buffalo, Attica and Arcade Railroad ceased to exist. Locals, concerned they might lose all rail service, quickly formed the Arcade and Attica Railroad and bought the dormant assets of the Buffalo, Attica and Arcade Railroad. (This entire section is condensed from a more comprehensive summary provided in Kenneth Springirth's book *Arcade and Attica Railroad.*[7])

Things seemed to go a bit smoother from then on. The Arcade and Attica Railroad was so successful during the Great Depression, it didn't need to lay off a single employee.[8] On the other hand, heavy rains in January 1957 caused the Tonawanda Creek to overflow its banks, washing out hundreds of feet of track.[9] With little business between North Java and Attica, the Board of Directors decided to abandon the line rather than rebuild it.[10] To this day, the Arcade and Attica Railroad operates only between Arcade and North Java.

In 1962, faced with declining freight revenues, the railroad decided to go into the steam engine passenger excursion business. This is where I enter the picture.

My parents knew I liked trains. I noticed them wherever we went. I got excited whenever we had to stop for one. I made crazy comments whenever

I'd see them. Once, when I was four, we were crossing Seneca Yard on the Ridge Road bridge in Lackawanna when, noticing the string of automobile laden cars, I turned to my mother and said, "when I grow up, I want to be just like the guy who owns that train. With all those cars he must be rich."

So it was no surprise that my parents took my brother Kenny and I to ride the Arcade and Attica Railroad soon after it opened its steam excursion. What was a surprise was that my mother convinced my father to allow my uncle to tag along. He's only three years older than me, meaning back then he was just as much a kid as I was, if not more so.

I don't remember how old I was, but I was old enough to remember the raw joy of riding on a real train for the very first time. And that it was a steam locomotive with bright orange cars made it all the better. We (well at least my brother and I) behaved well enough in the coaches for my father to agree to take us out on the open air gondola. My uncle got to go, too, but, apparently, he didn't have to behave.

When we went out to the low-sided railroad car, we had to be careful. It wasn't as if we had to be careful walking between the open platform cars. That was easy. We had to be careful of the soot and ashes coming from the engine's smokestack. Depending on the direction of the train and the direction of the wind, sometimes we'd get sprayed with very tiny, but still hot cinders. I don't remember ever getting hit by any.

What did strike me back then, as it does today, was the placid vista along the route of the leisurely-paced train. With the exception of a few obviously modern structures, very little has changed since the Tonawanda Valley Railroad first ran in the latter half of the nineteenth century. Slowly snaking through the gentle rolling farmland of Wyoming County, it was as if we were riding through a Currier and Ives setting.

Coincidentally, the excursion stopped at what I thought was an open field but now know to be the quaint hamlet of Curriers. We detrained and the engineer permitted us to inspect the locomotive and its cabin "as long as we didn't touch anything." My uncle touched something. Luckily, he didn't burn himself, but he did get good and greasy dirty. Boy was my father mad. He held it in. He even let my uncle ride in the gondola on the return trip.

Several decades later and with much greater knowledge, I took my own young family on that same trip. This time I knew more of the history of the Arcade and Attica, as well as the history of northeast railroads in general. For example, I now recognized the passenger cars we sat in were original Delaware, Lackawanna & Western "Boonton" coaches. These classic cars, which ran on the DL&W from the 1920's until the dreaded merger with the Erie in 1960, are much beloved by railfans. The Arcade and Attica also has several matching DL&W combines, an even rarer piece of rolling stock.

I could see the genuine excitement in my kids' eyes as we rode the train and toured the steam locomotive. It reminded me of a certain little boy's eyes some thirty or forty years earlier. I sigh now, just thinking about it. Anyone with the least bit of yearning for the nostalgia of yesteryear's yesteryear – the real hidden gem of the Arcade and Attica Railroad – must make it a habit to visit this jewel on a regular basis. It'll recharge your batteries.

The unfortunate truth about all things railroad is, eventually, they're gone. So it's important to experience them before a new future removes them from the physical world and consigns them to world of memories, just like it has done to our next hidden gem.

CHAPTER 19: A BRIDGE TOO QUIET

I never understood why trains lure me as much as they do. Don't get me wrong. I love trains. I just can't figure out why. I mean, I was born at the dawn of the Space Age, watched *Star Trek* when it was still on the air and followed NASA's lunar program with diligent pride. Heck, I even majored in physics and astronomy, served on the Strasenburgh Planetarium's 40th Anniversary Task Force and created an official astronomy outreach project (AstronomyTop100.com) that received the official endorsement of the United Nations during the International Year of Astronomy in 2009.

Many were the times when I thought I was finally done with trains. But, like the mob to Michael Corleone, they kept pulling me back in. Back to a past I never knew. Back to a past that was the past when my parents were kids. Indeed, it became an obsession early in my marriage. I would drag my wife (and eventually my children) across abandoned meadows to identify the architectural remains of our region's industrial past. I dreamed of creating a museum quality diorama in my basement as a tribute to Greater Western New York's railroads, with a special concentration on the spaghetti-like network of steel ribbon located from Blasdell Junction, through Lackawanna and into South Buffalo. Unfortunately, a chronic back injury kept me stalled. I never got any further than East Salamanca. If you can get as far as the real Medina, in Orleans County, you can actually see the largest HO layout east of the Mississippi River in the Medina Railroad Museum. The Museum also offers a 2-hour 34 mile seasonal train excursion through the Erie Canal Heritage Corridor between Medina and Lockport. We visited the Museum as my Father's Day gift once. The kids (and the dad) loved it.

Growing up in Blasdell, you couldn't help but like trains. You woke up each morning to the cheerful chime of today's arrivals. You went to sleep every night to the mournful cries of departing freights, their wailing whistles' slow *ritardando* fading along the twin lake shore lines of the New York Central and Nickel Plate railroads. On cold clear winter nights, the crisp air carried that fade to forever, or at least until a new horn signaled the approach to a nearer grade crossing.

At one time, counting shared rights-of-way, up to five Class One railroads crossed and crisscrossed through not more than a quarter mile of Lake Avenue. Each day I went to school, I crossed those tracks. Each Sunday I went to church, I crossed those tracks. Even now, for some reason, I go out of my way to cross those tracks, though the New York Central's High Line has returned to grade, GB Tower that once guarded the Erie-Nickel Plate crossing has left without a trace and history has consumed many of those wonderful truss monsters that long ago loomed like large catheters feeding the arteries of the Bethlehem Steel complex.

The Lackawanna Railroad has always been my favorite railroad, probably because that's where I first lived (Victory Avenue). It was only later in life I would discover, while each derived its name from the same Pennsylvania river, the railroad never ventured into the Steel City, as it terminated at the foot of Main Street in Buffalo. (Yes, I know the *Erie*-Lackawanna railroad traveled through Lackawanna, but, if you know me, you'd know what I think of that merger.)

Ah, the merger between the infamous Erie Railroad (ironically, given its many journeys into bankruptcy, nicknamed "Old Reliable") and the pristine Delaware, Lackawanna and Western Railroad (its moniker, "The Route of the Phoebe Snow," evoking a chaste purity found only through the burning of anthracite, rather than bituminous, coal). The October, 1960 merger represented the dying breath of a once proud – and routinely profitable – DL&W, done in by Hurricane Diane, from whose 1957 devastation it could never recover. Ironically, the Erie and the DL&W had once been allies in the New York City to Buffalo rail competition, with the DL&W transferring its Buffalo bound freight cars to the Erie in Binghamton. Then, in 1883, the DL&W, no doubt finally justifying the "and Western" in its name, completed its own line from Binghamton to Buffalo. From that day, the two railroads became bitter rivals.

By the way, do you know the biggest obstacle faced by the DL&W in its quest to build its link to Buffalo? None other than Dansville Hill. Rising nearly 900 feet from its base, this hunk of solid rock very nearly proved the undoing of the DL&W's version of manifest destiny. Still, the combined grit of corporate brass and (primarily) Italian immigrants – aided by the best explosives available at the time – blasted a rock shelf halfway up East Hill that "left a scar entirely across its fair face."[1]

Once the DL&W completed its standard gauge iron superhighway to Buffalo, it became the shortest route to the Queen City from New York City; thus, besting the Erie's broad gauge route in more ways than one. Time tables might not have made it the fastest, thanks again to the slow climb through Dansville, and, indeed, it would be the New York Central that would soon lay claim to the fastest train. And where would this speed record occur?

While pulling the Central's *Empire State Express*, Engine 999 became the first steam locomotive to pass the 100 mph barrier when it clocked a top speed of 112½ mph on a special run between Batavia and Buffalo.[2] Of course, the day before, on May 9, 1893, it had already become the first vehicle on wheels to surpass 100 mph when it travelled the 69 miles from Rochester to Buffalo in 68 minutes, with an average top-end travel speed of 102 mph.[3] Reporters and train officials recorded the official speed record the next day (May 10, 1893) on the return trip as Engine 999 passed through the village of Crittenden in Alden, Erie County.[4] Just to complete the Greater Western New York connection, the engineer of Engine 999 heading the *Empire State Express* was Charlie Hogan of Batavia.[5]

Unlike its most famous train, the *20th Century Limited*, which provided pretty much non-stop service from New York to Chicago (OK, OK, it did stop for refreshments at around midnight in Buffalo), the *Empire State Express* actually serviced the cities of New York State. The *Express* was the New York Central's "New York State" train, traveling from New York City through all the cities of the Erie Canal (that's from Albany to Buffalo) and on to Niagara Falls. Engine 999 still exists, but, poignantly, it sits like an anachronistic display within the Chicago Museum of Industry, a gateway to the museum's once famous (and now mostly outdated) model railroad. Perhaps one day Engine 999 will find itself in a more suitable location graced by a model railroad display depicting the true height of 20th century industry (hint: Central Terminal).

Just as the New York Central owned the northern tier of Greater Western New York, it was the Erie and the DL&W battling it out for supremacy in the southern tier. The DL&W had several advantages. Built two decades after the Erie, it could identify profitable municipalities and build a direct route to Buffalo. The Erie, on the other hand, had to re-gauge its track from broad to standard (i.e., the gauge modern railroads use today) and it had to build a reliable route to Buffalo (remember, it originally terminated in Dunkirk).

Therein lay the problem. Its original route through the undulating hills of Allegany County required trains to climb steep grades; hence, slowing them down. In 1905, the Erie Railroad, through its subsidy the Genesee River Railroad, began buying property for its new "River Line," a 34-mile cutoff between Portage and Cuba.[6] Along that line the railroad would have to cross the expansive mile long Genesee River valley in the Town of Caneadea just north of the Town of Belfast in Allegany County.[7] This deck girder bridge would rise 141 feet above the valley floor, extend a total of 3,121 feet and require 3,871 tons of steel,[8] making it, as near as I can tell, the longest railroad bridge ever constructed in Greater Western New York.

There's a more fascinating fact about the Genesee Viaduct. Stretching from one end to the other, this structure dominated the docile valley of the Genesee. In the otherwise tranquil setting of the slow snaking river, the man-made behemoth interrupted the otherwise placid fertility of this quiet preserve. Its twenty-five towers, each with two spindly steel legs resting on a blockish concrete foot, stood as a magnificent testament to progress, industry and economic vitality. Actually, there were only 48 feet, as one tower rose directly over the river. Rather than individual feet, both legs rested on a concrete pier. Except there's a problem with this particular pier. The company engineer who drew up the plans for the bridge assumed the Genesee River flowed to the south. As a result, the pier formed a point facing north. The river actually flows north, so the pier's south end should have had the point. When Harry Benjamin, who worked on the carpenter gang, pointed this out while the pier was being built, his observations were ignored because Harry "was just a farm boy, not an engineer."[9] As a result, the pier was built incorrectly.

Alas, time marches on, old industries fade, new methods take their place and short-sighted bean counters, perhaps inspired by short-sighted laws, made short-sighted decisions. The results of these decisions forever take away once wondrous and utile resources from all future generations. So, too, it has been with the railroads. When the Erie Railroad merged with the weakened DL&W, Erie management had the advantage of vigor, and it was the Lackawanna's lines that were torn up west of Binghamton. This included the track across the face of Dansville Hill; thus, stripping the chance for rail passengers to ever again experience the "never to be forgotten" view from the summit of East Hill, where, "as far as the eye can reach in almost every direction there opens a panorama that cannot be excelled."[10]

Fatefully, what the Erie Railroad did to the Lackawanna Railroad, Conrail did to the Erie-Lackawanna. Though I am a Lackawanna fan, this revenge tastes just as bitter. The last train on the River Line ran on Mother's Day in 1980[11] and the forever frugal Conrail razed the steel superstructure crossing the Genesee Valley the next year. This was before my mind turned once more to trains. I never got a chance to see with my own eyes the Genesee Viaduct in all its glory. The closest I've come is the similarly styled viaduct crossing the Genesee at the south end of Letchworth State Park. Historic in its own right, this former Erie Bridge is a gem you can still embrace.

As for much of the rest of the one-time heyday of railroads in our region, it's best to put on your archeologist's hat, as it will take some effort and a willingness to explore if you want to uncover anything of interest. And there are things to uncover. But it's not just the discovery that excites; it's the intrigue of the journey that lures you in.

There's something positively Indiana Jones-ish about walking through now overgrown fields searching for a clue to a former water tower's foundation. Of course, now, just unearthing the remnants of an ancient right-of-way brings a glow to my face. For instance, though the Genesee Viaduct no longer hogs the vista of the Genesee Valley between Filmore and Belfast like it once did, traces remain.

I know. I've gone there. I've travelled down Route 19, one eye on the road, one eye on the river valley. The steel may have been scrapped and sold to Japan[12], but the rock – or in this case, concrete – lingers. You can still see the wrong-way pier. And the cement feet, arranged in tidy rows two by two like oh-so-many midget Easter Island statues, still mark the path where the giant once walked, replaced today by an all too quiet ghost.

And speaking of rock, one of these days, while travelling on Route 390 above Dansville, take a peak across the valley. You'll see East Hill. And if the light's right, or if you're travelling in the winter, you'll see a stone scar athwart its face. Man might be able to take a bridge away, but only nature will remove that wound. The Dansville Cut endures on East Hill, a tribute to ingenuity, engineering and resolution.

Such is the nature of some hidden gems, like these, where rock best tells the story, both when man shapes rock, and, as we'll see in the next chapter, most especially when man makes rock.

CHAPTER 20: SEEDS OF A NEW MOVEMENT

The Erie Canal made Buffalo. Joseph Dart made Buffalo memorable. Through Joseph Ellicott and the establishment of Greater Western New York west of the Genesee River, we've seen the importance of the canal from before it was even drawn up. We've witnessed how its opening paved the way for the creation of America's first tourist destination: Niagara Falls. We'll discover in a few chapters how it allowed our region to become ground zero for a cultural and spiritual revolution.

The primary impact of the Erie Canal, however, was commercial. Soon after it began operation in 1825, the cost of shipping a ton of grain dropped from $100 to a mere $10.[1] Cities sprang up along its path with amazing speed. Rochester's population grew from 331 in 1815 to almost 10,000 by 1830, prompting Nathanial Hawthorne to comment (in 1835), "The town had sprung up like a mushroom..."[2] One wonders what the famed early-American author would have thought if he had found out one of the later architectural wonders in the Flour City would be called "The Mushroom House."

Buffalo, representing the western terminus of the Erie Canal and the eastern terminus of the midwestern Great Lakes, quickly developed into a transshipment center. Grain arriving from lake freighters was trans-loaded to canal boats in Buffalo. The City's growth exploded. Caroline Gilman, in *The Poetry of Travelling in the United States* (1838), said, "I had thought the other western towns great, but at Buffalo I almost rubbed my eyes to see if all was real."[3] Buffalo doesn't appear on the U.S. Bureau of Census list of urban places until the 1830 census, when it ranked #27 in the country with 8,668 (behind Rochester's #25 at 9,207).[4] Oddly, given its strategic location, Buffalo (at #16 with 42,985 residents) doesn't pass Rochester (at #21 with 36, 403 residents) until the 1850 census.[5] Incidentally, Buffalo would first break into the top ten (at #10 with a population of 81,129) in the 1860 census, when Rochester would be #18 with 48,204 people.[6]

What might explain Buffalo's leapfrog over Rochester between 1840 and 1850? For one thing, at the canal's outset, there was very little grain to be shipped (and that was primarily from Ohio).[7] However, by the late 1830s, Michigan and Illinois had begun to ship grain to Buffalo, causing concern the Queen City's harbor would soon become one big naval traffic jam.[8] From 1835 to 1841, the amount of grain transshipped in Buffalo increased from 112,000 bushels to more than 2 million bushels.[9] The train would come to Buffalo in 1843[10] and begin to steal traffic from the Erie Canal; thus, providing some relief from the bottleneck. But the real hero did his dirty work the year before, and that work would eventually make Buffalo world famous.

In 1821, Joseph Dart, aged 22 and unmarried, came to the Village of Buffalo (for those keeping score, its population at that time was a mere 1,800) and set up a retail store on the southeast corner of Main and Swan Streets.[11] Selling hats, caps and furs, Dart was quick to befriend the Indians, even learning their language, and it is said Chief Red Jacket visited his store often.[12] In 1842, Dart's cunning eye and business acumen sensed the coming congestion caused by the increasing grain shipments. In the fall of that year, he erected a storage facility for grain, and, in adopting a mechanical system he attributed to one Oliver Evans used in flour mills, Dart created the first steam operated grain elevator in the world.[13] Among the features of his invention, the now familiar "marine legs" that poked into the ships' holds like an elephant's trunk to automatically scoop out the grain.

As might be expected of Western New York ingenuity, Dart had his skeptics. Mahlon King, one of Dart's competitors, scoffed at the invention, telling Dart, "Irish backs are the cheapest elevators ever built."[14] But Dart would have his day, and, less than fifteen years later, with ten grain elevators with a storage capacity of 1.5 million bushels, Buffalo would exceed Odessa (Russia), London (England) and Rotterdam (Holland) to become the world's largest grain port.[15] Ironically, the success of the grain elevator likely led to the hiring of more Irish laborers than before.

As testament to the impact of Dart's invention, Samuel M. Welch, a well-known Buffalo attorney, military man and author, once wrote of Buffalo Harbor in the 1830s, "As said of canal boats, the vessels were of small tonnage and capacity as compared with the ships of the present, and were increasing in number. After a succession of westerly winds they gathered in such numbers in the creek that you could pass from one to another across the creek on any part of it from the light-house pier to the foot of Washington Street, thus materially impeding the process of docking and unloading the vessels; all of which is changed since 'Dart's' elevators came into use."[16]

But while the elevators quickly gained fame, that was about it. English novelist Anthony Trollope wrote of his visit to Buffalo in 1861, "over and above the elevators there is nothing especially worthy of remark at Buffalo."[17] As resilient as ever, Western New Yorkers were too busy to pay heed to this itinerant British subject. Business was booming, and, unfortunately, so were the elevators. Dart, who would eventually take to selling lumber, built his first elevator out of wood. In fact, most of the first elevators were made of wood. Grain tends to explode or catch fire easily and wood tends to burn. And so, too, grain elevators.

That last surviving wood elevator was the Wollenberg elevator at 133 Goodyear Avenue, although its lineage goes back further. Wollenberg was constructed using the wood left over from the demolition of Kellogg "A" in 1912.[18] Wollenberg lasted until October 2, 2006, when, you guessed it, it caught fire and burned. The City of Buffalo razed its remnants the next day.[19]

To thwart this combustible tendency, in 1897, both the Great Northern and the Electric elevators were constructed with materials designed to reduce the risk of fire and explosion. Each of these eliminated the number one cause of fire: fire. That's right. Remember, Dart's novelty was that he used steam to power the elevator. Steam requires boiling water and boiling water requires – you guessed it again – fire. The Great Northern and the Electric elevators were among the first to take advantage of the newfound resource available cheaply in Western New York: hydro-electric power. This eliminated the need for steam, coal, fire and the usual ingredients that led to conflagration. It also eliminated the space taken up by steam-related paraphernalia. That meant more room for storage and, indeed, with a capacity of 2.5 million bushels, the Great Northern elevator was, for at least a short time, the world's largest grain elevator.[20]

The Electric and Great Northern elevators were also among the first elevators built in Buffalo with materials other than wood. They used steel bins and, in the case of Great Northern, according to Timothy Tielman, Executive Director of The Campaign for Greater Buffalo History, Architecture & Culture, it is a "one-of-a-kind elevator" that "represents an important advance in the application and aesthetics of elevator technology."[21] Now, if you drive by it, you might think, "that doesn't look like a grain elevator." And you'd be right. Unlike like most grain elevators you see, the bins of Great Northern are enclosed in a brick building. This protects the steel bins (the ones inside Great Northern are the originals).[22]

Anyone taking the Skyway or Fuhrmann Boulevard or even Ganson Street can easily spot the Great Northern elevator, probably the most notable of the remaining elevators that once defined Buffalo's waterfront. Today, that view is marked by the vast bulk of the concrete elevators, which use a technology developed immediately after the construction of the Great Northern (and is why you don't see too many brick-sheathed steel bin elevators). The one unique characteristic about concrete is that it is, for all intents and purposes, rock. It might be man-made, but it's still rock. And rock, being structurally recalcitrant (a.k.a., "hard") is enormously expensive to remove. It's probably why those footpads and the pier still linger as the last vestige of the ghost of the Genesee Viaduct we spoke of in the previous chapter.

Hardness, of course, can be a good thing, and it may be the only reason these monolithic monsters remain standing. There are a couple of classic views you should try to go see first-hand (if you haven't already done it). You can take in these vistas from the comfort and convenience of your own (or somebody else's) automobile. As a matter of fact, I recommend it be someone else's automobile, or at least getting someone else to drive while you sight-see. The panoramic is awe-inspiring, so you really need to stare at it for a while before it sinks in. That's why someone else should be driving.

Classic View #1: The first classic view is from the Skyway. Unfortunately, the best way to view it is by going south on the north-bound side of the street (you can actually do this using Google Maps, or at least I was able to do it this way). Once you cross the Buffalo River (approximately above the old DL&W train sheds) start looking down the City Ship Canal. You'll see the General Mills elevator and Mill complex. This is the part that smells like Cheerios (assuming you have your car windows open. The elevator is the northern most building and is white. It also has the General Mills logo on it. The Mill complex is to the south and immediately abuts to the City Ship Canal. This is the building to focus on. In particular, pay attention to the three cylindrical towers sandwiched in between the Mill and another building. These towers are part of the Washburn-Crosby elevator built in 1903. We'll come back to that.

Going further south, You'll see from St. Mary's Cement (formerly Kellogg) and then Agway (formerly GLF). Kellogg is a traditional series of white cylinders in two separate groupings connected by a high bridge. The grayish GLF with its darkened windows looks like something straight out of a post-apocalyptic science fiction movie. Moving further south and butting up to the City Ship Canal is the famous Great Northern, whose aged brick façade looks more at home with the old Bethlehem Steel buildings found further to the south. Farther behind Great Northern, you'll see more grain elevators in the vicinity of the Ohio Street Bridge. But rather than strain our eyes from the Skyway, why not go straight to Ohio Street.

Classic View #2: Well, you could do that, and, having been there, the view looking towards the east up the river is fairly impressive. It looks as though the river cut a canyon through the grain elevators. But there's actually a better view. Go to the north end of the Ohio Street Bridge and turn right on St. Clair. Follow St. Clair to the end and turn right on South Street. Just before the railroad crossing stop and look southwest up the river toward the Ohio Street Bridge. On your right is the very long Standard Elevator. On your left, from closest to farthest, is the flat wall of the Lake & Rail, followed by the Perot Elevator, then the American Elevator and finally the 1940 extension of all that remains from the Electric Elevator. Remember the American Elevator.

Classic View #3: From almost any vantage point, you can see the quarter-mile long Concrete Central. With its 4.5 million bushel capacity making it the largest transfer elevator in the world when it was completed in 1917,[23] it's impossible not to notice the isolated gray mammoth hugging the banks on the bend of the Buffalo River. Abandoned in 1966, in 2003 Concrete Central was placed on the National Register of Historic Places.[24]

Perhaps you've passed by these towering stone shrines so many times, you've come to ignore them. What you shouldn't ignore, however, is their historical and internationally renowned import. Both Trollope in 1861 and later Rudyard Kipling in the 1880s, after visiting the Queen City, would describe Buffalo's grain elevators in terms of a beastly metaphor, a line of elephantine warehouses whose trunks sucked the life out of the passive lake boats docked by their sides. The Europeans would return after the turn of the century. This time, it was serious.

In 1909, Walter Gropius visited Buffalo and when his essay *"Die Entwicklung moderner Industriebaukunst"* appeared in 1913's *Jahrbuch des Deutschen Werkbundes*, it included images of two Buffalo grain elevators – Washburn-Crosby (see Classic View #1) and the Dakota (demolished in 1966).[25] Gropius then shocked the staid intelligentsia of European architecture by telling the world that America, not Germany, was the "Industrial Motherland."[26] Reyner Banham, in his 1986 book *A Concrete Atlantis*, says, "The Washburn-Crosby complex constitute the most internationally influential structures ever put up in America."[27]

In 1919, Swiss-born architect and theorist Charles-Edouard Jenneret-Gris, Le Corbusier asked Gropius if he could use his pictures of the Buffalo Elevators.[28] Le Corbusier's 1923 publication *Vers une Architecture (Towards a New Architecture)* featured these grain elevators as prototypes for an industrially rooted style, calling American grain elevators "the magnificent first fruits of a new age" and stating "American engineers overwhelm with their calculations our expiring architecture."[29]

With *Towards a New Architecture* fast becoming the bible of this new modern architecture, Erich Mendelsohn, taken by the pictures, visited Buffalo in 1924 to see the "elevator fortresses" first-hand.[30] So enthralled, in a letter to his wife he described Buffalo's grain elevators as "mountainous silos, incredibly space-conscious, but creating space… I took photographs like mad.

Everything else so far now seemed to have been shaped interim to my silo dreams."[31] Mendelsohn published *Amerika: Bilderbuch eines Architekten* two years later and included photographs of several Buffalo elevators.[32]

All this work was limited to the French or German-speaking world until 1929, when Bruno Taut published *Modern Architecture*, which, as you can guess from the title, was written in English. This book presented a new Buffalo elevator – Concrete Central – to the world. The power of this gigantic edifice is best captured by Banham, who describes his feelings upon approaching Concrete Central this way: "I was looking at one of the great remains of a high and mighty period of constructive art in North America, a historical monument in its own right."[33]

Walter Curt Behrendt in 1927's *Der Sieg des Neuen Baustils*, would summarize the feeling of these thought-leaders of modern architecture as follows:

> "To do justice, it is necessary to say, and this will probably surprise the reader, that it was the example of America that gave the impulse to the German architects when they first tried to clarify the problem of structure. To be sure, this impulse did not originate in the skyscraper . . . but the simple structures of industrial building such as grain elevators and big silos . . . These examples of modern engineering, designed for practical use only, and obviously without any decorative assistance from an architect, made a deep impression by their simple structure reduced to basic forms of geometry such as cubes and cylinders. They were conceived as patterns exemplifying once more the essence of the pure form of use, gaining its impressive effect from its bare structure."[34]

Sometimes the hidden gem isn't what you see in front of your eyes, it's what you don't see in front of your eyes. Forever silent, their colors ever so slowly blending with their surroundings, the ubiquitous grain elevators can seem to melt into the everyday background of our daily lives. Yet they carry within them secrets of a movement that defined twentieth century architecture.

Commuters pass through these great fields of modernist minimalism without a hint. In a similar way, our next hidden gem lies preserved, overlooked and noiseless beneath the feet – or, more appropriate, wheels – of a different city's workers.

CHAPTER 21: LIKE A BRIDGE OVER ROMAN WATERS

I t's proof of its importance that the Erie Canal seeps into many of our chapters. Personally, the Canal never really captivated me. As a kid, the only form of transportation that earned my attention were NASA's manned rockets. And the equally American-made 1964/65 Ford Mustang. (Yep, that's right. Even James Bond's famous Aston-Martin failed to draw but a mere glance of my eyes.)

Now, I did admit I liked railroads. But that really had more to do with the right-of-way and its adjacent infrastructure. Sure I liked the see the maroon, yellow and gray colors on those Erie-Lackawanna diesels that passed through the fields on the far end of the property of Big Tree Elementary School on the main-line of the former Erie Railroad's Southwestern Division. But I found the nearby bluntly black thick plate girders of the bridge spanning the dipping South Park Avenue attracted greater interest.

Definitely. It was the bridges I liked the best. And why not? Remember my earlier reference to Blasdell Junction? I would often travel through it multiple times a day. Within a mile or so of Lake Avenue, there were more than a dozen railroad bridges of all types. And on South Park just north of Fran & Ceil's (a favorite stopping place then and now), two heavily used railroad bridges (Pennsylvania and Lehigh Valley) crossed above this main thoroughfare. One of them even had wooden piers.

As you can guess from the chapter on the Erie Genesee River Viaduct, it was those bridges that crossed rivers and river valleys that I liked the most. I very faintly recall what I think was a rather impressive wooden trestle bridge somewhere in the Southern Tier of Greater Western New York. I must have been three years old or less, and my father took the family on a business trip to either Jamestown or Olean. I remember the bridge, though far away, as being clearly visible from the little motel we stayed in. I've tried to figure out what railroad used that bridge, but, to date, no luck. Do you know?

That's not my favorite bridge story. The bridge story that most delights me occurred in 1987, when I travelled to Italy with three of my college classmates. While in Firenze (Florence), the one who knew "all the places we had to see," insisted we saunter through the street of shops on the Ponte Vecchio. Built in medieval times, the Ponte Vecchio crosses the Arno River on three stone arches. On the bridge sit shops on either side, with only the center open for viewing the picturesque panorama. I really didn't appreciate the beauty of this view, which is also through stylistic arches, until the second time I visited the Ponte Vecchio with my wife and children in 2011.

But my tale takes place in one of the many jewelry shops on the first sojourn through the Ponte Vecchio. Now, I hate shopping, especially in jewelry stores, just as much as the next guy. Unfortunately, those classmates of mine weren't "the next guy" and they enjoyed perusing the shops. While waiting for them, I happened upon a mother and daughter arguing about what to buy. They were Americans. I don't know how I knew, but it's just one of those things you can tell. They must have noticed I was bored and not really doing anything, so the daughter, a slender brunette with a girl-next-door face, came up to me and asked, "Hey, you're a regular guy, right?" I answered in the affirmative, half wondering if I was about to become a victim of an elaborate sting. But my worries left when she told me she needed a guy's opinion on a piece of jewelry because she wanted to make sure her boyfriend would like it. For ten minutes I played fashion consultant, and the mother and daughter seemed genuinely appreciative. Still, as they departed I stealthily dragged my hand across my back pocket to make sure my wallet was still there.

It was then that I noticed my three friends had been staring at me with a weird stunned look and only tentatively approached once the two women were well out of hearing distance. The first came up to me and, pointing to the daughter, somewhat breathlessly asked, "Do you know who that was?" I didn't and I asked my friend to reveal her name. By now almost jumping up and down in excitement, he answered, "That was Carol Alt!" My response: "Carol Alt? Was she one of our classmates?" (Ever since my concussion sophomore year, I had a tendency to forget people's names.) "No," my friends shouted back in unison. It was then and there that I learned Carol Alt was a supermodel for some sort of woman's product. And that is my most memorable experience while standing on a bridge crossing a river.

It wasn't until I moved to Rochester that I learned something rather intriguing about bridges crossing rivers: sometimes even canals needed to do it. In fact, upon its completion in 1825, the original 40' wide Erie Canal, in addition to its 83 locks, contained 18 aqueducts.[1] When the original Erie Canal was widened in the mid-1800s to 70', the number of locks was reduced to 72 and, with the building of the "Barge Canal" in the early 1900s to replace the Erie Canal, the number of locks was again reduced to 57.[2] In addition, many of the aqueducts were taken out of service, including our hidden gem, the Broad Street Aqueduct in Rochester. Don't ask me why they call the Erie Canal Culvert in Orleans County a "culvert" instead of an "aqueduct." I guess it's all a matter of perspective. In Medina, the road goes under the Canal (as opposed to the Canal going over the road). Incidentally, this is the only instance of a road going under the Erie Canal.

The Rochester vicinity proved an engineering nightmare for the builders of the Erie Canal. Those pesky glaciers came down and either carved out immense valleys or redirected rivers and streams to do the same. To the east of Rochester, the glacier dug deep into the Irondequoit Creek valley, but was kind enough to leave what's called the Cartersville Esker at the edge of Bushnell's Basin in the Town of Pittsford.[3] Bushnell's Basin proved too deep for the Erie Canal. Workers, using only wheelbarrows, built a 70' high embankment (the world's largest)[4] across from the Cartersville Esker, creating a path for the Erie Canal.[5] The original embankment, called the Irondequoit Embankment, was actually one wall of an aqueduct which allowed the Erie Canal to pass over the Irondequoit Creek.[6] Incidentally, if you travel to Bushnell's Basin today, you won't see the Irondequoit Embankment. Instead, you'll see the Great Embankment, which was created as part of the Erie Barge Canal project.[7] Other than straightening the original Canal to improve distance and travel time,[8] the Great Embankment provides essentially the same function as the Irondequoit Embankment.

On the other hand, you can still see one relic from the era of the original Canal. Richardson's Canal House Inn began life as "The Bushnell's Basin Hotel." Initially used as a tavern (a.k.a. a "public house") when it was built circa 1818 and it remained so until the 1930's, when the then current owners sold it to a nudist group.[10] It was abandoned in the 1960's, but restored in 1979 when it was opened as a restaurant.[11] Considered the oldest surviving tavern on the Erie Canal,[12] in 1980 Richardson's Canal House was placed on the National Register of Historic Buildings.[13]

As impressive an engineering feat as the Great Embankment, and as old as Richardson's Canal House is, the real hidden gem sits above the Genesee River, to the west of Bushnell's Basin on the Canal in the City of Rochester. But you won't see it unless you're looking for it. Why? Because it lies beneath your feet, or, more appropriately, beneath your wheels. In fact, it's a viaduct built over an aqueduct built over a raging river.

No sooner had our brave engineers solved the problem of a 70' too low valley floor when another major obstacle presented itself. This one was called the Genesee River. This wouldn't be the first time canal builders would construct an aqueduct over a river. Indeed, not too far to the east they had just built the 94' three arch Mud Creek Aqueduct in the Village of Palmyra in

Wayne County. Mud Creek has a real name. It's called Ganargua Creek. You can see the mostly extant remains of this aqueduct if you go to Aqueduct Park in Palmyra.

The Genesee River Aqueduct would turn out to be a greater challenge than expected. The first attempt to build it proved fruitless. The crew spent the late summer/early fall of 1821 chiseling out gray limestone from the west bank of the River and mining red sandstone from the Lower Falls area of the River.[14] After bolting and cementing this stone to the River floor as a foundation, the crew called it a season, only to return the next spring to discover the River's turbulent waters had yanked the solid stone blanks from the bolts and washed them away.[15] They found a quarry of more reliable red Medina sandstone in Greece (NY) and used that stone to create an eleven arch aqueduct stretching more than 800' from one bank of the Genesee to the other, making it the largest structure of its kind in the world.[16]

There were a couple of problems. First, the red Medina sandstone demonstrated itself to be less than desirable. Second, the aqueduct was only 17 feet wide, creating a bottleneck in the normally 40' wide canal. If you don't think this is an issue, imagine the traffic problems when a normally two-lane highway is reduced to a single lane. Of course, there were no cars in the early nineteenth century and folks could apparently live with a "single lane" aqueduct, at least for a while.

"A while" turned out to be only a decade, and in 1842 a second aqueduct was built just south of the original. This seven arch structure was built from Onondaga Limestone (from a Syracuse quarry) and was 45 feet wide.[17] This aqueduct remained in use until the Erie Barge Canal went on-line in 1918, but saw new life as the roadbed of the Rochester Subway from 1929 to 1956.[18] With the increasing use of the automobile, city planners sought an alternative parallel route to Main Street. At the same time, there was a desire to get the street cars off the street. With Broad Street now considered a major artery, the last thing the city wanted to do was to see automobiles and trolleys share the old Erie Canal aqueduct. To solve this dilemma, the trolleys became a subway and, while they remained on the aqueduct, an automobile bridge was built over the railroad, creating a viaduct over the aqueduct.

To give you a sense of the durability of the second Erie Canal aqueduct, city engineers discovered in the late 1960s they had to replace the entire bridge superstructure of the then 50-year old Broad Street Bridge, but the then 130-year old Aqueduct required only minimal repairs.[19] Like its Roman forebears, you can still see the Erie Canal's Genesee River Aqueduct to this day. And like its ancient ancestors, it represents a heroic feat of engineering for its time. Though it lies dormant today, it may yet again find a new use and return to glory. Who knows? Maybe some future entrepreneur may turn it into a street of shops, making it Greater Western New York's version of the Ponte Vecchio.

And why not? I spoke to local businessman Neal Rudin, who is interested in seeing the aqueduct developed into a world-class attraction featuring Rochester's many Sister Cities, its remarkable history, culture and its industries making it comparable to the EPCOT Center in Disney World. Of the spacious Aqueduct, he estimates "about 3,000 or more could easily fit within it."

Would you believe me if I told you the Genesee Aqueduct was merely among the first such engineering accomplishments in Greater Western New York? If not – or if you want to find out more – simply proceed to the next chapter.

CHAPTER 22: WHILE STROLLING THROUGH THE PARKS ONE DAY...

My brother Kenny went to the University of Buffalo. While he majored in environmental design, he actually studied architecture. Like me, he's quite proud of his hometown, so when he discovered the widely recognized significance of several Buffalo buildings, he was quick to share his findings. He would take that passion and design and build houses, just like my father and his father and his father before him (at least that's as far as I know for sure).

During those wonderful snow days courtesy of living in the snowbelt south of Buffalo, when it came to snowball fights, my brother excelled at building the fort while I toiled at developing some grand game-winning strategy. Unlike all the other men in my family, building and construction never excited me. I never got excited about building houses or creating landscapes or rearranging furniture or anything having to do with home-related matters. I preferred a Spartan life, although marriage and children have (somewhat) tempered that. (I did like my vegetable garden, though, until the local deer population decided they liked it, too.) Rather than buildings, however, I like to build businesses. Yes, my name is Chris Carosa and I'm a serial entrepreneur.

But I've always appreciated my brother's knowledge of and appetite for art and architecture, especially as it pertains to Greater Western New York. Listening to the fruits of his scholarship made me aware of several hidden gems I might not have otherwise known about. Don't get me wrong. Two of my closest friends in college majored in architecture, so, just by being in the same room as them, I quickly picked up the names of significance. You know the ones I mean: Frederick Law Olmsted, Louis Sullivan and, of course, Frank Lloyd Wright. With all the publicity given to Wright and his structures, his gems cannot reasonably qualify as hidden. On the other hand, there are aspects of Olmsted and Sullivan that bear mention. In this chapter, I'll focus on Olmsted.

Frederick Law Olmsted is perhaps best known as the designer of Central Park, but when it comes to landscape design and architecture, his work and influence across the nation is without peer. By the time he retired, he and his firm had had a hand in more than 500 projects, including Yosemite Park, the grounds of the US Capitol Building and many urban parks and landscapes.[1] Among these were several in Greater Western New York. He worked on the Niagara Reservation, including the preservation of Goat Island (between the Canadian and the American Falls), after New York Governor Grover Cleveland signed the law that would create America's first, thus, oldest, state park at Niagara Falls.[2] In addition to several parks in Rochester, including the Genesee Valley Park, Highland Park and Seneca Park,[3] Olmsted designed "River Walk," a promenade of 197 oak trees between Elmwood Avenue and Intercampus Drive at the University of Rochester.[4]

More importantly, he created the first integrated park system in America in Buffalo.[5] After witnessing Olmsted's triumph with New York City's Central Park, city planners asked the famed architect to provide the Queen City with its own unique urban park. They showed him three different prospective lots and, when asked to choose the best one, Olmsted chose all three.[6] Originally called The Park (later Delaware Park), The Front (later Front Park) and The Parade (later Martin Luther King, Jr. Park), these three parks represent the inner ring (and first constructed) phase of The Olmsted Park System. The second phase of outer ring parks contains Cazenovia, South and Riverside Parks. The Buffalo Board of Parks Commissioners rejected Olmsted's original recommendation to place this park configuration on the waterfront because of the high cost, the potential for storm damage and because it was located too far from the residential neighborhoods it was supposed to support.[7]

Olmsted admired Joseph Ellicott's radial street design and once called Buffalo the "best planned city… in the United States if not the world."[8] The Park System and European-style tree-lined connecting parkways were completed in time for the 1901 Pan American Exposition, adding the moniker "City of Trees" to Buffalo's signature slogan "City of Light."[9] The Expo itself promoted Greater Western New York's access to low cost energy, thanks to the nearby hydroelectric plant in Niagara Falls. Its centerpiece exhibit – the Tower of Light – though torn down with all the other temporary buildings, in part inspired the building of the beaux arts neoclassical Electric Tower in 1912 (the other half of the inspiration came from the Lighthouse of Alexandria).[10] Anyone who lives in or visits Buffalo knows fondly the celebratory colors of light emitted from the top of Electric Tower upon the occasion of any significant event. The only building remaining from the Pan

American Exposition is the New York State Pavilion, now occupied by the Buffalo History Museum. Many think the Albright Knox Gallery, stylistically similar to the Buffalo History Museum, was also part of the Exposition, but it wasn't. Oh, it was supposed to be, but construction delays deferred its completion to 1905, four years after the event.

The Pan American Exposition, part of which took place in Delaware Park, is unfortunately best remembered as the site of the assassination of President McKinley. But that seemed so distant to me as a child. If you were to ask me back then what came to mind when I heard the words "Delaware Park," I'd have to say the zoo and a couple of really old turtles. I mean, these turtles were so old, they were probably around when Lincoln was shot, let alone McKinley.

As a kid, the name Olmsted and the idea of an "integrated park system" meant nothing to me. In fact, the concept of an urban park seemed a contradiction of terms. With family in Lackawanna and Hamburg, the last place we'd go to refresh ourselves in nature was the city. We went to Chestnut Ridge Park. Located in Orchard Park, Chestnut Ridge is Erie County's oldest county park.[11] We went there quite often. Apparently, I fell off the same rock two years in a row when I was one and two. Fell right on my head. Apparently I have a hard head, since I received no lasting damage, except perhaps those falls might be responsible for my fear of heights.

I always thought Chestnut Ridge Park was really cool. I loved the nature hikes, the famous 100 steps, walking along (and through) the shale shrouded creek (aptly called Shale Creek), collecting salamanders along its banks and, of course, the much talked of Eternal Flame. The Eternal Flame is caused by methane gas leaking through the rock fissures. The Eternal Flame wasn't so eternal when I visited it. I could smell, the gas, but the flame was out. That's why hikers more expert than I recommend you always bring a barbeque lighter just in case you need to relight the flame.[12]

While we viewed Chestnut Ridge as a playground, we considered the Botanical Gardens at South Park a hallowed museum. We would frequently pass by the triple-domed conservatory, styled after England's Classic Crystal Palace,[13] on our travels up and down South Park Avenue. The expansive glass and steel structure, which was totally rebuilt in 1930,[14] has the allure of the nineteenth century. It's just as alluring and as fascinating today as it was when I first saw it in the 1960s. And just as the exotic flora excited me back then, so has it enthralled my son today. In the same way, to many, Olmsted's work on Buffalo's integrated park system one-upped his efforts on New York City's Central Park.

In my naïve youth, I thought Buffalo's single architectural gem lay kitty-corner across the street just south of the Botanical Gardens. (Hint: There's a connection between it and the Eternal Flame at Chestnut Ridge Park.) Once again, my brother enlightened me, as I will do for you in the next chapter.

93

CHAPTER 23: THE MIRACLE OF LIMESTONE HILL

To anyone born and raised in Lackawanna, the stern threat, "You better behave or I'll send you to Father Baker's" remains forever burned into one's ears. It turns out, chances are that same phrase remains forever burned in the ears of a child *raised* by someone born in the City of Lackawanna. Like mine.

I can definitely see my grandmother shouting this phrase at my uncles when they were kids. The effect was no doubt the same on them as it was on me when my mother tried using it. Actually, it probably wasn't the same. By the time I was old enough to realize the truth behind "Father Baker's," it looked just like the school it was. The orphanage of my uncles' youth had been torn down before I was born.

To me, though, Father Baker's wasn't the school, it was the church and the amazing story behind it. Our regular church was St. Anthony's on Ingham Avenue, the proverbial "other side of the tracks" where my mother's family lived. We had cousins who were parishioners at Our Lady of Victory (the official name of "Father Baker's"). Every once in a while, we dressed up extra special, promised to behave (lest we be sent there forever) and journeyed to Mass at Father Baker's. Although I was yet to experience a European Cathedral, something inside my prepubescent heart told me this church would rival some of those in the old country.

But the story of Father Baker, as told by my grandmother to my mother and my mother to me, with incidental corrections from my grandmother, is as inspirational in their telling as it is in reality. This was the tale they told me. One day, the diocese assigned Father Baker to their orphanage on the corner of Ridge Road and South Park. No sooner had he arrived than he learned the institution was deeply in debt and was about to be closed. After a night of intense prayer, he took a stroll on the campus' vast grounds. Something told him to stop on a certain spot. It was on that spot that drillers discovered a natural gas well, and the money from that well saved the orphanage and allowed Father Baker to build the grandest church in all of Greater Western New York.

Pretty cool, huh? Kinda brings a lump in your throat, all that "God's way" stuff and everything.

There's only one problem.

It's not quite true.

Here's the real story. Indeed, in 1882 Father Baker was assigned to the diocesan protectorate atop "Limestone Hill" in what was then part of the Town of West Seneca. And, yes, when he arrived the creditors were waiting. But natural gas did not save that particular day. No. It so happened that Father Baker, when he was still simply Civil War veteran Nelson Henry Baker, was a very successful businessman. His partner was devastated when Nelson informed him he wanted to become a priest.[1] Father Baker convinced the debt collectors to hold off by giving them the remainder of his life savings and reminding them of his past business success.[2] Prayer gave him the inspiration to create The Association of Our Lady of Victory, and through this he raised the funds to pay off the remaining debt.[3]

A few years later, after learning how others had discovered nearby natural gas wells, Father Baker convinced the Bishop of Buffalo to provide $2,000 to him to drill on the property.[4] He then took drillers down his usual prayer path until he came upon a particular spot, whereupon his stopped, buried a small statue of Our Lady of Victory and told the workers to start drilling.[5] Going far beyond normal depths, skeptical drillers began calling the venture "Father Baker's Folly," but the Monsignor's insistence to continue paid off when they found gas at an incredible depth of 1,135 feet (compared to a typical depth of 600 feet).[6] The well continues to yield today, all the more amazing because wells typically run dry after only a few years,[7] making it truly an Eternal Flame.

See? The true story is even more amazing.

The church where the Basilica now stands was originally called St. Patrick's, at least until it burned to the ground in 1916, then it was probably called ashes. The 74 year-old Father Baker vowed to build a European-style cathedral and, again, relied on donations to fund it. To do this, he employed artisans from across the ocean and, in May of 1926, the same year Shea's Buffalo and the Buffalo Airport opened and coincident to the 50th anniversary of him becoming a priest, Father Baker opened the Our Lady of Victory church without incurring any debt.[8] Later in the year, Pope Pius XI declared it a minor Basilica.[9]

Because of its placement at the summit of Limestone Hill, you can see the Basilica from any one of many locations. It's especially impressive coming towards it from the south on South Park Avenue. Its green dome, 165 foot high and at the time of its construction second only to the U.S. Capital in size,[10] peers over the nearby buildings, enticing you to come toward it. The best exterior view of the baroque structure comes from the north side of Ridge Road. From this vantage point, its dressing of Georgia and Carrara marble, as well as its signature twin towers,[11] evokes wonder and awe. It makes you imagine you're in Rome itself. And if the towers awe you now, think how you'd feel if you saw them as originally built. Until a violent thunder storm damaged them in 1941, the towers stood more than 16 stories tall, equal in height to the dome.[12]

The story of Father Baker goes beyond his ability to raise money, find a new energy source and build grand buildings. During the depression, and into his 90s, Father Baker's vast complex served a million meals a year, provided clothing to more than 500,000 and offered medical services to 250,000,[13] all without the need of the Federal government. In addition, this kind man, for all his business acumen, had a unique ability to connect to people, too. To this day, the boys, now old men, of his orphanage remember him with a special fondness. As of May 2012, only six "Father Baker Boys" survive, yet the stories they tell of "Daddy Baker" speak to the authentic veneration of the only parent they ever knew.[14] Speaking of veneration, in January of 2011, Pope Benedict XVI elevated Father Baker to "Venerable" status, meaning his "heroic virtues" have been official recognized by the Church and he's moved a step closer to canonization as a saint.[15]

As brilliant as it is and as proud as we might be of Our Lady of Victory Basilica, many believe Louis Sullivan's 1896 Prudential (née Guaranty) Building to be the most significant (remaining) architectural asset in Greater Western New York. The National Park Service declared the building a National Historic Landmark in 1975 because it represents "the last collaborative effort of its architects" [Adler and Sullivan], stating it was "a triumph of early skyscraper design."[16] Sullivan himself called it the "sister" of the Wainwright Building, his prototype skyscraper built five years earlier in St. Louis.[17] The Prudential Building, located on 28 Church Street at the corner of Pearl Street in Buffalo, represents the capstone of Sullivan's "form follows function" philosophy, and, with its fine exterior ornamentation, is considered by some as a "refinement" of the Wainwright.[18]

Travelling down just a block to the east on the other side of Main Street stands the 10 story Ellicott Square Building. Built the same year as Sullivan's masterpiece, its terra cotta exterior has suffered in comparison to the Prudential's similar covering, thanks in part to Sullivan's more imaginative use of ornamentation.[19] The Ellicott Square building was built on the block encircled by Main Street, Swan Street, Washington Street and South Division Street. When he laid out the city of Buffalo, Joseph Ellicott set aside this parcel for himself and his family; hence, the name "Ellicott Square."[20]

At the time of its completion in 1896, the Ellicott Square Building, with 299,000 square feet of rentable space, was the largest office building in the world.[21] By 1897, the building saw 10,000 people coming through its doors every day.[22] For comparison sake, there were between 10,000 and 15,000 people working in the twin towers on September 11, 2011 (the total capacity for each tower was 25,000).[23]

By the turn of the nineteenth Century, Greater Western New York had established itself as a leading center for business, architecture, transportation and invention. But of all the inventions credited to our area, no one single product has produced so much money for so many for so long a time as the item we feature in our next chapter.

CHAPTER 24: THE GREATEST INVENTION IN
THE HISTORY OF THE WORLD

Here's a quick question: What popular fast food was invented right here in Western New York? Think you know the answer? I'll give you a hint: it's not chicken wings. OK, smarty-pants, with apologies to Frank and Teresa, "chicken wings" is a correct answer, but too obvious and not the correct answer. I'll give you another hint: it was invented at the Erie County Fair in 1885. If you know Western New York, then you may think you already know the answer. If you're not sure, you'll have to read on.

As I mentioned earlier, I can tell you stories about the Fair dating from my youthful days when I helped my grandparents hawk slices from the family's pizza stand. Recall, too, the Erie County Fair began in the city of Buffalo but had to move to the suburbs as it grew larger and larger. It remains one of the largest and most successful County Fairs in the country. Indeed, it rivals many state fairs, even New York State's own state fair.

Now, about the answer to my question… Here's one final hint: "Would you like fries with that?"

By 1885, the Fair had settled in the Town of Hamburg and locals soon began referring to it as the "Hamburg" Fair. Would you believe this wholesome setting was the background – and the cause – of perhaps the single most important invention ever, an invention upon which wealthy empires were built, million (and billions) were fed and many teenagers have to thank for their first job?

I do not speak in mere hyperbole, but with 100% U.S.D.A. certified all-American truth, for this invention is none other than the hamburger!

That's right, it's the hamburger, that staple of fast food franchises everywhere. I stumbled on this fact while researching a paper on the history of Buffalo as a senior at Yale University in New Haven, Connecticut. I rummaged through the multi-storied library stacks looking for source documents when I uncovered a still intact copy of a special edition of the Buffalo *Express*. (Does the name sound familiar? This paper merged with the Buffalo *Courier* to form the *Courier Express* in 1926.) The copy I found was printed sometime in the 1880s (I can't recall the exact date) and featured the Erie County Fair. One of the articles mentioned the popular "hamburger" sandwich – named for Hamburg, NY, the site of the Fair – which was first invented at the Fair a few years earlier.

Well, truth be told, there are several competing versions of the birth of the hamburger, but I believe Greater Western New York's claim represents the most credible for a number of reasons. First, two other stories take place more than a decade after ours.

Louis' (pronounced "Lew-EEZ") Lunch Wagon (ironically, located in New Haven, of all places), whose claim states its proprietor, Louis Lassen, flipped the first burger when an impatient customer – no doubt a college student cramming for his midterm – ran up to the counter and asked for something quick to go. For reasons unknown, Louis grilled a beef patty and slapped it between two slices of toast before serving it to his hungry customer.[1] Given this occurred in 1900, and given there are at least two earlier (and equally credible claims), for yet more reasons unknown, the Library of Congress has documented Louis' Lunch as the first place to serve hamburgers in the United States.[2] Unfortunately for Louis, his family and the credibility of the venerable Library of Congress, Louis' Lunch own website[3] states the establishment didn't start until 1895, a decade after our earlier claim.

Then there's Fletcher "Old Dave" Davis, of Athens, Texas, who lays his claim to inventing his hamburger "sometime in the 1880s"[4] (how convenient). His claim is actually only documented in a 1983 book[5] by fellow Texan Frank Tolbert (he even shared the same home county as Davis). Tolbert references a fourth hand account of a New York *Tribune* newspaper article of dubious reality (the original article has never been found) and places Davis' "invention" at the 1904 St. Louis Fair. According to Josh Ozersky, American food writer and historian and founding editor of New York magazine's food blog *Grub Street*, "The *Tribune* article, which does not exist, has been quoted everywhere; its real source seems to be Tolbert himself."[6] By the way, the McDonald's Corporation Hamburger University recognizes the St. Louis Fair as the birthplace of the hamburger, in part because of this phantom New York *Tribune* article. We'll be contacting them shortly to set them straight.

Again, the story occurs a generation after our claim or the other most credible claim.

That other 1885 claim involves the story of a Wisconsin teenager by the name of Charlie Nagreen who, at the 1885 Seymour Fair (now call the Outagamie County Fair), allegedly created the hamburger by flattening a meatball and placing it between two slices of bread.[7] OK, so this puts

Wisconsin in the same year as our claim, leaving us with the question, which Fair occurred first? A newspaper article celebrating "Seymour's first annual fair" appeared in print on October 15, 1885.[8] So, did our story occur before or after October 1885?

Let's first look at what the authoritative WhatsCookingAmerica.net has to say about our story:

> The family of Frank and Charles Menches from Akron, Ohio, claim the brothers invented the hamburger while traveling in a 100-man traveling concession circuit at events (fairs, race meetings, and farmers' picnics) in the Midwest in the early 1880s. During a stop at the Erie County Fair in Hamburg, New York, the brothers ran out of pork for their hot sausage patty sandwiches. Because this happened on a particularly hot day, the local butchers stop slaughtering pigs. The butcher suggested that they substitute beef for the pork. The brothers ground up the beef, mixed it with some brown sugar, coffee, and other spices and served it as a sandwich between two pieces of bread. They called this sandwich the "hamburger" after Hamburg, New York where the fair was being held. According to family legend, Frank didn't really know what to call it, so he looked up and saw the banner for the Hamburg fair and said, "This is the hamburger." In Frank's 1951 obituary in *The Los Angeles Times*, he is acknowledged as the "inventor" of the hamburger.
>
> Hamburg held its first Burgerfest in 1985 to mark the 100th anniversary of the birth of the hamburger after organizers discovered a history book detailing the burger's origins.[9]

It appears the Town of Hamburg rediscovered a book[10] written in 1970 by Jamestown native John C. Kunzog, once said to be "the number one circus historian of all time,"[11] which contains a reference to the author's 1920s interview with Frank Menches in which Menches describes the story related above.[12] Hamburg's first Burgerfest in 1985 merited national attention with papers as far as the West Coast picking up the Associated Press story.[13]

So, we have two competing 1885 claims, with Seymour coming in October. This leaves the question, when was the 1885 Erie County Fair? In the early years, the Fair was held in Buffalo in October, but changes began to occur once it moved to the suburbs, with the August date firmly established much later. However, we do have direct evidence the 1885 Erie County Fair occurred in September,[14] making it a month before the Seymour Fair and giving the Menches brothers first claim over Charlie Nagreen.

Here's why I think the Menches brothers' story is the truest of them all. First, having worked in a food stand at the Erie County Fair, I can tell you first hand you don't stop selling when you run out of product. As long as there are Fair-goers going to the Fair, you find something to sell. Anything. Picture us selling cigarette lighters from my grandfather's pizza stand. So it makes sense for the Menches brothers to go through all the machinations to find a suitable substitute for pork sandwiches.

Second, the derivation of the name "Ham" burger is best explained by the name "Hamburg" Fair. At the time of the 1885 Fair, the Erie County Agricultural Society was basically run by Hamburg natives[15] and their promotion of their home town would soon have everyone calling the Erie County Fair the "Hamburg" Fair within a few years. It makes sense "Hamburg Fair" banners would be flying within easy seeing distance of the Menches brothers. This best explains why a couple of pork sausage sandwich vendors may have inadvertently named the famous ground beef sandwich after a pork product.

Third, again based on my experience working at the Fair, the popularity of the Fair meant it was THE event for vendors, carnies and itinerant salesmen in general. This explains why two brothers from Akron, Ohio (the Menches' hometown), would travel to Western New York to set up a pork sausage sandwich stand for a few days. This is what they, and many others, did. They'd travel from town to town, no doubt together with other venders, to earn their living. Along the journey, and even at the county fairs they visited, they likely took some time to sit down and talk with each other, sharing stories of what people bought and what people avoided. These word-of-mouth stories can travel really fast (think "viral" in today's terms). So, it's very possible Charlie Nagreen heard of the Menches success and, a month later, duplicated it as best as he could.

One thing we can't argue about the hamburger is that, at least according to USA Today, Greater Western New York has one of America's best burger joints[16] and certainly the best in all of New York State.[17] Indeed, so popular is Livingston County's Tom Wahl's that in the summer of 2011, in another widely covered Associated Press story, the Wahlberg brothers licensed the name "Wahlburger" from the Avon eatery to open their own restaurant.[18] Seriously, this was big news. It was even carried by the Wall Street Journal.[19]

Thus, arguably the greatest invention ever (as judged by the amount of money people have made off of it), the All-American Hamburger – a hidden gem from Western New York – was first concocted at another hidden gem from Western New York: the All-American Erie County Fair, or, again, as us natives like to call it, the Hamburg Fair. And just to make all things equal when it comes to picnic foods, we should note *Woman's Day* magazine named another native culinary creation, the Zweigle's hotdog, among the "8 Best Boardwalk Foods in the U.S."[20]

Incidentally, that copy of the Buffalo *Express* I discovered in the stacks of Sterling Library apparently was also a hidden gem. When I returned it, the librarian asked me – in a rather accusatory tone – how I had managed to take it out of the hallowed halls in which it was housed. I told her the truth. She then told me it belonged in the rare books library. I guess this means I'm probably the last person to have read it.*

And lest you think the hamburger was the last world-wide phenomenon to debut at the Erie County Fair, there was another, more recent, event. It involved one of America's most popular candy treats. We'll take a bite out of this story in the next chapter and reveal the origin of "America's Favorite Dessert," which, as it turns out, is just a hop, skip and a jump from Tom Wahl's Avon location.

* This may have been truer than I expected. When I returned to the Beinecke Rare Book and Manuscript Library some thirty years after writing my original paper, that Buffalo *Express* supplement, though still listed in the Yale Library catalog, could not be found by the library researchers. I was told it was probably purged, which astounded me. After all, who in their right mind would "purge" a "rare" book or manuscript? Unfortunately, Yale now has a need for the artifact for one of its new collections. I did discover the Buffalo Library has eight versions of this newsprint document, but when I went to read them, they seemed too big (in terms of number of pages) than what I remembered. Who knows? Maybe I miswrote the bibliography (remember, it was an "easy A" course being taken by a second term senior who was about to graduate).

CHAPTER 25: OUR JUST DESSERTS

They disappeared without much fanfare in 2005. I barely noticed it, but, then again, I don't often buy M&M's®. When I did, I usually did it only to fill treat bowls for the holidays. But Crispy M&M's® remained my favorite of the brand. You'd think they might have been the favorite of the manufacturer, since, according to the Wikipedia entry (as of July 18, 2010), they brought in more profit than any other M&M® variety (caveat emptor, Wikipedia contains no reference for this "fact").

Just in time for Christmas – is that why I first noticed them? – Crispy M&M's® came into being in December 1998, the company's first new flavor since 1954, when it introduced Peanut M&M's®. Most folks, though, probably remember the debut of the paranoid "Orange" character in an ad that aired during the 1999 Super Bowl.

In 2010, M&M/Mars decided to create an alter-ego to the Crispy M&M's® in similar blue packaging. These faux-Crispy M&M's® are, in reality, chocolate covered pretzels. Now, like any honest American, I like pretzels and I like chocolate, but I loathe chocolate covered pretzels. There's something seriously disturbing about that (to allude to an old M&M's® commercial). I say, boycott the pretzels and bring back the Crispy! Who's with me?

While you're pondering that piece of passion, consider this fascinating M&M's® fact that has a local twist:

Do you remember the "Cows on Parade" phenomenon that swept the country and the world? It started right here in Greater Western New York.

In 1990, the prototype for the Cow Parade – dubbed "Candy" – made its global debut at the Erie County Fair. This famous fiberglass female was featured at the M&M® exhibit at the Fair. Covered with 66,000 M&M® chocolates, the cow brought the candy manufacturer more than $1 million in free publicity. *Newsweek* call the eight-foot bovine "udderly amazing." Regis Philbin even "interviewed" the chocolatine model.[1]

Fair goers waited in line for up to thirty minutes to view the year's most popular exhibit. Were you one of them? Candy inspired the Cow Parade mania, when some of the world's largest cities surrendered to the fad, including Zurich, Taipei, Rome, Hong Kong, Chicago, New York, London, Sydney, Houston, Las Vegas, Atlanta, San Antonio and even Lima, Peru.

And to think it all began in our neck of the woods.

But when it comes to sweet treats, Greater Western New York is the home to one of the most delicious hidden gems that actually looks like a shiny jewel (albeit one that wiggles). It turns out, this hidden gem really is hidden. And it also contains a hidden gem within it. Pretty cool, huh?

The story begins in 1897 in Genesee County at the Leroy home of Pearle Wait. A carpenter by day, Wait dawdled in patent medicines by night. This hobby introduced him to Peter Cooper's 1845 patent for gelatin. Peter Cooper invented America's first steam locomotive and founded New York City's Cooper Union. He's often credited with inventing Jell-O. He didn't. He didn't even invent gelatin (the Frenchman Denis Papin did in 1682). Cooper did receive the American patent for gelatin, which Wait later purchased.

Thanks to his work in medicine, Wait knew had to add colors and flavoring to Cooper's gelatin recipe. What Cooper's gelatin didn't do, though, was gel into the familiar moldable wiggly solid we know of today as Jell-O. Wait discovered how to do that, and its first flavors were orange, lemon, strawberry and raspberry. His wife Mary named the product. Although no definitive explanation exists, it's possible she named it after another Leroy product Grain-O.[2] Mr. Wait, try as he might, failed to develop Jell-O into a profitable product.

Along comes Orator Francis Woodward (the "Orator" refers to his first name, not his job, which was an attorney, which meant he was probably a good orator, which ends up only confusing things more). Woodward was already wealthy when he purchased the Grain-O company in 1896. So popular was his product, that by 1897 he was spending much of his money defending the trademark rights of Grain-O.[3] About the same time, Wait couldn't "wait" any longer and decided to sell Jell-O to Woodward for $450. Perhaps it was Woodward trying to protect Grain-O's "-O" ending,[4] but it looks like Wait's wife Mary had a pretty good idea of what she was doing when she came up with the name Jell-O.

Woodward, dissatisfied with Jell-O's progress, tried to sell it. But, like the product itself, no one would buy. He then had a brainstorm that changed everything. His 1902 ad campaign in *Everybody's, Boston Cooking School Magazine* and *Ladies' Home Journal* cost $336,[5] but by the end of the year, Jell-O had generated $250,000 in revenues.[6] From then on, Jell-O was off to the races and, as "America's Most Famous Dessert," became engrained in American culture. Not only did it quickly become a mealtime sensation, but its unique characteristics soon found their way to Hollywood. Cecil B. DeMille used Jell-O to create the parted Red Sea in his 1923 version of *The Ten Commandments*, and the "horse of many colors" in *The Wizard of Oz* was really multiple horses dyed with Jell-O.[7]

The marriage of Jell-O and the entertainment industry is well documented at the Jell-O Gallery,[8] located in the classic two-story stone walled former Leroy High School.[9] The Gallery, also called the Jell-O Museum, is hidden behind the Historic LeRoy House on Main Street. The Gallery is connected to Main Street by the "Jell-O Brick Road," located just to the left of the LeRoy House, itself a treasure for those interested in the history of LeRoy. The LeRoy house was built before 1812 and was the land office for the "Triangle Tract," a vestige of the Phelps and Gorham faux pas resulting from a surveying accident that eventually landed the triangular shaped property into the Morris Reserve, who then sold it to Herman LeRoy, William Bayard and John McEvers.[10]

But wait! There's more! Located below the Jell-O Gallery we find yet another hidden gem of sorts: the Transportation Exhibit of the LeRoy Historical Society. This is a great exhibit for kids because it's short, informative and has real vehicles of all sorts in it, everything from classic "horseless carriages" (a 1908 Cadillac Model S) to actual carriages (sans horses), and some sleds, too. It's in this exhibit we learn about Henry Ford's one and only visit through LeRoy. According to a poster at the exhibit, on August 1, 1922 while traveling with his chauffer, Henry Ford was issued a speeding ticket. Although he paid the $30 fine, he nonetheless accused the Village of operating a speed trap. To reflect his anger, he posted "Speed Trap" signs just outside the Village limits warning tourists.

But not all celebrities disdained Leroy or, in particular, its most famous product. Jell-O (through its sponsorship) virtually launched the career of Jack Benny. And who can forget Bill Cosby's long-standing role as spokesman for the product (which, together with his stint for Kodak, made him the spokesman for not only one, by two classic Greater Western New York products). The Jell-O museum does a fabulous job of highlighting Jell-O's connection to Hollywood (beyond the special effects department).

It's not often we have a single site featuring a nest of hidden gems like we have in LeRoy. It sort of makes it easier if you're looking to take a break and make a day trip of things. Speaking of taking a break, Greater Western New York happens to be the origin of an important workplace tradition. So important was it, the United Auto Workers once threatened to go on strike over it. So, sit back, relax, and turn the page to discover why you should thank your Western New York predecessors for being able to sit back, relax and take five (or ten) at work every day. Oh, yes, and don't forget to pour yourself a cup of that all-American beverage.

CHAPTER 26: THE GREATEST BUSINESS TRADITION

On the evening of December 16th (there's that date again), 1773, dozens of New England colonists, dressed like Mohawk warriors, boarded three ships in Boston harbor and unceremoniously dumped the contents of 340 chests of tea into the water below.[1] It's been said Americans have preferred coffee ever since.

I don't. When I happen to go to a meeting in the morning, they'll ask me if I want coffee. I say, "No, but I'll take a Diet Pepsi if you've got one."

Disclaimer: Unfortunately, I received no compensation (nor permission) from Pepsi to place their product name in this musing. Of course, had I thought to sell them this space, I would gladly have, and, if they are so kind as to later offer me free Diet Pepsi for life (or any other reasonable time period), the reader is well advised that I would be more than happy to accept such offer. Furthermore, if Pepsi is in a really charitable mood, I would be amenable to any offers on their part for the benefit of my readers, too.

There. We got the legal mumbo jumbo out of the way. But, seriously, as anyone who has ever gone to a restaurant with me can attest, I'm Pepsi through and through. When I order a Diet Pepsi for lunch and the waitress kindly smiles and asks, "would a Coke be OK?" I say, "No." and ask for an iced tea. When I was in Italy that first time with my college classmates, we once spent an entire afternoon scouring Rome looking for a Pepsi. I eventually found a place that served fountain Pepsi. Mmmm, there's nothing as tasty as fountain Pepsi. I learned that working at the Erie County Fair.

But, alas, America has an irreplaceable fondness for coffee. Every morning starts with a cup. Every lunch ends with one. Even the Jell-O dessert we have after dinner features fresh brewed coffee. Employers (though not me) throughout the land offer coffee to clients and workers alike.

Ah, but that has not always been the case. The idea of the "coffee break" became memorialized, as near as anyone can tell, by the Pan-American Coffee Bureau when the South American industry advocacy group ran a promotional campaign in 1952 advising coffee drinkers to "Give yourself a Coffee-Break – and Get What Coffee Gives You."[2] In 2002, NPR reporter Susan Stamberg authored a story on the history of the coffee break. In that report, Stamberg quotes Wayne Stevens, then CEO of Barcalounger, who claimed his firm's predecessor company, Barcalo Manufacturing Company of Buffalo, in 1902 was the first company to offer workers a coffee break.[3]

At least one industrial historian doubts Stamberg's source. Dr. Howard Stanger, Donald E. Calvert Distinguished Professor at Canisius College who specializes in labor relations, human resources, management and business history, was interviewed by NPR for Stamberg's report. I spoke with Dr. Stanger to get more clarity and was surprised by what he told me:

"I was asked by an NPR producer to discuss what working conditions were like in factories and large workplaces around the turn of the last century. She indicated Stevens said Barcalo Manufacturing 'invented' the coffee break in its Buffalo plant in 1902. I recalled from my archival research that Larkin provided free coffee to its employees in 1900 or 1901. This was the first time Larkin Co. mentioned a break in which it provided coffee to its employees."

Dr. Stanger told me, in all his research, he never came across anything mentioning "free coffee" save for the Larkin records, and he wondered how Barcalo came to NPR's attention. "I do not recall getting a good answer from the NPR producer as to how she found the Barcalo CEO in North Carolina and why he believed his company was the 'first' to provide a coffee break for employees," he wrote me via e-mail. "As an historian," he continued, "I am not sure that being the first really matters so much. I would contend that companies like Kodak and Larkin in Greater Western New York were more significant that Barcalo in a number of ways, especially in their employee relations initiatives (and of course marketing)." To give you a sense of the impact Kodak had, by 1955, three years after the Pan-American effort to promote the coffee break, at its Rochester plant, Kodak had 100 coffee machines that sold 280,000 cups every month.[4]

Larkin did many great things, besides making soap and bringing Frank Lloyd Wright to Western New York. According to Dr. Stanger, the Larkin Company introduced several novel marketing techniques that echo through to today. Its "Larkin Clubs of Ten's" was a club-based system that predates Tupperware's now famous (and much copied) "2 party plans" (which date from the post-war era). In addition, the company created a "strong corporate culture" of "Larkinites" (does this sound like Apple?) that created a social network of employees, management and Larkin Club Secretaries (who were unpaid and scattered around the country), an impressive achievement before the advent of e-mail, Facebook and social media in general.

Perhaps most impressive, though, is Larkin's commitment to what Dr. Stanger calls "welfare capitalism" a movement he says "emerged in progressive firms in the last few decades of the nineteenth century and peaked in the 1920s." In a paper he wrote on the Larkin Company, Dr. Stanger noted the leading edge employer created many new types of benefit categories, including educational, financial, health, recreational and sports. "Providing breaks to workers was a part of welfare capitalist initiatives to provide an array of benefits (some small and symbolic) in order to retain (mostly skilled) workers, to avoid unions, to build loyalty and esprit de corps," he says, adding, "In Larkin's case, welfare benefits were initially directed to the office force that was largely young and female, a common target of progressive employers during the Victorian and Progressive eras."

Alas, Dr. Stanger admits, despite the best efforts of NPR, "In all my reading about welfare capitalism, I never recalled coffee being used as an inducement, but that's not to say it wasn't offered as a stimulant to goose efficiency." Still, he wonders. He says though "It's not a research question historians would seek to answer. On the other hand, it likely was part of welfare capitalist offerings to employees that attempted to achieve important management outcomes. I wonder if the Great Atlantic & Pacific Tea Company, which branched out from teas to include coffee, provided coffee breaks to its employees. Larkin expanded its product line after 1900 to include teas and coffees and that could explain its offering it to employees."

Ironically, the coffee break, once a proactive policy to avoid unionization, almost lead to a union strike. In the heat of negotiations in the summer of 1964, United Auto Workers Vice President Leonard Woodcock said, "You have coffee breaks on assembly lines all over the world. Only the U.S. has no coffee breaks on the assembly line."[5]

In either case, unlike the hamburger, at least it appears the fight to claim the origin of America's first corporate coffee break is between two Greater Western New York companies. Or is it?

Our good friends in Stoughton, Wisconsin (really? Wisconsin? again?) allege the first coffee breaks occurred there on aptly named Coffee Street in 1880.[6] This one isn't well documented (to be honest, only the Larkin Company has documentation), but it supposedly involves women, hired seasonally by a tobacco company, going home for a short break to tend to domestic affairs, and possibly drinking a cup of coffee during that break.

Whatever the real story behind the origin of the coffee break, the hamburger and Wisconsin's apparently incessant need to one-up Greater Western New York, there is one thing we can say for sure: We stole the next hidden gem from Kentucky, by way of France and the Emperor Constantine. It represents perhaps the most amazing fact very few people know about our region, although it's very possible this fact is right at their fingertips, or at least in their toaster.

CHAPTER 27: GREATER WESTERN NEW YORK'S BREAD OF LIFE FILLS BOTH SPIRIT AND STOMACH

We quivered before the unmarked heavy wooden doors. Their darkness – and the lack of cars in the parking lot – evoked a certain caution. After several rounds of "no, you open it," I took a deep breath and pressed hard on the right door. Once encouraged, its own momentum propelled it, ever so slowly, open. It didn't creak like we expected. We stepped inside and, with one whiff, all earthly thoughts escaped from our heads. It's the advantage every bakery has over its distributors, and with distributors like Wegmans, Tops and Wal-Mart, we're not talking about some mom and pop bakery here. We're talking about one of a higher Order...

Brother James looked just the way I would picture a monk looking. Tallish with an angular face, he wore the kind of retro heavy-rimmed glasses that aren't really retro, merely that old. His soft caring voice spoke with the peaceful contentedness so appropriate for the part you'd swear a Hollywood casting agent placed him. Only you wouldn't swear here – and here is about as far from the superficial celebrity of Tinsel Town as you could get.

Where exactly is "here"? It's the Abbey of the Genesee located in the hamlet of Piffard in the Town of York, Livingston County. About a mile west of the Genesee River, this community of Trappist monks belongs to the Roman Catholic order of Cistercians of the Strict Observance. In 1949, Porter (a cousin of the Wadsworth family) and Gabrielle Chanler, donated land to Dom James Fox, abbot of the Abbey of the Gethsemani in Trappist, Kentucky. The Wadsworth family had lived in the area since 1790, and the Chanlers wanted to bring a monastery to the Genesee Valley. James Kearney, then Bishop of the Diocese of Rochester, embraced this request and the Abbey of the Genesee opened its doors in May, 1951.

We traveled to the Abbey on a hot, sunny, summer solstice. As the crow flies, it's only a few miles from Route 390, although, in keeping with the monastic theme, it's located on a road less traveled. Lack of confidence in our maps had us eschew the direct flight of the crow, opting instead for the more circuitous route of the vulture. An attempted short-cut transformed a twenty minute hop into a forty-five minute excursion. Apparently roads less traveled also mean roads less likely to have road signs. Did I mention the car lacked air conditioning? On the bright side, in our never ending search for River Road, we did discover an old B&O baggage car sitting by itself near some grain silo. In the false rush to get to the Abbey – no doubt inspired by the suspicion we were lost – we failed to record a picture of that piece of railroad history.

Upon arrival, though, any tension derived from driving blind immediately dissipated… once we figured out what entrance was the correct one. Except for an incidental sign which modestly admits "Bread Store," there are no other indications of such a shop, let alone the proper door to use for entry. We guessed the dark wooded double doors might provide the answer. Once we entered, though, the overpowering aroma of the freshly baked bread sucked any temporal concerns from our minds, lifting the spirit and drawing the body towards the humble shop. We could taste the bread as we made our way through the lobby. We eagerly sought to purchase our consignment.

But not before we had a chance to speak to the tranquil Brother James. I asked him for a brochure and he gave me a computer generated trifold paper promoting the Abbey's various retreats. With 2,400 acres of unspoiled woodland in the heart of, well, nowhere, the location had the quiet solitude of "retreat" written all over it. In fact, "quiet" seems a quite appropriate modifier, since one of the retreats features a silent house, where talking is limited only to the Speaking Room. When I queried if he had anything more substantive – and perhaps something that spoke of the famous bread – Brother James directed us to a seventeen minute movie.

The movie filled in more blanks. For example, we learned once the Roman Emperor Constantine I declared his Christianity, the Age of Martyrs passed but the need to emulate the martyrs had not. This in part led to the monastic movement. Soon, the rules of St. Benedict (he wrote a book on the monastic tradition called, appropriately enough, *Rule*) became the standard. In 1098AD, however, a group of monks left the French Benedictine monastery of Molesme and established a reform at Citeaux. For this they were later called "Cistercians." They wanted to devote their lives to a greater degree of solitude, ease and self-reliance than had been common at the time. (Here's a piece of interesting trivia: These are the guys who gave us St. Bernard.)

Naturally, I thought the name "Trappist" derived from their Kentucky origin. Silly me, I should have realized the Kentucky town derived from their name. It turns out, in the late 1600's, while French trappers were beginning to rile British settlers in the New World, the abbot of La Grande Trappe, Dom Armand de Rance, gave the order some much needed leadership. His followers became known as "Trappists." They didn't move to America (and their Kentucky location) until 1848, long after a young George Washington and the British rooted out the French fur trappers from the wilderness.

The movie's only mention of the famous Monk's Bread, though, was it represented the "work" side of the "work and prayer" equation. The film also mentioned a fascinating aspect about this work: since the monks have no money, they can't buy gifts to show appreciation. Instead, they offer work.

But I was really more interested in the bread, so I cornered Brother James and got him to spill the beans. Apparently, the whole bread thing started as an in-house only venture. But then more and more people in the outside community began concocting ways to obtain the bread (no doubt lured by the luscious smell of the bakery). The monks decided to sell it to the public as a fundraising effort. Today, sales of the bread support the Abbey.

The process of making the bread starts at midnight and goes until five o'clock in the morning. The monks work in shifts so no one has to pull an all-nighter. The monks offer several different varieties of loafs. We bought the white bread, the maple cinnamon, the raisin and the sunflower bran. We couldn't wait until we got back, so we started eating them on the way home. The white bread tasted just like the monastery (or was it the monastery smelled like the white bread?). The maple cinnamon reminded me of French Toast, although with a lot less of that annoying syrupy stickiness. My son finished that loaf the next day. After eating a slice of raisin bread, I decided it was perfect for toasting and buttering and I wouldn't waste any more of it 'til the next morn. The sunflower bran was purchased for a friend, so I didn't have any of that one, but, judging by the other three, I'm sure it was yummy.

Although the monks sell the bread nationally through the Internet and at their Abbey, Brother James told me nearly 98% of their sales occur through their distribution partners. This would include stores like Wegmans, Tops and Wal-Mart locations throughout Greater Western New York (primarily Buffalo and Rochester) and as far east as Syracuse. Still, there's nothing like buying bread from the bakery and traveling through the heart of Western New York just to get it makes it all the more worthwhile. If you're traveling to visit Letchworth State Park, be sure to include the Abbey of the Genesee on your itinerary. Just remember one thing: get a good map and don't take any "short-cuts" unless you're absolutely positively sure it really is a short cut.

Many are surprised to hear of a monastery right in the middle of Greater Western New York. If you count yourself among them, then the next chapter might surprise you even more, for, thanks again to a familiar friend, our region found itself the epicenter of America's Second Great Awakening.

Part III

PATHOS

– Passionate Thoughts –

Chris Carosa

CHAPTER 28: A MODEL OF CHRISTIAN SPIRIT

E ver since John Withrop's famous "city upon a hill" sermon aboard the *Arbella* in 1630, it's been tough to separate religion from the spirit of America's founding. Indeed, some say the evangelical movement of the mid-eighteenth century known as The First Great Awakening played a key role in America's strive for independence.[1] And don't think the whole "separation of Church and State" thing in the Constitution came about because the Founding Fathers felt the First Great Awakening was a tad too much. I'll remind you the whole purpose of the First Great Awakening was to rebel against the Church of England and to recognize broader religious freedom. This is the very philosophy embodied by our constitution.

Our focus in this chapter, though, isn't the *First* Great Awakening, but the *Second* Great Awakening. The Second Great Awakening began in 1790 and lasted for about 50 years. It featured traveling preachers leading revival camps where "hundreds and sometimes thousands of people would gather for miles around in wilderness encampment for four days to a week."[2] One such preacher was Charles Finney, who, from September 1830 through June 1831, led various revival campaigns[3] in Rochester, Buffalo and "the intermediate towns between there."[4] And what facilitated this travel? Why, none other than our old friend the Erie Canal. For example, Finney and his family arrived via canal boat with much fanfare in Rochester on the morning of September 10, 1830.[5]

The Canal proved a convenient mode of transportation for revivalists. For Greater Western New York as well as other parts west of Albany, it quickly became an information superhighway for the Second Great Awakening. Attracting all types of evangelicals, the region was so saturated with spiritual awakening Finney referred to it as the "Burned-Over District" in his 1876 autobiography.[6] Finney's legacy to our region, though, goes far beyond coining a term for it. The Second Great Awakening incited social activism, and Finney himself was a well-known abolitionist and advocate for women's suffrage,[7] two issues Greater Western New York has become noted for.

The fiery sermons of the Burned-Over District forged two hidden gems that continue to shine to this day.

The first and most famous is the birth of the Mormon Church, a.k.a., the Church of Jesus Christ of Latter-Day Saints or "LDS." Around 1818, the Smith family moved to Manchester, New York, in Ontario County. Each morning, young Joseph would go to his special spot deep in the woods to pray. On "a beautiful, clear day, early in the spring of 1820," fourteen year-old Joseph Smith, Jr. saw a vision of God and Jesus Christ.[8] The teenager kept what's now called his "First Vision" to himself for three- and-a-half years until, while praying to God, the angel Moroni appeared before him to reveal divine truth.[9] Moroni told Smith to find the Golden Plates that contained the Book of Mormon on a nearby hill, and the young man went to this hill each year for four years until he was allowed to retrieve the plates.[10] The Book of Mormon itself was first published in the Grandin Building in the Village of Palmyra in Wayne County.

It is this hill, unnamed at the time, where we find our hidden gem. While the locals soon began calling it "Mormon Hill," the LDS eventually christened it "Hill Cumorah." Each July, thousands of LDS volunteers come to the hallowed site and stage the annual Hill Cumorah Pageant, an extravagant production with a "cast of 700, 1,300 costumes, 10-level stage and thrill-a-minute special effects" that, according to a *New York Times* review, evokes Cecil B. DeMille.[11] While Mormons initially starting coming to the site in the 1920s, the first show was held in 1937 and carried the title "America's Witness to Christ."[12]

I'm told the Hill Cumorah Pageant is an event everyone should experience. At least that's what my parents told me after they went. The spectacle attracts Mormons and non-Mormons alike. Its cast has even included well-known celebrities. In 1997, Donny Osmond appeared in the show as a Mormon prophet.[13] Osmond would return with his family in 2010, this time as spectators.[14] Who'd a thought Greater Western New York would have been the Jerusalem of the New World?

Just to the east of the Town of Palmyra, and still in Wayne County, lies the Town of Arcadia. Towards the end of the Burned-Over days, a small hamlet called Hydesville existed. In it was a small house. In that small house lived two teenage girls, Maggie and Katy Fox. Maggie and Katy one day in the winter of 1848 decided to scare their mother by making ghostly noises.[15] But the prank backfired as the mother panicked and brought in the neighbors to confirm the eerie origin of the strange sounds. The girls hid the truth to avoid getting into trouble and, as news spread, their older sister Leah, who was living in Rochester, saw a money-making opportunity.[16]

It's not clear from the records when the girls concocted the story that the sounds came from the ghost of a murdered peddler buried in the cellar of their home, but the neighbors searched the foundation and came up with no real hard evidence, apparently torrential rains thwarted their efforts.[17] With Leah as their manager, the girls soon gained international notoriety for their ability to speak to the dead. Alas, in their old age and perhaps due to acute alcoholism, the sisters had a falling out, and Maggie spilled the beans of their hoax in 1888.[18] She tried recanting her confession the following year to no avail. The sisters died in 1892.

Now, here's the real strange thing about the story. In 1904 that same water problem that stymied curious neighbors in 1848 undermined a false foundation wall in the Fox sisters' former home. The fallen wall revealed a hidden chamber containing human remains.[19] Amazing, right? Too bad skeptics have since refuted this claim.[20]

Nonetheless, that Maggie and Kate Fox started the modern Spiritualism movement cannot be denied. Spiritualism believes, after the body dies, the personality of that person lives on as a spirit. Spiritualism grew quickly once the Fox sisters hit the stage. Within a decade of their initial claim, the nation could count more than a million practicing Spiritualists.[21] Like their predecessors in the Second Great Awakening, they would often meet in camps for weeks at a time. In 1871, one such group began meeting on the shores of Cassadaga Lake[22] in the town of Pomfret in Chautauqua County. A few years later this group would formally organize themselves as the Cassadaga Lake Free Association, although in 1906 their gated community would become known as The Lily Dale Assembly in honor of the great many lilies flourishing in the nearby lake.[23]

In 1916 the childhood home of the Fox sisters was taken from its Hydesville foundation and moved to Lily Dale where the spiritualist village used it as a museum (it burned to the ground in 1955, taking Finney's Burned-Over District metaphor to a new level).[24] Hydesville has since built a shell of the original house above the still intact foundation of Maggie and Kate's childhood home. Still, Lily Dale, remains the center of the Spiritualism movement.

The ashes of the Burned-Over District may have been quite cold, but they must have provided fertile nourishment for the blossoming of our next hidden gem. The very same year of the first meeting of spiritualists in Chautauqua County, another religious assembly would meet for the first time. It would take a vastly different direction that reverberates to this day.

CHAPTER 29: THE SHINING CITY ON THE LAKE

Lewis Miller first entered the United States in Greentown, Ohio on July 24, 1829 as a new born baby. Not many people lived there then. And not many people live there now. Miller himself moved to Akron, Ohio, where he died on February 17, 1899, having lived a full and productive life. So full and productive was his life, that in 2006, he was inducted into the National Inventors Hall of Fame. He had 92 patents to his name, the most famous being the Buckeye Mower and Reaper, the antecedent of the modern lawn mower.[1] Oh, yeah, he was also the father-in-law of some guy by the name of Thomas Alva Edison. Yeah, THAT Thomas Alva Edison.

But our interest in Miller has nothing to do with his mechanical genius, wealth or the discriminating tastes in men his daughter must have had. No, our interest deals with a common trait of many well-to-do businessmen. Miller's philanthropy knew no bounds, and he often volunteered his time, talent and treasure to the Methodist Episcopal Church of Akron. In 1864, he didn't just form a Sunday school for his church, he was pivotal in helping to create an integrated solution of space and curriculum that was to become known as the "Akron Plan."[2]

Just as Miller was completing his Akron Plan, John Heyl Vincent was returning from his Grand Tour of Europe, the Middle East and Africa. Born on February 23, 1832 in Tuscaloosa, Alabama, Vincent, unlike Miller whose religious and educational pursuits were avocational, chose to make a career of both areas. Upon his return from overseas, he quickly established himself as "the" specialist in Sunday schools, seeking to incorporate "all the most advanced methods of the public school" into the Sunday school syllabus.[3]

Vincent soon developed a curriculum and began what today we might call "faculty meetings" for Sunday school teachers.[4] What Vincent wanted most, however, was to create a platform to teach all Sunday school teachers. In

1864, the Union Sunday-School Institute for the Northwest started and Vincent helped start (and publish) *The Northwestern Sunday School Teachers' Quarterly* magazine.[5] In 1871, he held 29 Institutes across the county, attended nine Annual conferences and travelled more than 17,000 miles.[6]

That Miller and Vincent would eventually meet, given their growing acumen in identical subject areas, seems predestined. After all, they shared a similar vision. They soon began discussing an idea for an "Assembly," the purposes of which would be, as Vincent would later attest, "to distinguish it from ordinary Sunday School institutes and conventions."[7] It was Miller who would suggest the secluded woodland of Fair Point, New York (in the Town of Chautauqua in Chautauqua County) on the shores of Chautauqua Lake as the ideal location for what they would soon be calling "The Chautauqua Idea."[8] Vincent did not immediately like the location. He wanted to avoid the allusion to the religious camp meetings of the recent past and would have much rather had a city location.[9]

As luck would have it, the Methodist Association already owned Fair Point – a protrusion of land into Chautauqua Lake a few miles south of Mayville – and they had been holding camp-meetings there since 1871,[10] the same year the folks right up the road in Lily Dale began doing their thing. With Miller able to convince Vincent to give Fair Point a look-see, our two heroes ventured to the "Fourth Erie Conference Camp-Meeting of the Methodist-Episcopal Church" held at Fair Point, Chautauqua County, New York from Tuesday, August 12th through Friday August 22, 1873.[11] The duo decided Fair Point was the place and held their first "Assembly" there the following year. Vincent later wrote, "the Assembly was totally unlike the camp-meeting. We did our best to make it so."[12]

Here's an objective contemporary account made in 1875:

> "There are, on the grounds, 135 cottages, 1 hotel, 1 general office, 1 dining hall, 1 bath house, ticket offices, etc. Preparations for the contemplated assembly in August, were commenced early in the spring, and carried forward rapidly. An invaluable work, designed as an aid to Sunday School instruction, was the Holy Land, in miniature, laid out on the shore of the lake. It exhibited the more prominent features of Palestine – villages, cities, mountains, valleys, rivers, seas, and plains, almost perfect in detail. The first session of the assembly, in respect to numbers, was a great success. Thousands, from great distances, were attracted thither by the announcement of the names of distinguished speakers from different religious denominations. Thus encouraged, the directors were determined to make the second session [in 1875,] an improvement on the former; and it is by many believed they were successful.

Whether the same degree of interest will be kept up in
succeeding years, time will determine. The fame of 'Chautauqua
lake and its surroundings,' has become almost world-wide; and
there are, as yet, no signs of their becoming less attractive as a
summer resort."[13]

Andrew Young, the author of this passage, needn't have worried about the
future of the event. Within a decade, the "Chautauqua Movement" as it was
then and still is called, had more than 40 "Chautauquas" in the United States
and still more in at least a dozen countries.[14] By the end of the nineteenth
century there were "well over 200" "daughter Chautauquas" and in 1904 we
saw the advent of a series of "Circuit Chautauquas," essentially a traveling
road show that brought the Chautauqua experience to rural communities.[15]
Incidentally, although Young mentions the ships that carried President Grant
to and from Fair Point in August of 1875, he fails to acknowledge the reason
for the President's travels was to visit the Assembly, something Vincent called
"the most important event of the season of 1875."[16]

Though from a single denomination, from its very beginnings, Miller and
Vincent intended their "Chautauqua Idea" to be presented "on a broad and
catholic basis."[17] Miller has said "Chautauqua was founded for an enlarged
recognition of the Word" with "the original intention to make Chautauqua an
international center – a place where the highest officials in all spheres of life
should come to give the Book that recognition which would magnify it in the
eyes of all the people, so that every citizen through the land should have a
higher appreciation of the church and church-school in their midst."[18]

More important than its inclusiveness was the events immersion of
temporal affairs with religious matters. As Miller explains, "It was the purpose
that the scientist and the statesman, the artisan and the tradesman, should
bring their latest and best to this altar of consecration and praise; that the
tourist and pleasure-seeker should here stop and find their respective fields,
and there, through the year, weave into the fiber of the homework the newly
gathered inspiration and strength…The men of trade, factory, or field need
the association of the theorist and the professions; the theorist and the
professions need contact with the arts and artisan."[19]

If the bell doesn't ring quite right in the telling of this story, then you're on
to something. Through the years, the names have changed. In 1877, Fair
Point rechristened itself as "Chautauqua"[20] and formally changed its name to
"Chautauqua Institution" in 1902.[21] The Chautauqua movement peaked in
the 1920s, the public's fascination with cars and radio made "getting away"
easier and the need for road shows in general to diminish. Chautauqua
Institution itself went bankrupt in 1933 and, although it reopened its doors in
1936, it was but a shell of its former self, the realities of economic Depression
and world-wide war taking the shine off the luxury of intellectual relaxation.[22]

The concept, and the facility, of Chautauqua had a resurgence in the 1980s and today provides its popular program mix of arts, education, religion and recreation to 170,000 people each summer.[23]

The Institution is a throwback. Until May 2006, alcohol was forbidden. According to the Chautauqua Property Association Board Meeting minutes of June 28, 2006, "Steeped in Methodist tradition, many deeds specified that if alcohol were consumed on the premises, the owner would forfeit his ownership in said property."[24] Despite this little concession to modern living, the Institution really does recreate a time when America was a much simpler place. And I'm not talking about a time when anyone could pop the hood of a car and fiddle with the engine (you know, before they put all those anti-pollution laws in place that make it impossible for you not to go to the dealer to get your air filter replaced). No, I'm talkin' 'bout a time afore them fancy automobiles even had the temerity to grace our peaceful countryside.

That's right. Chautauqua would love to count you among its 7,500 or so summer residents or tens of thousands of visitors, but please, leave your car on the other side of the gate.

Yes. Chautauqua Institution is a gated community and, during its nine-week season, there is an entry charge. Except sometimes. On Sundays.

I went on a Sunday. It was a warm summer Sunday. Once I walked past the residences, I came to the campus proper. It's laid out in the "City Beautiful" style of its founding era. The lawns rolled in green as the attendees strolled at a leisurely pace. Just beyond, the blue lake sparkled under the cloudless sky. I sauntered through the famous Anthenaeum Hotel, although not through all 157 of its rooms. Overlooking Chautauqua lake atop a hill shaded by elegant trees, this Victorian masterpiece (built in 1881), just oozes of a time when "hurry" was a rude word. Some might argue the Greek-Revival houses that dot the area in and around Jamestown might offer greater architectural significance, by the grandeur of the Athenaeum lures like a Lorelei. Perhaps one day I should like to take my wife there for a well-earned respite, (after the kids are through college and we've saved a tidy sum).

I must admit, in all honesty I had never heard of the place until I met my wife, a Jamestown native. I guess that's why *Forbes* calls Chautauqua Institution "one of America's best-kept secrets."[25] You'd think, having grown up in nearby Buffalo and attending a school like Yale, the name would have fallen upon my ears at least once. And I can't even lay it on the fact I tended to associate more with the carnies of the Hamburg Fair than with the artsy crowd. (To find out why, ask me about the Albright-Knox Gallery art class I once took as a ten-year old.)

But, despite my plebian roots, I was aware of the existence of art and the arts. In fact, growing up, everyone always talked about our next hidden gem with such awe that I always wondered what all the fuss was about. Then I found out. Turn the page and you can, too.

CHAPTER 30: I'LL HAVE ONE FOR THE ROAD
AND TWO FOR THE SEA

> And let me the canakin clink, clink,
> And let me the canakin clink.
> A soldier's a man;
> A life's but a span;
> Why, then, let a soldier drink.
> – Othello

The reason James Fenimore Cooper strode into Hustler's Tavern has disappeared into the hazy mists of history. By 1821, his life had been less than pristine. Kicked out of Yale after three years as a trouble-maker (he blew up a classmate's door), the son of a (probably embarrassed) Congressman who founded the City of Cooperstown did what any other lost teenager trying to find himself did in the early eighteenth century: he joined the Merchant Marine.[1]

Perhaps he remembered his earlier, albeit brief, stay in the Niagara Frontier just before the War of 1812.[2] Serving mostly overseas, he saw some of his best crewmates taken from their ships and forced to serve aboard British warships against Napoleonic France. Like the rest of America, he detested the idea of England treating his country like some nautical farm team. He joined the Navy, fought for his homeland, married his loyal sweetheart and… and what?

Just a year earlier, in 1820, his wife challenged him to write a better novel than the one she was reading. He did. But only she thought it was better. His first novel, *Precaution*, failed.[3] So bad was this initial effort years later his eulogist would purposely ignore it during Cooper's funeral.[4] Contemporary critics condemned his choice to model his characters on his European acquaintances and thought the novel "to be an unpatriotic vein."[5] Maybe, just maybe, they felt Cooper, as children so often do, was rebelling against his patriotic father. He wasn't. But just what could he do to confront these detractors?

So he found himself in the Town of Lewiston in Niagara County during the summer of 1821. This was no ordinary town. Before the Erie Canal later in that decade would grant Buffalo the title, Lewiston was considered the Gateway to the West.[6] Since the time of the French traders, it had been considered a strategic port city. The French were good friends of the Seneca Tribe, especially after the latter wiped out the Huron and the Erie Tribe to gain control of the Niagara Peninsula. In 1719, the Seneca Tribe granted permission to Chabert Joncaire to build a trading post in Lewiston.[7] When the British booted the French as a result of the French and Indian War, the peace treaty also stripped the famous "Mile Strip" (or "Mile Reserve") along the banks of the Niagara River from the Seneca Tribe and ceded it to the British.[8]

As we've seen in our chapter on Pre-Emption Line, the Revolutionary War left many questions unanswered in terms of Greater Western New York. Even the Treaty of Hartford in 1786 failed to address the issue of ownership of the Mile Strip. Eventually, the Jay Treaty of 1794 would determine the international border between the United States and Canada to be the middle of the Niagara River, and the British finally abandoned Fort Niagara and Lewiston to the Americans. Until the Jay Treaty, many British Loyalists, including their Seneca Tribe allies, continued to reside along the Mile Strip, though after the Jay Treaty was signed, they began their exodus to Canada.[9]

The Jay Treaty only delayed the inevitable war with Britain. The first engagement of the War of 1812 would occur along the Niagara River. But it was that fateful battle of December 1813 that would deal Lewiston a cataclysmic blow. Remember our earlier story about the burning of Buffalo? That was revenge for the Americans burning the Canadian city of Newark, at the time the capital of the British province and today called Niagara-on-the-Lake. Unfortunately for its residents, Lewiston fell directly in the path of the vengeful British on their way to torching Buffalo. The march from Canada left Lewiston in ashes, an omen to what was about to happen in Buffalo.

Like Buffalo, one building was spared: Thomas and Catherine Hustler's inn.[10] Maybe that curious fact prompted Cooper to visit the Inn. We'll never know. Today, Hustler's Tavern no longer exists, which, as we shall see later, is too bad.

If you're like me, the first thing that comes to mind about Lewiston is the bridge into Canada. The second thing that comes to mind is the New York State Park named in honor of Earl W. Bridges. You might recognize it by the name "Artpark." It may have come about to fill the void left by the Chautauqua Institution (remember, the Institution's renaissance was still a few years away). Dedicated on July 25, 1974, it was meant to be the summer home of the Buffalo Philharmonic Orchestra as well as the venue for important artistic events and cultural history. By way of example, the opening night featured actress Cicely Tyson and comedian James Coco and finished with the Buffalo Philharmonic's rendition of the *1812 Overture*, complete with canons.[11]

Today, New York State has contracted with a private firm to run the shows, some of which are free and open to the public. Artpark contains several historic sites including a Hopewellian Indian Burial Mound (this culture dates from the birth of Christ to 500AD), remnants of the Oak Hill Mansion (the home of the "old and eccentric" Starkweather sisters, said to be the model for their one-time guest Joseph O. Kesselring's play *Arsenic and Old Lace*),[12] the original location of Joncaire's trading post (it's a parking lot now) and Owen Morrell's "Omega" (actually, the 1981 sculpture isn't the historic part, it's the two stone support columns of the old *Queenston-Lewiston Suspension Bridge* that offer historic value).[13] Artpark continues to be the site of popular celebrity acts and its placement overlooking the Niagara Gorge is spectacular.

That very view might have inspired James Fenimore Cooper to write his first – and America's first – best-selling fiction novel *The Spy*.[14] To appease critics, Cooper choose the Revolutionary War as its setting. In many ways, it's a tribute to the many unheralded patriots of that day. And, as he would do again in the future in even more successful novels, he heeded the advice of his friends following the debacle of *Precaution* and chose people he met in real life as models for his characters.[15]

Thomas and Catharine Hustler earned a place in *The Spy* as Sergeant Hollister and Betty Flanagan.[16] Cooper's characters Hollister and Flanagan resemble the real life of Thomas and Catharine with eerie precision. During the Revolutionary War, Hollister was a soldier and Catharine was "sutler" specializing in the provisioning to the soldiers their daily allotment of liquor.[17] Sutlers were civilian merchants who followed the army with a peddler's wagon and sold necessities to the soldiers. In *The Spy*, Hollister was regular army while Betty followed the troops in her wagon filled with liquor. It is Betty's character that holds our interest. Here's a short piece from the novel describing one of her talents:

> "Added to these, Betty had the merit of being the inventor of that beverage which is so well known, at the present hour, to all the patriots who make a winter's march between the commercial and political capitals of this great state, and which is distinguished by the name of "cocktail.""[18]

Indeed Catharine Hustler is credited with inventing the term "cocktail" to describe mixed drinks. She concocted a "gin mixture" that "warms both the soul and the body and is fit to be put in a vessel of diamonds."[19] For effect, she placed the tail feather of a male fowl in the glass; hence, the name "cocktail."[20] The term cocktail (specifically pertaining to a mixed alcohol drink) first appears in 1806,[21] coincidentally the same year the Hustlers moved to Lewiston to open their tavern.[22] It's very plausible Catherine has earned her place in the history of mixology. It's been suggested the invading Britons, possibly remembering the fine times they had sipping Catherine's mixed drinks at Hustler's Tavern, left it unscathed in hopes of quenching their collective thirsts at the conclusion of their raid.

Is there any question that James Fenimore Cooper left that same Tavern duly impressed with the quality – and perhaps the quantity – of the libations so served? It's very plausible Catherine has earned her place in the history of mixology, however circumstantial the evidence may be. One thing were sure of, Betty (or Betsy) Flanagan did not invent the cocktail outside New York City while serving George Washington and his troops during the Revolutionary war. You'll find many sources claiming this as fact, but we know it as fiction written by James Fenimore Cooper in *The Spy*. One wonders if the wordsmith left something more than a tin coin in the tip jar of the famous barmaid.

The wording on Catherine's gravestone is hard to read, but with patience you can decipher it:

> "Traveler, as you are passing by –
> As you are now, so once was I –
> As I am now, so you must be,
> Prepare for death and follow me."[23]

As travelers pass, so, too, do eras. And along with the currents of time, the spirit of those bygone days grows thinner and thinner. Our next hidden gem reflects one man's successful attempt to capture the essence of a then vanishing, now vanished, classic American epoch before the revisionists forever tarnished all that was great about it. Strangely, though given plenty of opportunities to choose a more appropriate venue, he opted to keep his memorial right here in Greater Western New York. Most conveniently for you, dear reader, I have translocated that memorial to the very next pages.

CHAPTER 31: PUTTING THE "WEST" IN GREATER WESTERN NEW YORK

In order to smooth the acculturation of what might be viewed as the most dramatic change in a teenage life, college freshman tend to congregate around a common evil. Sometimes it's a national figure. Sometimes it's a piece of particularly abhorrent popular culture. More often than not, it's a University administrator, usually the President. It's a silly practice, one that parents seem unable to appreciate, but it allows an otherwise diverse group of randomly selected eighteen-year-olds to rally around a common bond, namely, a common enemy.

It seemed the tradition of my school, particularly in the 1970s as chronicled by Gary Trudeau in the early incarnations of his once relevant strip *Doonesbury*, to select the University's President as the *ennemi du jour*. Our target was therefore the newly installed President of Yale: A. Barlett Giamatti, (yes, the father of Paul Giamatti and once the Commissioner of Major League Baseball – the one responsible for banning Pete Rose for life). The well-spoken Giamatti, however, disarmed our Freshman class from the outset when he admitted his lower stature by telling us at the inaugural Freshman Address he was the only one to make it in from the wait list. Such was the natural self-effacing amiability of his character.

So we selected an alternative antagonist to unite against, the Dean of the College, Howard Lamar. It didn't help Lamar's case that our class still had the taste of Mel Brooks' *Blazing Saddles* in our brains. The evil Hedley Lamarr, played with such delicious dislikability by Harvey Korman, sounded too much like the name of our Dean. Little did we know Lamar was (and remains) a much admired historian of the old west, having gained a reputation as a debunker of much of the mythos of the classic west. Of course, it wouldn't have mattered to us back then. Or now. No, Howard Lamar will forever be remembered as the evil administrator who banished Bladderball from the hallowed halls of Yale.

Bladderball? That was a game invented by young Elis no doubt to test the concept of Social Darwinism, or at least the survival of the fittest. Imagine putting 5,000 college students in a courtyard the size of three football fields – the Old Campus – walled in by vintage late nineteenth and early twentieth century architecture trying its best to look like some even older European century. Now, imagine splitting those students into four equal sized teams, each guarding a corner and each trying to push a heavy six foot diameter leather ball into the opposite corner. The only rule: There are no rules.

If this sounds like mayhem, you only know the half of it. I've been in the middle of the scrum. This is where the survival of the fittest thing comes in. It's hard to breathe. If you trip, you risk being trampled (think: Cincinnati Who concert). But winning the battle of the scrum is the only way to win the game. I should know. My team won the contest all four years I participated. My sophomore year, atop the shoulders of some varsity athlete I barely knew, I personally hit the ball into the opposing goal. Senior year I was a co-Captain and led the team to victory, a victory I attribute to a rallying pregame speech. Picture Knute Rockne's famous "win one for the Gipper" speech combined with the opening monologue of the movie *Patton*. Actually, you don't have to imagine it, that was the opening speech. As a veteran disc jockey and sports director of the radio station, I had access to old movie tracts and the technology to transfer them for mass audience broadcast purposes. It's amazing how much a well delivered oration can inspire folks, but it does. And on that particular fall morning, it did.

Sadly, during the autumn game after my graduation, several students earned their badges of honor via broken bones and other dramatic but non-life threatening injuries. University officials deliberated and apparently concluded Yale students had an unfair disadvantage as it pertains to natural selection (i.e., they weren't all fit). Apparently too many arm chair quarterbacks thought they could leave the armchair and proceeded to break their arms or legs or whatever. Little did they know, to invoke another perhaps more appropriate movie character, Dean Wormer from *Animal House*, the administration had placed Bladderball on Double Secret Probation.

Following the injury-plagued game in the fall of 1982, Dean Lamar banned the game. Make that, the evil Dean Lamar banned the game. If we didn't hate him as first year students in 1978, we vilified him as first year graduates.

Why do I remember all this stuff from a college career more than thirty years old? Much to the chagrin of my wife – and the incessant needling of my own children – I collect things, including the trinkets of my life. Some of my collections are actual collections, to the dismay of my son, who has yet to use his closet as a closet is intended to be used.

But, apparently, I share this "collecting" trait with others.

Unless you're from Steuben County, you probably don't recognize the name Bob Rockwell. Bob was born just over the border in Bradford, Pennsylvania, but grew up on his family's Colorado ranch.[1] He came to Greater Western New York to help his grandfather oversee the family's chain of department stores in Corning, Hornell, Wellsville and Perry.[2] He married a local girl and, after serving three and a half years in the Seabees during World War II, returned to Corning, where he ran the local store (the family would sell all the others) and raise his own family.[3]

And begin collecting.

Bob always loved the west. His collection of western arcana soon grew beyond the borders of his home and spilled over into his store, various museums (on loan) scattered throughout the west and even a temporary art gallery he set up in the former Baron Von Steuben Hotel.[4] Remember, he grew up in the west. He knew real cowboys and admired them. The romance of the West continually inspired him.[5] He meant to collect pieces that would reflect that philosophy.

When it became known his collection was busting out at the seams, the museums he had worked with, including the Cowboy Artists Hall of Fame and the Denver Art Museum, approached him for a bequest.[6] But Rockwell stayed loyal to his adopted home town. "Corning was where I made my money and raised my family," he said, adding "I wanted my collection to remain here."[7]

Corning Glass Works, the city's biggest employer, approached Rockwell with the idea of creating a museum in Corning. The company agreed to purchase and restore a suitable building if Rockwell would then donate his collection to the museum. Rockwell consented and Corning Glass Works purchased the abandoned (due to damages sustained during the Hurricane Agnes floods of 1972) Romanesque-Revival-Style former City Hall. The building has an architectural style similar to the pseudo-European buildings surrounding the Old Campus, which isn't surprising because it was built in 1893, around the same time as most of those Yale buildings. Corning Glass Works paid one dollar for the building.[8] It cost $3.5 million to renovate it.[9] It wasn't until 1982 – the same year Dean Lamar banned Bladderball – that the building was opened as the new and permanent location of the Rockwell Museum of Western Art.[10]

Visitors to this museum often say walking past the displays sends them back to a time they've only read about in books. Those from the west swear they can smell the rocky mountain air as they meander through the various exhibit halls. Good art does that. Good American art does that even more. Whether we recognize it or not, the fabled past of our nation courses through our veins. A good art collector can feel this in the pieces he seeks. For those visiting the Rockwell Museum, to hear them describe their experience in this manner, only attests to the success of Bob Rockwell. He wanted to capture that special inspiration only the American West can offer. He has succeeded.

And no less an expert on our western heritage, and author of the definitive *Encyclopedia of the American West*, one Howard Lamar, who made his academic name exposing the warts and scars of the old west, has, among his many highlights of the old west, included a listing of Bob Rockwell and the Rockwell museum, an institution dedicated to celebrating the Romantic aura and uniquely American persona of the Old West.[11]

By strange coincidence, the original Chittenden part of Linsly-Chittenden Hall on Yale's Old Campus was built in 1889. Similar to the Rockwell museum, it was constructed in a Neo-Romanesque style.[12] If you go to room 102, you'll notice a stained-glass window facing on the High Street side of the building. Rockwell, who also collected colored Steuben glass (another famous product of Corning), would have certainly appreciated this window. Inscribed on the bronze plaque beneath the window you'll find this biblical quote:

> "Through wisdom is a house builded, and by understanding it is
> established, and by knowledge shall the chambers be filled with
> all precious and pleasant riches."[13]

Nothing better sums up the will and intent, as well as, ultimately, the wisdom of Bob Rockwell and the Rockwell Museum. The "precious and pleasant riches" contained within the Museum's Romanesque walls will impart the knowledge and understanding of a time long ago, when the American West captured the destiny, the drive and the desire of a young nation. It is America. And it is right here in the Heart of America's first western frontier: Greater Western New York.

Incidentally, the stained-glass window, entitled *Education*, was created by a fellow by the name of Louis Comfort Tiffany, the same Tiffany of Tiffany lamp fame. If you're surprised to learn the creator of Tiffany Lamps also created fine stained-glassed windows, you shouldn't be. President Chester B. Arthur refused to move into the White House until it was redecorated by Tiffany.[14] The glassmaker installed two large stained-glass panels at the Entrance Hall doors.

Greater Western New York also features a wide array of Tiffany stained-glass creations. But two stand out, and they'll lead us to yet another hidden gem in our next chapter.

CHAPTER 32: DINNER AND A MOVIE

Recall how two members of the Methodist Episcopalian Church worked together to form Chautauqua Institution. Although Lewis Miller and John Heyl Vincent brought their "Chautauqua Idea" from the Midwest shortly after the Civil War, Methodists and Episcopalians began establishing themselves through Greater Western New York following the War of 1812 and the many revivals of the Second Great Awakening. Inspired by such revivals, a "small band of hardy pioneers organized the first Methodist Church Society in Erie County's East Aurora on March 9, 1822.[1] The church was already almost fifty years old when Miller and Vincent held their first event on the shores of Chautauqua Lake. At the time, the Reverend Chauncey Steele Baker served as the pastor of East Aurora's Methodist Church, and a very successful one at that.[2]

When need arose for a bigger church, Carrie Baker Maxwell donated the money to build it, and it was completed in 1928.[3] She asked that it be named in the memory of her father, the Reverend Baker.[4] The sanctuary features 17 Tiffany stained-glass windows, of which six are signed.[5] It is cited as "the only house of worship in Western New York whose windows are all Tiffany."[6]

But let's not leave the Episcopalians out. In the Town of Brockport (Monroe County), St. Luke's Episcopal Church, built in two sections in 1855 and 1903, entered the list of the National Register of Historic Places in 1990.[7] The facility contains three Tiffany stained-glass windows, but it is the three paneled window over the altar which has the most claim to fame. Called "The Nativity," its subject and beauty dazzles the viewer. So much so, in 1955 the Eastman Kodak Company used it as the subject of their famous Grand Central Station panoramic for Christmas.[8]

Next, we'll travel to the east end of Greater Western New York to Seneca Falls in Seneca County. There, in 1886 after nearly fifty years as an established

130

congregation, the Trinity Episcopal Church built its new building.[9] Like many of the Tiffany windows displayed in our local churches, they came through donations in memory of a loved one. One of Trinity's three Tiffany stained-glass windows – "The Savior Knocking at the Door" on the east wall– was offered in 1931by Carrie Dobbyns Garnsey in memory of her two children.[10] The significance of this particular window is the year it was installed. It might have been one of the last created by the company, as Tiffany Studios (née Tiffany Glass Company) shuttered its doors in 1932.

Greater Western New York is home to two of the three (why do these things keep coming in threes?) rare Tiffany "Last Supper" mosaics (the third being in Baltimore). Of the two local masterpieces, the most accessible is the one at Christ Church in Rochester. The more publicized one (if you are to believe the *New York Times*[11]) and certainly the one with the more interesting backstory sits inside the former Sanitarium of a seldom-used chapel in Ontario County's Village of Clifton Springs.

Originally called Sulphur Springs for its waters,[12] Clifton Springs straddles the Towns of Manchester and Phelps. In 1849, Dr. Henry Foster chose the town as the site to establish a facility to practice his soon-to-be famous water cure.[13] In 1850 Foster opened the Clifton Springs Sanitarium Company.[14] The facility today operates under the name Clifton Springs Hospital and Clinic. Of course, another source implies the Sanitarium, now closed and operating as the Spa Apartments, was built in 1896.[15] In either case, we are certain the chapel was built in 1856.[16] The Tiffany mosaic is currently being restored, but it is open to the public on weekdays.[17]

At least one self-acclaimed expert believes St. Paul's Church has the most Tiffany stained-glass windows of all churches in Rochester.[18] Those same authors relay an interesting story that bears repeating here. George Eastman lived across the street from St. Paul's and occasionally attended worship services there. His suicide made him ineligible for an Episcopal burial, but the Bishop declared Eastman was not of sound mind; thus, absolving him of any sin and allowing Eastman's funeral service to take place at St. Paul's.[19]

Which connects us to yet another hidden gem. Eastman willed his home to the University of Rochester for 10 years and, upon the conclusion of World War II, the University transferred it to a board of trustees formed to establish a museum of photography.[20] In addition to still photography, the museum is considered "one of the major moving image archives in the United States."[21] With 30,000+ titles, the museum has an unrivaled collection of silent era (1895-1928) and Hollywood golden age (1920s-1940s) films.[22]

Hmm. If, in visiting both these gems together, have we given new meaning to the phrase "dinner and a movie"? As we're about to discover, Greater Western New York is not merely Hollywood's archive, it has also produced and influenced the entertainment industry in many ways. We'll start with perhaps its greatest – and most denied – impact ever.

CHAPTER 33: THE HOLLYWOOD IDEAL?

We drove down "Main Street" into Seneca Falls trying very hard to capture in our eyes the wholesome virtue of Frank Capra's fictional Bedford Falls. Many people believe the Seneca County village was the inspiration for Capra's town in the Christmas classic It's a Wonderful Life. Some say you can see the obvious resemblance just by driving down the main street of Seneca Falls. It was tough to do. First, a lot of things have changed since Tommy Bellissima remembers cutting Capra's hair in late 1945. For one thing, urban renewal, while not overly disturbing the buildings on Falls Street (the real name of the main thoroughfare through town), did change the layout of the road on the east side of town.

On the other hand, it was summer and hot. It's hard to conjure up the comforting warmth of a tranquil blanket of freshly fallen snow when you've got the air conditioner cranking inside a hermetically sealed automobile.

Plus, I couldn't figure out where the dang bridge was. Seneca Falls has three bridges. The east end bridge – on Ovid Street – obviously participated in the aforementioned urban renewal. The west end bridge – Veterans Bridge on aptly named Veterans Bridge Street – lay on the only other street that crossed Fall Street (a.k.a, 5 & 20 for all you veteran Greater Western New York drivers).

Frustrated, sweaty and starting to grow hungry, we seeped down the part of Fall Street immediately following 5&20's escape from it for a couple of quick shots of Van Cleef Lake. They were working on the road, further infuriating us. We parked, took a few pictures, then headed back to the car, thinking maybe we'd take the bait and try lunch at the Hotel Clarence (OK, that wasn't the original name of the place).

That's when we noticed it.

Nestled in the corner of this beaten down portion of Fall Street sits a museum within a museum, sort of like what we found at the Jell-o Museum.

Except, this time, the real gem isn't the headliner, it's the supporting actor. Of even greater coincidence, the building is Seneca Falls first movie theater.

OK, so here's the scoop. On the outside you'll see above the arch of the grand entrance the words "Center for the Voices of Humanity." Beneath it, and much smaller, a plastic banner hangs precariously pinned. On it reads "The Seneca Falls *It's a Wonderful Life* Museum." It's almost as if they're embarrassed to admit it. But don't mistake this for the quality of both the exhibit and the exhibitors.

We tentatively knocked on the door. They were closed, but we saw someone moving inside coming ever so slowly to the door. They opened it, but just a crack. "We're sorry, but we're closed," was all we heard. We explained we were there researching this book and they kindly let us in, apologizing for the state of things. Monday – the day we were there – was normally their day off, but they received word that morning of a water leak on the second floor and it was dripping into their space. Fortunately, it was far away from the fine exhibit they had set up in the front corner of the building.

The curator, Anwei Law, was so kind and inviting. Her husband, Henry, was, too, but his more important job at the moment was to fix the water leak. We asked only for the chance to get a couple of good shots for the book's video, but she insisted on giving us the grand tour. We looked at each other and, without saying a word, agreed lunch could wait a little longer. Law went through the entire litany of "proof" that Seneca Falls was the model for Bedford Falls: The coincidence of the street layout; the similarity of the buildings (go to 32 Cuyahoga Street and tell me that doesn't look like George and Mary Bailey's home on 320 Sycamore); and, the mention of all those New York towns and cities EXCEPT for Seneca Falls. She even explained how Seneca Falls, like its fictional kin, had a large Italian population that lived in a neighborhood called "Rumseyville," named after John Rumsey, a successful factory owner who built cheap and affordable housing for his immigrant labor force. She was speaking to the choir.

But what about the bridge?

She then showed us the exhibits, movie posters, collectors' items and even some still photos. Much of the movie memorabilia has been provided by Karolyn Grimes, the actress who played Zuzu in the movie and who has written eloquently of her experiences visiting Seneca Falls (and the museum).[1] Law explained how people have written their feelings about the movie on a banner in the museum. She even told us – and showed us – envelopes people addressed to "Bedford Falls" that somehow have found their way to Seneca Falls. Does the post office know something Tinsel Town doesn't?

But I kept wanting to get back to the bridge.

Law then offered, again apologetically despite our clear enjoyment, to show several news stories and a short film about the museum and the movie. We happily sat through. Then, she came out of the blue and said, "those in

Hollywood who know Frank Capra insist he did not model Bedford Falls after Seneca Falls. They don't offer an alternative. They just say it's not Seneca Falls. And here's the truth: There's no way to know for sure." In fact, Capra never mentions Seneca Falls ever. In his memoirs. In his notes. In this personal archives.

My heart sank.

"Except," she continued, "for the strange coincidence of the story of the bridge."

My eyes lit up! The bridge! The bridge! I knew it. It was the bridge all along.

The story begins in 1945 with Frank Capra in New York City trying to convince Jean Arthur to play the part of Mary. We know this took place in November of that year. We also know he had an aunt in Auburn, NY and, given the most direct route at that time, driving from New York to Auburn would have taken Capra directly through Seneca Falls. It's not outside the realm of possibility he stopped in Seneca Falls and decided to tidy himself up for his aunt by getting a haircut.

Tommy Bellissima didn't know Frank Capra from Adam when he cut his hair. Only after the movie came out the next year did Tommy recognize his most famous fare. Bellissima said he remembered Capra because they spoke of Italy and because Bellissima (which mean "beautiful" in Italian) made fun of Capra's name (capra means "goat"). Bellissima's only significance is that he places Capra on the other side of the bridge.

Ah, the bridge. The bridge Frank Capra must have crossed to go to his aunt's house. The bridge with the conspicuous bronze plaque with the following inscription: "Here April 12, 1917 Antonio Varacalli gave his life to save another. He honored the community. The community honors him." Ironically, Varacalli rescued a young girl attempting to commit suicide.

It was from this bridge, the bridge on, I'm not kidding, "Bridge" Street, the bridge that appears identical to the bridge in Bedford Falls, the bridge that George jumps from TO SAVE ANOTHER's life (or at least so he thought), that a real person duplicated the same feat. And Capra was there to read this plaque.

Coincidence? Wait. There's more.

We know, a few weeks before, Capra had just signed the contract to make *It's a Wonderful Life*. We know he's in New York at this time to convince an actress to take the lead role. It makes sense he's still in the very early planning stages of story boarding the movie, at least in his mind. In "The Greatest Gift," a short story by Philip Van Doren Stern on which the movie is based, George Bailey contemplates committing suicide by jumping off the bridge, *but never actually jumps!* Clarence appears on the bridge and convinces George not to jump. The movie changes the story. In the film, Clarence jumps in, forcing George to follow in order to rescue him.

Voilà! There's your smoking gun. After learning of the Varacalli's story, it's plausible Capra, still in the story board phase, adjusts the plot line of "The Greatest Gift" to the more powerful one used in *It's a Wonderful Life*. It's just one too many coincidences to believe Capra did not have Seneca Falls in mind when he created Bedford Falls.

Yet, all this speculation doesn't matter. The very fact we're even having this discussion provides further evidence that, just as Walter Cronkite once said about our "accent" representing the heart of America, *It's a Wonderful Life* shows Greater Western New York represents the character of America's heart. And that, certainly, is the greatest gift any area can give to its country.

For all this make-believe show business brings into Greater Western New York, you might be surprised to learn how many real entertainment artists our small (and not so small) towns have produced. We'll give you a bit of a taste in the next chapter.

CHAPTER 34: OUR HIT PARADE

I'll be honest. I have no intention of naming every single person with Greater Western New York lineage who ever appeared in a movie, television show or Ivory Soap commercial. That would fill an entire book. I also don't want to play up too much those Greater Western New York "wannabes" who supped, dined, edited or even wrote here. Besides the aforementioned James Fenimore Cooper, such literary luminaries as F. Scott Fitzgerald, who spent his boyhood here,[1] Carl Sandberg, who wrote poetry here,[2] Jack London, who, charged with being a tramp, once spent 30 days in the Erie County Penitentiary,[3] and Mark Twain, who did just about everything everywhere and whose original manuscript of *Huck Finn* resides in the Buffalo Libarary,[4] all stepped into our midst at some point in their careers. OK, OK, Elimirans, I give! As home of the Center for Mark Twain Studies, Chemung County's Elmira can boast a greater claim to Samuel Clemens than the Queen City.

Nor do I have space to dabble in times too far back, like the mid-nineteenth century when Edwin Pierce ("Ned") Christy invented the minstrel show in the then seediest part of Buffalo (Canal Street where the Erie Canal met Lake Erie).[5] Though the infamous black-faced entertainment remained popular for nearly a century right up through the early Disney years, there's a reason why I preface the term "black-faced" with the modifier "infamous" today. Incidentally, a "tamer" (if you accept the bawdy humor) version of the minstrel show morphed into the vaudeville acts that spawned acts into the television era. There's a reason I mention Christy, though, and it has to do with our last chapter. One of the more noteworthy scenes in the movie *It's a Wonderful Life* has George and Mary singing the song *Buffalo Gals*. Christy wrote the catchy tune in 1848 to pay homage to his days in the Canal Street district.[6] Although Christy – and the Canal Street district in general – owed much of their opportunity to the Erie Canal, I don't have to tell you the occupation of those particular gals had nothing to do with anyone named Sal.

I'll also ignore those Greater Western New Yorkers who, like Tom and Catharine Hustler and like Richard Tobias Greene, found themselves personified as fictional characters in the books of famous American writers. The same goes for the character Benjamin Franklin Gates, Nicholas Cage's character in the *National Treasure* movie series. He should not be confused with the real Benjamin Franklin Gates, a pioneer who was the first to settle in the Town of Barre, Orleans County and whose 1830 Greek Revival home (on Route 31A – Lee Road) is now listed on the National Register.

Huh? You don't know who Greene was? Greene saved Herman Melville's career as an author just as it was getting started. In Melville's first novel, *Typee*, he tells the story of two deserters – Tommo and Toby – who lived among cannibals on a South Pacific island. The publisher had doubts about going forward after initial reviews doubted the plausibility of the story. Melville insisted it was not only possible, but true, as he and another shipmate had experienced what happened in *Typee*. Along came Greene who, in an open letter published in the *Commercial Advertiser*, confirmed to the whole world he was Toby to Melville's Tommo.[7] Melville's career was saved.

More interesting, however, is Anna Katharine Green, who was born in Brooklyn in 1846, and, after living a portion of her childhood in Buffalo, moved back to the Queen City in 1887 and stayed until her death at age 88 in 1935.[8] She is considered "The Mother of American Mystery," having published a total of 36 books in her career.[9] In 1878 she published her first novel, *The Leavenworth Case*, the first ever mystery novel written by a woman.[10] For reference, Arthur Conan Doyle would not produce the first Sherlock Holmes book, *A Study in Scarlet*, until 1887. Doyle would end up making an appointment to meet Green in Buffalo during his 1884 trip to the United States.[11] Doyle, a spiritualist, also visited Lilydale.[12]

A bestseller, *The Leavenworth Case* would become the first of 20 books to feature the bumbling, but sly, detective Ebenezer Gryce (think Peter Faulk as Columbo). She was called "the world's foremost detective story writer" and was considered a friend of both Theodore Roosevelt and Woodrow Wilson.[13] Unfortunately, the name Anna Katharine Green has become forgotten, displaced as the matriarch of her genre by Agatha Christie, although Christie herself admitted it was Green's works that first inspired her to write mysteries.[14] And, even after discovering the Yale Law School once regularly used *The Leavenworth Case* to show students the problems of relying on circumstantial evidence,[15] if you read the book today you'd decry it as nothing more than a collection of stale clichés. Of course, you'd be missing the whole point. Those stale clichés of today were first invented by Green, whom *Time Magazine* once called "a born story teller."[16]

But let's get right to the nitty gritty of our Hit Parade, that cavalcade of stars born in Greater Western New York that touched the lives of millions through song, personality and art. We'll start with this factoid. Of the four seminal television shows that defined the dawn of the age of the silver screen, two of them featured natives of Greater Western New York. Coincidence? Perhaps if we believe Walter Cronkite's statement that these two stars came from the place between Buffalo and Cleveland that represented "the classic American accent," then maybe it's not a coincidence at all.

Emil and Emma Schmidt were just glad to be away from the coal mines of Illinois when their son Robert was born on November 27, 1917 in Buffalo. Emil had been one of three survivors in a coal mine collapse, and the event – and his wife – convinced him to quit the business and move to the growing city of Buffalo to work as a carpenter.[17] His parents encouraged Robert to play the piano and organ, and when he was fifteen, he joined WGR, appearing as a member of "The Cheer-Up Gang,"[18] He also formed a three-man vocal group named the Hi-Hatters. It was through this group that he met Kate Smith who suggested, with nary a coincidence, he change his name to Smith.[19] On Kate Smith's advice, Robert Schmidt changed his name to Robert E. Smith, but the familiarity of radio soon had him known as "Buffalo" Bob Smith.

Nothing says "Western New York" more than "Buffalo" and no talent is more associated with Buffalo than "Buffalo" Bob Smith, the host of *The Howdy Doody Show*. The first children's show broadcast in color[20] and television's first smash hit,[21] it boomed in popularity as the babies boomed after World War II. The show helped launch the career of Bob Keeshan, a.k.a., Captain Kangaroo, and added the terms "peanut gallery" and "cowabunga" to our cultural lexicon.[22]

By coincidence, one of the other Hi-Hatters was Foster Brooks, famous for playing Hollywood's loveable lush, who, in his early career, worked in radio in both Buffalo and Rochester. And speaking of Rochester, it's the birthplace of Cab Calloway, a Christmas present Santa brought to the family on Christmas Day, 1907. Of course, he moved away when he was still a kid, so let's focus on that other Rochester music legend, Mitch Miller.

Miller was also born on a holiday – July 4th – but being that George M. Cohan had already (falsely) claimed that date some years before, Miller would have to select another aspect of music. Called "an absolutely first-rate oboist – one of the two or three great ones at that time in the world," his choice of instrument fell to chance: it was the only free instrument left unclaimed when he joined the orchestra at Washington Junior High School in Rochester.[23] He would later graduate cum laude from the city's world-class Eastman School of Music.[24] Despite his success as a musician and as a record producer in the 1950s, Miller would achieve his greatest fame with his "Sing Along With

Mitch" albums. Begun in 1958, this series appealed to the older generation, who sought a way to escape the burgeoning rock and roll movement.

If Mitch Miller is Greater Western New York's top music producer, we have to consider Hyman Arluck Greater Western New York's top music writer (with apologies to Ned Christy). Born in Buffalo in 1905, by the time he was a teenager, he had formed two successful bands that performed on the Crystal Beach lake boat "Canadiana" and then at the Lake Shore Manor.[25] He also found time to write his first song, using the name "Harold" Arluck on the copyright papers.[26] The band grew in size and in popularity. The eleven member Buffalodians began playing in better clubs, and it was at Geyer's ballroom restaurant in Buffalo's theater district that Arluck first met Ray Bolger (originally from Boston and soon to be the Scarecrow in *The Wizard of Oz*).[27]

Arluck moved to New York City at the age of 20, where he worked with lyricist Ted Koehler to write such hits as *Stormy Weather*.[28] By that time, his name was Harold Arlen, and he would soon create his greatest hit, one he would win an Academy Award for: *Over the Rainbow*. For all the other great songs he wrote – *Get Happy, I Love a Parade, I've Got the World On A String, That Old Black Magic, One for My Baby (And One for the Road)*, and *The Man That Got Away* – it is *Lydia the Tattooed Lady* that most strikes me, even more than *Minnie the Moocher's Wedding Day*, which Arlen wrote for Cab Calloway as a follow-up to his hit *Minnie the Moocher*. He wrote *Lydia the Tattooed Lady* for the Marx Brothers' movie *At the Circus* (not a great one), and for the rest of his life, Groucho Marx (and not *Hooray for Captain Spalding*) would consider this his signature song.

But *Over the Rainbow* remains Arlen's signature song, and if there would be anyone who could see bluebirds flying over the rainbow, that would be Roger Tory Peterson. Actually, his "first" bird, assigned to him by his seventh grade teacher Blanche Hornbeck, was blue: it was a blue jay.[29] Peterson was born in Jamestown, on August 28, 1908. He began a lifelong study of birds and nature. In 1934, his book, *A Field Guide to the Birds*, was published. It would be the first of many field guides. His paintings would also receive much acclaim.

Several years ago the City of Jamestown held a contest. Citizens were asked to vote for its most famous native. Roger Tory Peterson won by just one vote.[30] The city contains a fitting memorial to its "most famous native" in the Roger Tory Peterson Institute of Natural History, which contains much of Peterson's body of work and seeks to continue its namesake's "understanding, appreciation and protection of the natural world."[31]

Which reminds me, do you know the name of the actress known for being the first to do this? Do you know what the "this" is? Chances are, it's not who you're thinking of and it's not what you're thinking of. If you think you can handle the surprise, then go directly to the next chapter. Do not pass Go. Do not collect $200.

CHAPTER 35: AMERICA'S FIRST SUPERMODEL

In the 1915 silent film *Inspiration*, Audrey Munson did something that no other movie actress before her had ever done. Audrey was not famous for being an actress, she was an actress for being famous. Yet, for all the "Grecian perfection" of her figure, her life story reads like a Greek tragedy.

The marriage between Edgar Munson, a descendent of a long line of New England Methodists, and Katherine "Kittie" Mahoney, the daughter of Irish Catholic immigrants, on January 7, 1885 must have caused quite a stir.[1] The newlyweds soon moved to Rochester, working for a wealthy family in their home on East Avenue.[2] Six years later, on June 8, 1891, Kittie gave birth to what would be the couple's only child, Audrey Marie Munson.

Alas, things would not go well between Kittie and Edgar and, following a move to Providence, Rhode Island when Audrey was still young, the couple divorced. With the judge granting sole custody of the seven year old Audrey to Kittie, Edgar moved back to their original hometown outside of Syracuse, remarried and started a new family.[3] Audrey learned her skills as an entertainer in Providence and, following the completion of her education, moved with her mother to New York City.[4] Here is Audrey's own account of her discovery at the age of fifteen on the streets of New York:

> "I was standing in front of a department store window on Fifth
> Avenue in New York, wondering if, when I grew up to have
> money of my own, I could afford to buy some of the expensive
> hats I saw in the window. A young man came up to me, raised
> his hat, and said he was a photographer and very respectfully
> asked if I would like to come to his studio and pose for him –
> he said he would like to make some studies of my face. I was
> pleased, of course. He gave me his card, which read Ralph

Draper, and asked me to talk it over with my mother and bring her to his studio. His suggestion that I bring my mother seemed to show that he was sincere. Mother was interested, and flattered, too. She took me along and I posed for a number of photographs."[5]

Andrea Geyer, who researched Audrey Munson, found no records of a "Ralph Draper" anywhere in New York City Records, but did find early photographs of Audrey with another photographer's signature: Oscar Sholin.[6] Sholin's studio was located at 51 West 10th Street, the same location as the studios of Beaux Arts sculptors Isidore Konti, Adolph Weinman and Daniel Chester French.[7] For those interested in such things such as Red Herrings, the Beaux Arts style was a neoclassical architectural movement the evoked Renaissance and Classical styles. Whoever the photographer was who first spotted her, he then introduced her to sculptor Konti.[8] Konti asked her to pose for him. Of course, "pose" to an artist generally means "sans clothing" and Konti first had some convincing to do. "To us," he is reported to have said, "it makes no difference if our models are clothed or draped in furs. We see only the work we are doing."[7] Although initially circumspect, Kittie eventually gave in and allowed her daughter to pose.[9]

Considered her first work, Konti would go on to create *Three Graces* in 1907, a sculpture that adorned the Hotel Astor until it was demolished in 1967.[10] Over the next fifteen years, Audrey would live the life of her (and anyone else's) dreams. She became a much sought-after model among the elite sculptors and her likeness appears in civic statues across the nation (including up to nearly two dozen in New York City alone). Daniel Chester French, who appears to have used Audrey as a model for at least ten of his statues, including *Wisconsin* atop the Wisconsin State Capitol dome, once said of her, "I know of no other model with the particular style that Miss Munson possesses. There is a certain ethereal atmosphere about her that is rare. She has a decidedly expressive face, always changing."[11]

Like *Wisconsin*, Audrey's most famous New York City piece *Civic Fame* stands at the pinnacle of the Manhattan Municipal Building. At three times life size, it's second only to the Statue of Liberty in terms of dimensions in all of the Big Apple.[12] For this, Audrey would earn the label "Miss Manhattan" in the summer of 1913 (at least according to the *New York Sun*).[13] Adolph Weinman sculpted *Civic Fame*. You might also know him as the designer of both the popular "Mercury" Head dime and the "Walking Liberty" half-dollar. There's some speculation that Weinman used Munson as the model for both coins, although Elsie Stevens, wife of lawyer and poet Wallace Stevens, may have been the model.[13] It's been said Weinman may have been inspired by Robert Ingersoll Aitken's rendition of Liberty in the 1915 Panama-Pacific International Exhibition ("PPIE") medal. We know Weinman was at the PPIE where he contributed several pieces with Munson as his model. We also know Munson posed for Aitken's coin.

Ahh, the PPIE. Meant to celebrate the opening of the Panama Canal as well as the 400th anniversary of Balboa's discovery of the Pacific Ocean, its organizers appointed A. Stirling Calder as Chief Sculptor. You might recognize the name of Calder's son: Alexander. (If you don't recognize his name, you'll certainly recognize his modernistic mobile sculptures.) The elder Calder invited Audrey to come to the PPIE as the primary female model. In all, she posed for 75% of the statues and murals, including both female figures on Aitken's coin, earning her the nickname, the "Exposition Girl."[14]

Well, if you're famous and you're out in San Francisco, there's a good chance Hollywood might come calling. And that's exactly what happened to Audrey. The budding movie industry (as the mature movie industry still does today) was looking for some known talent it could capitalize on. They decided Audrey, who did learn to sing and dance in Rhode Island, was just that talent. But, they wondered, could she act?

Not to worry. If you can't act, then Hollywood creates a movie story where you don't have to act – you just play the same part that you do in real life. So Audrey's first movie, *Inspiration*, featured her in the role of a sculptor's model. Pretty easy, right? Well… not so fast! It turns out sculptors' models have a rather unique occupational requirement. They need to disrobe. In the retro-Puritan era of the Comstock Commission, public nudity was a no-no. Under threats of censorship, the film's producers were able to convince the powers-that-be not to censor their movie. After all, given this was not a porn film but an homage to art, to censor *Inspiration* would be to censor all renaissance and classical art.[15] ("Oh, that's why you went out of your way too define 'Beaux Arts' a few paragraphs back," said the knowing reader.) Thus, Audrey Munson became the first legitimate film actress to act without the need of a wardrobe department. She went on to play in three more movies which, despite receiving mixed reviews apparently generated enough revenue to justify making more.[16] Of the four movies, only a single copy of *Purity*, the second one, still exists (in France),[17] although we do have a playbill from *Inspiration*.[18]

Her modeling and movie careers over, she returned to New York with her mother where she resumed her writing career. Audrey began writing articles in 1915 for *New York American* and those articles were picked up nationally by other newspapers.[19] I've read some of her work, a serialized autobiography entitled *By the "Queen of the Artists' Studios*, published in 1921. Written at the relatively young age of 30, it struck me as much wiser and more insightful than I would have expected. In fact, part of it was downright spooky given what was to happen to Audrey later in her life.

Things started going downhill in 1919 and would only get worse. That year, Audrey and her mother were forced to move out of their apartment because their landlord's wife was jealous. Later, while the two were in Canada on business, the landlord, one Dr. Walter Wilkins, killed his wife, claiming he wanted to be with Audrey.[20] Out of the country and hard to find, suspicions grew until police found Audrey and her mother in Toronto. Audrey was eventually cleared, but the damage had been done. Audrey herself felt the straw that broke her career's back occurred when she spurned an unwanted advance from "a man prominent in the theatrical world."[21]

Running out of funds, the mother and daughter had no choice but to move back to Mexico, NY and live in a series of properties Edgar was slowly selling. Life in Mexico, a small town just outside of Syracuse, was worlds apart from New York City. There was no place for Audrey to disappear into the crowd and everyone knew – and didn't necessarily approve – of her career exploits. Her lawsuit for movie royalties failed. An attempt to form the Audrey Munson Producing Corporation in Rochester would fail. Finally, after a nation-wide search for "the perfect man" failed, Audrey tried to end it all by swallowing a solution of bichloride of mercury.[22] (It would have been ironic for the model of the winged head of Liberty on the "Mercury" dime to have died by consuming mercury.)

Still, things would become quite worse, as hinted at by Audrey's odd insistence on referring to herself as "Baroness Audrey Meri Munson-Monson" just prior to her attempted suicide.[23] Within a decade – and on the exact date of her 40th birthday no less – she would be institutionalized at the St. Lawrence State Hospital for the Insane in Ogdensburg, New York.[24] There she would stay for the rest of her life. It would be decades before she would have a visitor – her niece – and by then she was well into her 90s. She appeared happy and lucid, and expressed no desire to leave. She would die just shy of her 105th birthday in 1996 and she's buried next to her father in an unmarked grave, an ironic twist of fate for someone whose legacy endures in Beaux Arts stone.

Speaking of living to 100, did you know what Jamestown did to celebrate Lucille Ball's 100th birthday in 2011? (Yes, she was the Jamestown native who lost to Roger Tory Peterson by one vote.) They had a huge 5-day party at the Lucille Ball-Desi Arnaz Center, located right next to the Lucy Desi Museum. People from all over the world, including as far away as Australia, Japan and the United Kingdom, converged on the famous red-head's hometown. But don't fret if you missed this party, every year the city hosts its annual LucyFest. And if you can't make it, you can still drive through the city and try to find the huge murals depicting famous scenes from the old *I Love Lucy* show not so hidden on the sides of the even older down town buildings.

Well, speaking of old and speaking of Jamestown, have I got something for you. It's about twenty minutes southwest of Jamestown, or, for those of you not in your vehicles, it's right in your hands in the next chapter.

CHAPTER 36: WATCH OUT FOR THAT HOLE!

A s I've said, I've always like geology and the study of rocks. Growing up in Hamburg – and in Greater Western New York in general – the proliferation of and easy access to limestone deposits made finding trilobites a snap. What we didn't have were volcanoes. I had three childhood wishes related to the topic.

First, after reading a book about volcanoes in third grade in the library at Woodlawn Elementary School, I decided I wanted to climb a cinder volcano to see how hard it really was. I eventually did this in California while driving back from a week of skiing at Mammoth Mountain with my cousin and his friends. I now use that inspirational story to show people how they can achieve their Lifetime Dream.

Second, after seeing an advertisement in the back of a comic book, I always wanted to build one of those "working volcanoes." The closest I came to achieving this (as a kid) was Miss Palmer's fourth grade class at Woodlawn Intermediate. The anticipation proved far more than the actual event. All I remember is the disappointment and getting wet. With a better understanding of kitchen chemistry and equally enthusiastic offspring, I was finally able to recreate one of nature's furies for my own children as a part of their class projects.

Finally, after reading about history's worst earthquakes and volcanic eruptions in various books just about anywhere I could get my hands on them, I decided I needed to climb Mt. Vesuvius in Pompeii. The first time I went to Italy in 1987, our itinerary failed to include anything south of Rome. It turned out it didn't matter. The path to the top of Vesuvius was not accessible to the public then. It was open the summer of 2011 during a family sojourn to the Mother Country. I didn't realize the top of Vesuvius was a cinder cone. But it was one big hole

Natural disasters excited me as a youth. In addition to volcanoes and earthquakes, I read about hurricanes and tornadoes. I didn't have to read about snowstorms. As anyone living in Greater Western New York can attest, snowstorms are our bread and butter extreme of nature. All these other disasters occurred in other places. But we own the snowstorm market.

I did read a lot about the Ice Age, particularly in the 1970s. That was all the rage. Both *Time* and *Newsweek* (where it also made the cover) ran stories on it. It was the subject of many popular books. Those pesky glaciers from the last Ice Age did a lot of things, among them being our next hidden gem.

With 500 people, the Village of Panama lies within the Town of Harmony. We visited Panama Rocks over the July 4th weekend in 2012. We spoke with Shelly Johnson, Town Clerk for the Town of Harmony, who used to work in the snack bar when she was a teenager. Back then, two busloads would visit regularly every day. As a kid she used to play on the rocks. Her favorite area of the rocks is the Ice Cave because it has snow at the bottom no matter what time of year it is. She felt the most interesting thing was the wide variety of people from different parts of the country. Especially those from Chautauqua Institution. Shelly suggested we speak to Pamela A. Brown, Panama (both Town and Village) Historian and co-author of the book *Remembering Panama – Glimpses of the Past* (History Press, Charlestown, South Carolina, 2011).

We caught up with Pam and found out her family once owned Panama Rocks and, like Shelly, she worked there each summer. She told us the rocks are famous because they are so unique to the area. Pam noted the area was originally a farmer's field and the farmer couldn't farm it, so he thought he'd make money by offering it as a tourist attraction. George W. Hubbard and a partner had a proposal to make it a summer resort.[1] In 1885, Hubbard bought what was then called the "Rock Farm" and established Panama Rocks Park.[2] Pam's favorite part of Panama Rocks is also the Ice Caves. She' also interested in (and lives in one of) the many Greek Revival houses we mentioned earlier in our chapter on Chautauqua Institution. She feels it's likely the popularity of the Institution, as well as Panama being a stage coach stop for those traveling to Erie, helped push attendance at the park.

"By the 1960s," said Pam, "business had slowed down." She thinks this was because, before the automobile, Panama Rocks was a day trip for those in and around Jamestown and, with the advent of a more mobile America beginning in the 1950s, people could travel further. It was in the late 1960s that six area families, including Pam's, bought and operated the park. Pam was one of twenty children spread among those families to help with chores during the park's busy season. "I did a little bit of everything," she told us. One of the more important things they did was clean up and clear the trail, including removing many of the wooden stairs and other rotting structures from the trail itself.

About the trail: Here's the short summary of what you need to know about visiting this site. The trail is marked by small red triangles painted on trees that bring you down to the base of the formation. You'll see passageways opening into the rocks as you go. This is where the scenery is most dramatic and where it's easiest to go exploring into the passageways in the rock. After about a half mile into the trail the rocks end and you begin to ascend as you make your way to the upper level switch back that eventually takes you back to where you started. It is this upper level that offers the most intrigue – and danger. Shortly after you make the turn, the rocks reappear. Only this time they're below you. But be warned, as you'll start to see holes in the ground. There are no railings and some of the cracks, crevices and cliffs are up to forty feet deep. Some of these are right next to the trail and you need to be most careful. The trail takes about one to two hours to complete. We did it in one.

Numbers mark some of the more amazing sites, but age has taken a few of those markers away or they've been concealed others with overgrown vegetation (the Sierra Foundation calls this area an ancient forest). Speaking of overgrown vegetation, the trail is covered with trees, protecting hikers from both the sun and, to an extent, rain. You'll have to watch out for many exposed roots. They're easy to trip over. As you descend, you can't help but listen to the tranquil chirping of nature and the soft voices of the other hikers.

The rock formations fascinated me. At various points, it looked like God shook them in His hand and dropped them like dice. That's not the way it happened, though, for we know the helter-skelter appearance of the Panama Rocks formation came about from the descending ice sheet during the most recent Ice Age. The rocks themselves are a kind of natural concrete called quartz conglomerate formed, like more of the rocks in Greater Western New York during the Devonian Period of the Mesozoic Era. Their formal name is "Panama Conglomerate,"[3] in keeping with the Devonian Period naming convention we discussed earlier whereby rock types were named after the location where they were first discovered. If you look closely at the rock, you'll see small rounded pebbles. Those pebbles have been smoothed over by the waves of the prehistoric sea that once covered Greater Western New York.

And speaking of names, not only are the Rocks named after the Village, but the Village is named after the rocks. Unlike neighboring Ashville, named after the four asheries that once operated in the village,[4] the origin of the name "Panama" owes more to legend. One source says Moses Cushman Marsh, a wealthy Cuban trader who built the first house and store in the area, after being named the Village's first postmaster, dubbed the Village "Panama" on March 22, 1826.[5] Pam Brown cites the legend of "Panama Joe" as the origin of the name. It's been said when Panama Joe saw Village's famous rocks, he said, "Those look like the rocks I saw in Panama." The rocks had been known as "Panama Rocks" ever since. She goes on to say when it came time to name the new village, an argument ensued between naming it "Lewisville" (after the Lewis family) or "Smithville" (after the Smith family). Someone then suggested the new Village be named after the Rocks, because "The Rocks were here before the Smiths or the Lewises and they will probably be here longer."[6] And so the Village became known as "Panama" and the unique Devonian conglomerate discovered among the Rocks became known as "Panama Conglomerate."

Of the many formations – and, again, the best pictures come from the lower level – I have room to discuss only two, and they're both crevices best viewed from the upper level. The first is the Ice Cave mentioned earlier by both women. The haphazardly strewn rocks have created many deep fissures and, not quite tunnels, but enclosed passageways. If you recall the atmospheric impact of the Underground Cave of Lockport, the longer and deeper the crevice, the more stable the internal temperature. At one point at the lower level, there's a longer crevice that feels like a wind tunnel. If you stand in front of it, you experience the refreshing coolness of what I can only call a "natural air conditioner." The Ice Cave only exaggerates this low temperature phenomenon, and one can regularly see snow at the bottom of it, even in the dog days of summer. Unfortunately for us, we visited the park following a particularly mild winter. Alas, there was no snow to be found.

The second is Counterfeiters' Den. Pam told us there are plenty of stories and legends associated with Panama Rocks. These include everything from bank robbers hiding their loot and then forgetting which hole they put it in, to the Mormons hiding the Golden Plates somewhere deep within one of the many crevices. There is one story, however, that appears to have some credibility. Like the other stories, this predates the use of Panama Rocks as a park. According to Pam, it's a known fact "counterfeiters were producing and circulating their money during the 1880s in this area."[6] Although she's never seen them, she is confident dyes and plates were actually found in Counterfeiters' Den at some point during the history of the park.

Upon completion of our spiritually and physically invigorating hike, I had a chance to speak to Craig Weston, the owner and operator of Panama Rocks. You see, Panama Rocks, for all its natural beauty and very long history – it's been open to the public as a park since 1885, the same year Niagara Falls became the nation's first; hence, oldest, state park – is a privately-run enterprise. Craig and his wife Sandy bought the property in 1979 when they decided to move out of the city. They just drove by and "saw a for sale sign and a creative realtor." Craig, who received his undergraduate degree in psychology and did his graduate degree in geography, always liked land and the couple had a piece of property nearby. Still, he says the whole thing was somewhat accidental. The family expects to continue to operate the facility for the foreseeable future as he expects his son to take over in a year or two.

Panama Rocks, though in the extreme Southwest corner of Greater Western New York (it's about twenty minutes from Jamestown), seems to be the intersection of many of the material we covered in this book. Not only do we see Greater Western New York's geology exposed, but artifacts for the Erie Tribe have been found, too. More recently, and more mysteriously, a small "medallion" was found in the Park in 1986. The Weston's speculate, given its heraldry includes both a beaver and a griffin, the brass piece might date back to LaSalle's original exposition through Greater Western New York (recall from an earlier chapter LaSalle sailed out of the Niagara peninsula on the ship *Le Griffon*).[7]

Despite, or especially because of, its seeming isolation, Panama Rocks stands out as a perfect place to visit with your family, scout troop or organization. The mile hike is not that challenging (but that doesn't mean there aren't places you need to be really alert). It offers an otherwise peaceful interlude – at least for a moment – in this otherwise hectic world. The geology is amazing. This is because, unlike Olean's Rock City Park in the Enchanted Mountain region of Cattaraugus County, the formation at Panama Rocks is not the result of erosion or tectonic action, but the result of a glacial assault (the glacier of the last Ice Age never made it as far south as Olean). It's the glacier that gave Panama Rocks its disheveled look, a look that has inspired for eons and continues to inspire today.

Not that there's anything wrong with erosion. In fact, melting glaciers can also contribute to not only substantial, but epic, erosion, as we'll find out in our next chapter.

CHAPTER 37: GOLD. BLACK GOLD. CUBA TEA.

Does the name Joseph de La Roche Daillon ring a bell? Unless you're from the Town of Cuba in Allegany County, or a graduate of St. Bonavenure University in the City of Olean in Cattaraugus County, you likely haven't. But you should. He was a very kind man. If you're a native Greater Western New Yorker, you've probably gotten an earful of gloomy weather questions from, well, just about anywhere in America. Ol' Joe, though, well, he really liked our weather. He once said our region "is incomparably larger, more beautiful and better than any other of all these countries," that our winter "is not long and rigorous as Canada. No snow had fallen by the 22nd of November, and it never was over two feet deep, and began to melt on the 26th of January. On the 8th of March there was none at all in the open places, though there was a little indeed still left in the low grounds (woods)." De La Roche said a stay here "is quite recreating and convenient... so that I have no hesitation in saying that we should settle [here] rather than elsewhere."[1]

Think our local tourist bureaus and relocation agencies ought to employ de La Roche? Here we have an obvious foreigner (he's actually from France) saying great things about our weather. I mean, a winter that doesn't start until November 22nd and ends by March 8th? Holy North Carolina, Batman!

Oh, wait. I forgot to mention the year. The letter was dated July 18th, 1627 and he was referring to the previous winter. Those paleoclimatologists out there in TV land might recognize this as the time just after the Spörer Minimum and just before the Maunder Minimum, periods when sunspot activity was nearly non-existent and the global climate experienced the "Little Ice Age," when temperatures were the coldest since, well, the last Ice Age.[2] During that space between the two Minimums, temperature spiked almost as high as the era known as the Medieval Warming Period when it appears the earth's temperatures were nearly as warm as they are today. I wonder if La Salle and company thought le Roche might have drank some of that funny water he found outside of Cuba (more on this in a moment). As you may recall from earlier, La Salle ventured through Greater Western New York nearly fifty years after la Roche, while the Maunder Minimum was well under way and the Little Ice Age had begun, when worldwide temperatures dipped to their lowest since the last ice age carved up Panama Rocks, Dansville's East Hill and a few other choice locales we have yet to visit.

Joseph de La Roche Daillon was a Franciscan missionary priest sent from France to convert the Indian tribes in and around the Niagara Peninsula.[3] He may have been the first European to see Niagara Falls as he lived among the Huron before being escorted to the Neutral nation through the Petun Tribe, who grew tobacco – that's how warm it was around these parts back then (take that, North Carolina!).[4] La Roche tried to establish trade with the Neutrals and find the mouth of the Niagara River.[5] This apparently displeased the Huron, who then proceeded to spread nasty rumors about La Roche to the Neutral, who then proceeded to try to kill the priest.[6] Fortunately he escaped, lest we would not have his Chamber of Commerce description of our region. Nor would we have known the following story.

According to his letter, the Neutrals occupied the territory from the Niagara Peninsula into the interior of Greater Western New York as far east as the Genesee River. Before they decided to kill him, the Neutrals actually adopted La Roche into their tribe. The Neutral Chief Soubarissen, so trusting of La Roche, agreed to take the priest to a sacred place northwest to what is today the Village of Cuba. There, Soubarissen introduced La Roche to a natural spring with a black substance called "Atouronton" bubbling up through it. The Neutral, and later the Seneca Tribe, assumed these tainted waters contained medicinal properties. The black ooze was, of course, oil, and La Roche thereby became the first European to lay eyes on the resource and Oil Springs became the first place in North America where oil was discovered.

Before Cuba became "Cuba," it was called "Oil Creek."[7] According to one account, the oil spring was original "a muddy, circular pool of water 30 feet in diameter, the ground low and marshy immediately surrounding it, and the pool without apparent outlet or bottom."[8] Today it is part of the smallest Seneca reservation, a square mile straddling both Cattaraugus County and Allegany County. As late as the nineteenth century, the Seneca would spread blankets over its surface to absorb the oil, the wring the oil out into vials sold as "Seneca Oil."[9] I suppose "Seneca Oil" has more of a ring to it than the more accurate name of "Neutral Oil," but, as they say, to the victor goes the "oils." (I'll pause while you roll your eyes.) The spring no longer yields oil and today it is surrounded by a "large open-headed cask."[10]

Incidentally, the "De La Roche" in Joseph De La Roche Daillon means "of the rock." The word "petroleum" derives from Latin and loosely translates to "oil of the rock."[11]

We're pretty sure La Roche was the first European to step deep into the interior of Greater Western New York. We're not sure who the first humans were. But they left traces, one mysterious, one not so mysterious. You can find the mysterious one by traveling east on Route 86 from Oil Springs, then turning north on Route 54 in Bath and finally veering left on 54A, taking it all along the western leg of Keuka Lake's "Y" and into the town of Jerusalem in Yates County. There's not much to see there now. Most of the Bluff Point Stoneworks, as it is called, has disappeared over the century-and-a-half since it was first discovered. There's been much speculation its builders were anything from pre-Columbian Europeans (think Vikings) to ancient Indians.[12]

Of greater certainty lies the site just on the other side of Keuka Lake in the Town of Tyrone, Schuyler County near Lamoka Lake. Now owned by the Archeological Conservancy,[13] the site was discovered in 1905 and surveyed by Rochester Museum and Science Center archeologist William Ritchie in 1925, 1958 and 1962, who determined its occupants – the Lamoka culture – dated back some 5,000 years from between 3350-3100 BC.[14] Listed on the National Register of Historic Places the Lamoka Lake Site is considered the first archaic site in America.[15]

I wouldn't be a good astronomer if I didn't add this. Remember the Maunder Minimum? Jupiter's famous Red Spot disappeared during the Maunder Minimum. It also seems to have gone dim in two other periods: the early 1800s and the early 1900s. Another period of low solar activity occurred in the early 1800s – the Dalton Minimum – a period which featured 1816 as "the year without a summer." Most scientists blame the titanic eruption of Mount Tambora, a volcano in the Indian Ocean, not the sunspot cycle, for the year without a summer. I blame the sun's magnetic fields for everything. Why? Sunspots are magnetic storms and the earth, with magma forever circulating deep in its interior, act like one big magnet. You think of things like this when you major in astronomy. And when you like volcanoes. Oh, by the way, the Red Spot's late 1800/early 1900 fade coincided with another low period of low solar activity, but apparently not low enough to earn a name.

Of course, the strangest story of the year without a summer deals with a writers group summering – if you can call it that given the damp, dismal meteorological conditions of 1816 – in Switzerland. The dreary climate led them to a challenge: who could write the darkest story. The wretched weather thus inspired Mary Shelley to write Frankenstein, considered to be the first work of science fiction. Not the alien worlds kind, the other kind.

If you're looking for alien worlds, though, you need travel no further than the shores of Lake Ontario in Wayne County. I'll tell you exactly where – and why it's so alien – in the next chapter.

CHAPTER 38: GROUND CONTROL TO
COMMANDER TOM

I magine if you will an outlandish landscape as pictured by one of those ubiquitous 1950s sci-fi artists. It's the kind you see in movie mattes, comic books and even legitimate science magazines (when the issue deals with the future). It's a scene of a desolate planet with huge hairy spiders that munch on pretty actresses, with ugly multi-tentacled monsters who kidnap pretty actresses, with seemingly logical robots (too) loyal to their evil scientist masters who sacrifice themselves to save pretty actresses,... are you beginning to see a common theme here? Yeah, it's that same spooky panorama of sharp jagged rock mountains piercing like knives into the alien atmosphere.

Well, there's good news for those too old for Space Camp. You don't have to hitch a ride on some Soviet space bucket and fly to the moon to see an eerily fantastic setting like this. All you need to do is slip on your hiking boots, pack a lunch and get behind the wheel of your car. Destination: Wayne County. Specifically: the Town of Huron just east of Sodus Bay on the shores of Lake Ontario.

Just what are these creatures from another planet? Once again, we have our friends the glaciers to thank for this particular geological formation. According to the Chimney Bluffs State Park Brochure, the Bluffs "form the north end of a glacier-made hill called a 'drumlin.'" Think of a glacier as a big snow plow picking up "sand, clay, silt, gravel, cobbles and boulders" – called "glacial till" – as it oozed across the land. The Brochure goes on to say "drumlins were created when the overriding glacier worked glacial till into hills that ran parallel to the direction of the ice movement." Returning to the snow plow analogy, it's like the big snow bank on the side of the road created by the passing plow.

The cool stuff doesn't start happening until after the drumlin was formed six to ten thousand years ago. The Wayne County Tourism brochure picks up the story. After the glacier melted, the "large clay drumlin" was "eroded by waves and weather" to create the "150 feet" spires of barren rock and raw cliff we see today. Debris continues to melt down each year, especially in the wet spring season when one can often see rivers of mud creeping slowly down from the face of the cliffs to the beach and into Lake Ontario.

Now, here's where I get serious (as I will in the next couple of chapters, too). Although they look like solid rock, the Chimney Bluffs are really just heavily compacted till. That's why they weather so quickly and dramatically. And because they weather so quickly, there's no time for vegetation to grab hold and grow. That's why the rock is barren. If you try to climb the face of these cliffs, especially after a period of wet weather, chances are you won't be able to grab on to anything either. The short of it: Don't climb the cliffs.

But it gets worse. If you look up at the Bluffs from the beach, you'll likely see a lip of vegetation hanging over one of the cliffs. It appears as if the very ground gave way, leaving the forlorn grass hanging alone in the air, attached only to its more firmly rooted neighbors. That's more than a mere appearance. It's probably what happened. Whole sides of these Bluffs have been known to collapse with the mudflow, sometimes taking a tree with them.

Here's the scary part. There's a trail that meanders along the top ridge of the Bluffs. It's great for getting pictures, but it's not for the faint-hearted. Sometimes the trail goes precariously close to the edge of the cliff. This is where you have to use your head. If it's the wet season and you see the Bluff's crying rivers of mud, there's a good chance you might see a small chunk of the ledge go down. Don't be on that ledge. The mud is not likely to cushion the 150 foot drop.

According to a June 30, 2003 court filing in Syracuse, on April 5, 1999, a 25-year-old man was on that ledge, seeking a picture of the perfect sunset, when it gave way.[1] The man, who had earned his Eagle Scout as a boy, died in the resulting 50 foot fall.[2]

There is another park where campers would regularly wander off into the night only to fall to their deaths because the 400 foot gorge was not fenced off. Making matters worse, this was a popular summer camp for the flower children of the 1960s. It also featured Greater Western New York's only nude beach. The mixture of sex, drugs, rock and roll and steep unfenced cliffs meant only one thing: The State outlawed overnight camping in this park. What is it? Where is it? and How do I get there? are only some of the questions answered in the next few pages.

CHAPTER 39: SHANGRI-LA OR DEATH VALLEY?

Zoar Valley lay within miles of where I grew up, yet I had never heard of it until a few years ago. I regularly traveled over its gorge. I long admired its lone now abandoned railroad trestle. I'm sure I must have even been there one or two times. But I never remembered it being called anything.

After deciding to write this book, I wanted to include a chapter on Zoar Valley. It seemed the perfect operational definition of a "hidden gem" as I could imagine. Then I started doing research. Suddenly, I began to understand why the Zoar Valley has been such a secret, even to those within shouting distance. A stream of second thoughts suddenly flowed through my brain. *Perhaps*, I thought, *this was one secret that should stay secret.* Then, like the warning of Chimney Bluffs, it struck me that revealing the secret of Zoar Valley's existence might actually save a life.

So here it is.

Let me first describe the area itself. Zoar Valley is located within the deep canyons cut by the main branch of the Cattaraugus Creek and by its South Branch. It straddles the borders of Erie County and Cattaraugus County placing it in Erie County's Town of Collins and the Towns of Persia and Otto in Cattaraugus County. It's not really a park. In 2007, New York State, which owned the land since the 1960s, designated it a Multiple Use Area. Within that MUA lays a Natural Resource Protection Area which pretty much follows no less than 300 feet of the Creek's two branches. The MUA is open only from sunrise to sunset.

With that comes our first warning. The State banned overnight camping and motor vehicles in 1971 due to "irresponsible behavior" on the part of campers.[1] Let's see, that puts us right around the time of the hippies. I wonder what they might have been doing. After all, the place does have a tradition of skinny dipping going back to the 1800s. I'm beginning to understand why my parents never really told me about this place.

The real issue, though, deals with safety. The Zoar Valley gorge contains cliffs ranging from 150 feet to 500 feet, according to New York State. The rock is a form of loose brittle shale that crumbles easily and gets extremely slippery when wet. Walking on the cliff ledges can be dangerous and often fatal. In addition to falling from the ledge, visitors are warned to also watch for falling debris. That can be fatal, too. Finally, New York State says the area about 900 feet upstream from the Forty Road parking lot on the South Branch converts to private property. Apparently, this is a relatively recent event, as many visitors remember strolling freely up the South Branch to Big Falls. You can't do that anymore, and the private owners and New York State regularly patrol the area to prevent trespassing.

But you don't need to trespass to experience the true meaning of the Zoar Valley. Heck, I got it just driving through it on its one public road. Here's the thing: There's no there, there. Zoar Valley is not developed in any way. In fact, the state has undeveloped it more than developed it, allowing any semblance of civilization (like roads) to slip away into nature. Along these lines, there are plenty of access points to the Zoar Valley, but no formal entrance. Going there gives one the feeling you're entering the land that time forgot. As I descended into the Valley, while conveniently ignoring modern housing on the Area's boundary, it seemed as though I had found the Lost Paradise. Milton would have appreciated that the name Zoar, like his poem *Paradise Lost*, derives from the same source, the Book of Genesis.[2]

Now, here's the real secret of the Zoar Valley: It's not there. In the two hundred years of its recorded history, any attempt to civilize it failed. The trees were too difficult to get to, so, unlike 99.9% of the eastern forests, they were left uncut. They tried drilling for oil there and came up dry. They tried mining the shale but that didn't work. The Niagara, Lockport and Ontario Power Company considered building a hydroelectric dam in Zoar Valley, but that same shale that breaks apart so easy for hikers was also too brittle to sustain the dam.

So, at each turn, Nature defeated Man at Zoar Valley. Considering its level of danger, a case can be made that Nature continues to defeat Man at Zoar Valley. But, it has left one treasure, only recently discovered. Among its nearly 3,000 acres are at least five old growth tree stands totaling almost 600 acres. These old growth forests contain the tallest trees in New York State (and among the tallest of their variety) and date back to nearly 350 years[3] – about the time LaSalle launched *Le Griffon* from the shores of the Niagara River.

Zoar Valley, though, is only the first act. Our next gem is the granddaddy of them all – the Grand Canyon of the East. You might be surprised to discover what you don't know about it!

CHAPTER 40: A MORE CIVILIZED NATURE

O ther than how I ever managed to pass, let alone get good grades, one of the few things I remember of high school English was the opening line of Thornton Wilder's *Bridge Over San Luis Rey*:

On Friday noon, July the twentieth, 1714, the finest bridge in all Peru broke and precipitated five travelers into the gulf below.

Perhaps I remember it because the vivid detail and the alluring imagery make it impossible to forget. Maybe I remember it because the date mentioned falls on the same date Man first stepped foot on the Moon. Maybe it was because the date was within a few days of my own birthday. I used to think it was the word "precipitated" that caught my fancy since, at the time, I was in the middle of keeping a daily weather journal (which I kept up for my entire high school career).

But as much as the first line I remember how Brother Juniper, the Franciscan missionary, who, as luck would have it, stopped to rest and looked up just as the bridge snapped to see it "fling five gesticulating ants into the valley below."

I think I know the real reason I recall Wilder's masterpiece so intensely. It's because I'm afraid of heights. It gets worse. Like the chess master I once pretended to be, I tend to see life a few moves ahead of real time. Whenever I go to a high place, whether it be in an airplane, the Empire State Building or even crossing the New River Bridge in a car, I am at once Brother Juniper and one of those "gesticulating ants" as my mind forces me to imagine myself "precipitating" from whatever false bottom has just given way.

Such are my many experiences with Letchworth State Park, a 17 mile long canyon from Portageville to Mt. Morris. Like Zoar Valley (but more dramatic with its breathtaking cliffs rising some 600 feet from the valley floor), Letchworth State Park's river serves as a boundary for two counties – Livingston County and Wyoming County –and pieces of it fall into several towns – Mount Morris, Perry, Castile and Nunda. In a park that contains New York State's tallest (but not always active) waterfall – the 350 foot Inspiration Falls flows only during or after a heavy rain – folks with acrophobia might feel a special "something" during their visit.

I noticed it the first time I visited the place. We had just moved to Rochester (Chili, for you purists). Every summer our family would picnic with the families of my father's two childhood friends. This particular summer, we went to a place I had never heard of, a place called "Letchworth." My parents promised me I would like it as, they pointed out, it's called "the Grand Canyon of the East."

I had always wanted to go to the Grand Canyon, almost as much as I had wanted to climb a cinder cone volcano. I loved reading books with pictures of the Grand Canyon. When we got to Letchworth, I discovered one thing immediately: This was not the Grand Canyon. For one thing, it had trees, tons of trees. For another, it had no continuous sheer rock gorge (again, too many trees). Finally, it had waterfalls, lots and lots of waterfalls.

But what stood out in my teenage brain was the chain link fence, or, rather, the hole in that chain link fence. For all the great picnic food we brought I couldn't eat. I spent most of the time watching that hole, making sure no loose ball, unleashed pet or small child wandered too close to it. Mind you, and in keeping with our literary theme, this was no Holden Caulfield moment. I had no intention of catching any mindless person, place or thing before it could fall through the hole and into the rye grass of the valley below. Heck, I wanted nowhere near that fence, let alone the hole in it.

And so it's been, every time I've visited since. It's so bad I insisted my son stay away from the rock retaining wall overlooking a particularly scenic point of the gorge by the 107 foot Middle Falls. Myself, I stood a good twenty yards away. *You never know how much land will give out when the land finally gives out*, I thought. My son, Peter? He would get snug up to that two foot rock wall and take a picture of the valley. "You could see the same thing from back here!" I shouted angrily to him. His reaction? He taunted me and posed for a picture by sitting on the rock. My inner Brother Juniper sent my heart racing, only this time in my three-moves-ahead imagination, the "gesticulating ant" wasn't me.

I survived. My son survived, although not until after a good tongue lashing. My friend, an old college roommate who accompanied us on this endeavor, suggested I stay on *terra firma* while he and my son ventured down the 120+ stairs into the Lower Falls. I stayed high above and strolled down the trail – keeping a safe distance from the fenced ledge – until they returned.

About those fences, steps and trails. They definitely show signs of wear. The rock walls have crumbled in places and some of the trails have washed out, the orange "police" tape offering little comfort or protection. Although I saw many death-defying people use them, by the Lower Falls' stairs are remnants of earthen steps along the rim I dared not approach. These signs of age are not surprising considering most of the park's infrastructure was built in the 1930s courtesy of Franklin Roosevelt's Civilian Conservation Corps (CCC). At the time, the park had been in New York State hands for almost three decades, and the then roughly 6,000 acre park (it's now 14,350 acres) needed some work. It wasn't always that way.

William Pryor Letchworth bought what is now the Glen Iris and the surrounding 1,000 acres in 1859 after visiting the site a year following the opening of the Erie Railroad's famous Portage Bridge in 1852.[1] Letchworth immediately fell in love with the gorge and, after he purchased the property, improved the estate. But you can read about the origins of Letchworth Park elsewhere. Here's what you might not know. When built, the Portage Bridge was the largest wooden bridge in the world. It burned to the ground in the rainy wee morning hours of May 6, 1875.[2] By the time Letchworth woke from his bed at 3:45am, the fire had been burning for almost 3 hours.[3] He watched as the inferno consumed and destroyed the very thing that brought him to the gorge. In an account he provided to the *Buffalo Courier*, he wrote "the hoarse growl of the flames and crackling of the timbers sounded like a hurricane approaching through the forest".[4]

Here's an amazing fact. After the wooden bridge "precipitated" its burning timbers into the valley below (I assume they these lifeless logs were not gesticulating), the Erie Railroad built its wrought iron replacement in 53 days.[5] The celerity of completion did cause doubts as to its ability to carry heavy weight, especially given its superstructure's spindly appearance versus the bulk of its predecessor. It's likely quite a few breaths were held when the first test of its strength was conducted by sending a freight train pulled by six solid steam locomotives across it.[6] Rising 245 feet above the upper falls, this 820-foot-long deck truss viaduct remains as it was in 1875, save for a strengthening enhancement in 1903.[7] Today, Norfolk Southern – its current owner – says its 10 MPH speed limit and weight restrictions make it obsolete.[8] They've offered to build a new span and give the old bridge to New York State for use as a pedestrian bridge. Ironically, shortly after it first received the Park property, the New York State Senate in 1913 passed a bill appropriating $10,000 to build a pedestrian bridge "across the Genesee just north of the present Erie Railroad high bridge."[9] Apparently the Assembly did not agree as no such bridge was ever built.

Letchworth willed his 1,000 acres to New York State and, when he died in 1910, the state took control. By the early 1930s, the park needed some infrastructural improvements. Enter the CCC, the remnants of whose camps (which once housed German POWs in WWII), can still be seen today.[10] Such were their efforts that, save for a few augmentations like indoor plumbing and electricity, their works stands today. Well, most of it. Time does take its toll. Because of this, although Letchworth is obviously more civilized than Zoar, it remains dangerous in spots. In 2010, a nineteen-year-old man accidentally slipped from the rock wall above the Lower Falls and fell 300 feet to his death.[11] Nature, unfortunately, has a way of showing who's boss.

The gorge itself stands as a monument to nature's relentless fury – and I'm not just talking about the river's role in eroding the various Devonian Period (remember that?) shales, sandstones and siltstones. I'm talking about something bigger, something stronger, something with powers and abilities far beyond those of mortal men! Yes, I'm talking about our friends the glaciers, who can – and in this case did – change the course of mighty rivers. Prior to the last Ice Age, the Genesee River had a (much larger) east branch called the Dansville River flowing northwest down the Dansville valley and a (weaker) west branch flowing from Portageville to Nunda and then northeast from Nunda (probably through the gulch formed by Keshequa Creek). At Sonyea, southeast of Mt. Morris, the branches converged into one river that flowed through the present course of the Genesee River until the Town of Rush, where it abruptly turned east, following the present day Honeoye Creek to the Town of Mendon where it merged into the present day Irondequoit Creek and proceeded to flow up the Irondequoit Valley.[12] From there it cut into the Valley – a trace of the this gorge can be seen today – before meeting up with the Ontarian River in the middle of what is now Lake Ontario and draining into the Mississippi.[13]

With the coming of the glaciers, though, our world changed. The retreating glacier left several moraines (rock deposits formed along the terminal edge of the glacier), in particular, one that surrounded the Dansville Valley on three sides (only the north end would be exposed) that cut off its supply of water and one from Nunda to Portageville.[14,15] The blockage at Portageville redirected the Genesee River on a new route that cut the Letchworth gorge we see today.[16,17]

On a final note, the Portageville moraine was not the only pile of glacial till to have an impact on the course of the Genesee River. The path was also blocked by glacial till in Mendon, causing the river to redirect to its present course, the course that carved much of the scenery we see in the Genesee River Valley in the City of Rochester, scenery which has inspired many community activities, events, and lore. And all because of glacial deposits in Mendon. But let's return to the present day and an example of the sense of community many small towns throughout Greater Western New York share. And since we're already in Mendon...

CHAPTER 41: LIFE IS A (SMALL TOWN) CARNIVAL

L ike any kid growing up in the snowbelt otherwise known as Blasdell, I looked forward to three things each summer. The beginning of summer would signal going to Fantasy Island to celebrate a good report card, ride the steamboat and watch the live shootouts. The end of summer meant going to the Erie County Fair to see the vast array of other-worldly side shows on the Midway, the acrid smell of burnt oil and rubber at the demolition derby and the taste of my grandfather's sumptuous pizza. Sandwiched in between, both chronologically and geographically, was the Big Tree Fireman's Carnival. I think it was actually called the Big Tree Firemen's Annual Field Days. But for kids (and headline writers short on space) it was the Big Tree Carnival.

Here's the real difference between Fantasy Island, the Erie County Fair and the Big Tree Carnival. Fantasy Island served the broader community. In professional baseball terms, it would be considered AAA. The Erie County Fair, despite its commonly used "Hamburg Fair" nickname, served an even greater region. It was the Big Leagues. That it was in our backyard only made us prouder.

The Big Tree Carnival, on the other hand, well, that was home cooking. A sandlot game, if you will. That it was small made it better. It was for the local community. It was an event shared by everyone who mattered, and no one beyond that. Sure, outsiders could come, but they would be our guests. The Big Tree Carnival was the perfect place to catch up on the summer doings of our friends, ride a few rides and maybe win a gold fish that might actually remain alive by the time we got home, no doubt late into the night (but not as late as our parents).

There was a time when every community held these carnivals. They were quiet, yet raucous festivals, and if you don't know how they could have been both, then you've never gone to one. In those days, every weekend provided a local carnival – or field days – at some venue. For example, the weekend I was born, the Woodlawn Firemen held their Field Days while the next weekend Big Tree held theirs.[1] Each event held its own parade. When the Big Tree Firemen hosted their own Field Days, the Company marched 35-40 times a year.[2]

That was then. Today, the Big Tree Volunteer Fire Company only marches five to 10 times a year.[3] Insurance rates make it difficult for smaller carnivals to raise the funds they were intending to raise. The Big Tree Volunteer Fire Company decided long ago to pursue alternative fundraising strategies and the carnival, along with the community bonding it often brought, vanished into the realm of memory.

There remains, however, bastions of this bygone spectacle. Today I live in a small town. It's called Mendon. It's on the south end of Monroe County abutting both Livingston County and Ontario County. It's got about 6,000 people. It's not the most rural town in Monroe County, but it's close. The Thruway runs through the north end of town, but with no on or off ramps, all it does is take up space. There's no direct interstate access. There's only one other east-west road through town, but we do have two north-south roads.

We might not have many roads, but we do have a fireman's carnival. The Mendon Fire Department was established in 1932,[4] four years before the Big Tree Volunteer Firemen's Association.[5] They've been having carnivals for as long as I can remember. In fact, I started attending in the 1980s when the Fire Department was still located in the old Mendon Academy, a two story cobblestone former school house with space for only two bays. There wasn't any room at all, not even for a carnival. The lower parking lot of St. Catherine's Parish consumed all the land immediately behind the Firehouse and, back then, the church itself nearly abutted the firemen's abode.

For the firemen to hold a reasonable carnival required the effort of the entire community. The Parish had to permit the use of the parking lot, volunteers from all facets of the community had to join with the efforts of the firemen to put the whole thing together. And, remember, everything had to be torn down on Saturday night in order for the area to be clear in time for eight o'clock Mass. It always was. I was still young the first time I went and living in my parent's house. (Mendon was not yet my community until I bought my own house there a few years later after doing a short stint in the Park Avenue district in the City of Rochester.)

I moved back to Mendon because of the community spirit I witnessed in that first carnival. In my mind, working together as a community, crossing organizational lines and placing common sense ahead of bureaucratic red tape spoke to a character well worth becoming part of. That was Mendon. That is Mendon. That remains the spirit of the Mendon Carnival.

The Carnival has the luck of being one of the first such events of the year, occurring annually the first week of June. It coincides with youth baseball playoffs, the slowing down of school and the beginning of summer. Nearly every community organization is involved in some way with the Carnival. They gladly work with the Fire Department and the Fire Department gladly shares. The Mendon Fire Department moved a couple miles down the street to a new Fire Hall in the 1990s, one with a much larger field. This made for both a bigger carnival and a longer parade.

Unlike the Big Tree Carnival, where it seemed the parade kicked off festivities, the Saturday night parade at the Mendon Carnival occurs on the last day and gives one the impression of a climax, rather than a beginning. As the area's first summer carnival, the Mendon Carnival attracts fire departments from across the region. Sometimes the parade takes three hours before the last sirened vehicle turns off its flashing lights. I've had the honor to march in these parades with Pack 105 of the Cub Scouts, Troop 105 of the Boy Scouts and even CougarTech Team #2228, the High School Robotics team. Seeing all varieties of townsfolk along the parade route – not to mention the many picnics hosted in the nearby homes – only reaffirms the sense that the Mendon Carnival brings the whole community together.

But it's not just the parade, it's the actual carnival. Various local volunteer groups occupy the many booths and food stands along the Midway leading up to the rides. You can relax as you walk through the grounds, knowing everyone around is your friend, knowing most of the money you are spending is going to some worthy local effort, knowing the smiles of the kids you see are genuine, etching memories they will forever cherish. This is the "quiet" I referred to earlier.

The raucous? Well, it's a carnival. And Saturday night after the parade, when each fire department's band "competes" with the other, that's raucous. And that's part of what the fun of a carnival is all about. And everybody is your friend, even if they are from a few towns away. That's the essence of a small town carnival, and the Mendon Carnival captures it oh so well. If you have a small town carnival, then go. If you don't, then comes to Mendon's. We'll be glad to have you.

The small town community atmosphere reflects a certain American persona. It's special. It's ours. But don't take my word for it. Our next chapter trumpets what folks around the nation are saying.

CHAPTER 42: THE BEST SMALL TOWNS IN AMERICA

I learned at a young age the difference between a beauty contest and one based on skills. I'm sure we've all experienced the same. In school, the best and the brightest always lag behind the most popular. That's why I liked sports and games requiring quick thinking. If you won, you earned it. It meant something.

On the other hand, as I've seasoned with age, I've also learned not to look a gift horse in the mouth. There's no sense in turning down the lottery if you win it. You didn't earn it, but, heck, neither does anyone else.

So it goes with these national "best town" contests. Even with the ones using "experts" to rate the contestants, it all comes down to subjective analysis. In reality, the only way to rate the success of any municipality is population growth. If you're gaining population, you win. If you're bleeding population, you lose. Greater Western New York has counties, cities, towns and villages that fall on both sides of this assessment.

But this chapter celebrates the nationally recognized winners. Shucks, if we're going to make hay out of being selected among the best board walk foods or the best burger joints, why not trumpet our "best of" towns?

We'll start with the Town of Amherst in Erie County. Somehow, CNN categorized this town as one of the best small "cities," ranking it as #50 in its 2012 Best Places to Live list. We'll take it any way we can get it. But we'll take this one with a grain of salt, especially after reading the "winning" description." CNN touts Amherst's benefits as being "a stone's throw away from Niagara Falls and within driving distance of skiing and snowboarding," but it then says residents must "put up with over 90 inches of snowfall a year" and incredulously wonders why "folks seem loath to leave."[1] With friends like that, who needs enemies?

The Town of Lewiston in Niagara County fairs a magnitude better, both mathematically and descriptively, in Rand McNally's 2012 Best Small Towns in America ranking. Coming in at #5, it's described as "the perfect setting for picnicking, hiking and white water rafting. Visitors often come to boat and fish as well, with biking, cross-country skiing, Frisbee golf and swimming also available."[2] Hmm, I guess there's no winter in Lewiston. No wonder why it's ranked higher than Amherst. Lewiston also scored #5 in the same survey's "Best of Food" category (and, rather interestingly, Corning in Steuben County ranked #3 in its "Most Fun" category).[3]

A website going by the name "SmallTownGems.com" lists the Town of Chautauqua in Chautauqua County among the nation's top "theme towns" (ranking with Saratoga and Lake Placid as the only such towns listed in New York). In either case, their site shouts that it "EARNS OUR HIGHEST RECOMMENDATION" (yes, this sentence is written in all caps on the site).[4] The site emphasizes the major role Chautauqua Institution plays in the town. It also gives you advice on how to pronounce the name of the town. Beneath the name "Chautauqua," the site adds the phonetic spelling "sha-talk-kwa." Apparently the webmaster speaks with a stutter, because the correct phonetic spelling would be "shuh-taw-kwuh" (at least per Dictionary.com).

But the big winner is the Village of Hammondsport in the Town of Urbana in Steuben County. It tied for first place in *Budget Travel* magazine's 7th annual 10 Coolest Small Towns in America.[5] This is the first year the contest, open to towns with populations of less than 10,000, ended in a tie. The entry description played up Hammondsport's tradition of producing wines and its "placid atmosphere" of "gentle rolling hills," "picturesque views above Keuka Lake" and "its two public beaches."[6] Hmm (again), not a snowflake in sight.

There you have it. For what it's worth, we've got a town listed among the nation's top "small cities" and a village listed as one of America's coolest "small towns." Like I said, they're just beauty contests, but, hey, at least we're getting noticed!

Discovering the special small town soul doesn't require a carnival. It doesn't require outside recognition. There are many ways our communities both celebrate themselves and their character. We'll explore a few in the next chapter.

CHAPTER 43: FESTIV-AL-US FOR THE REST OF US

My writing has been publicly available for quite some time. I wrote a weekly "Commentary" column for the *Mendon-Honeoye Falls-Lima Sentinel* during the first couple years of its existence. Subjects included topics ranging from local to national, from the solemn to the silly, from the practical to the playful. Since 2009, most of my writing appears on the web, although you can still find me in print (mostly in the financial press).

Once, after writing about the special camaraderie of small towns, a woman contacted me and suggested I write about Colonial Days in Painted Post. Something about the Village of Painted Post has always intrigued me. It's located in the Town of Erwin in Steuben County just west of Corning. There really was a painted post. As early as 1779, an actual post marked where the three rivers (Cohocton, Tioga, and Canisteo) formed the Chemung River.[1]

The site held great strategic importance as it was a much fought-over piece of property. During the summer of 1779, under orders from Washington, General Sullivan marched up the Chemung River Valley, to lay ruin – in a style reminiscent of Sherman's March to the Sea – to Iroquois tribes who sided with the British. It was Cornplanter, the Seneca Tribe Chieftain who tried to keep the Iroquois neutral during the Revolutionary War, who reluctantly fought against the colonists when outvoted and who negotiated the ultimate peace with the victorious Americans. In his mid-1780s, Cornplanter gave us the best explanation of the origin of the painted post. Upon retreating from a battle against Sullivan, they came to a stop at the north side of the mouth of the Cohocton River, where "a great chief and brave was there taken sick, died and was buried under the shade of an elm" and, together with others of the council, "he placed over the grave a post, stained with the juice of wild strawberry, to mark the spot."[2] A monument now stands in place of the original post.

By strange coincidence, the first settler in Painted Post, William Harris, arrived there in the year 1786 on December 16th, (there's that date again!).[3]

With a rich history dating from the Revolutionary War and early America, Painted Post has a right to celebrate. That's what the aptly named "Colonial Days" festival is all about. Held for four days in early June, Colonial Days is a history lesson and community gala all in one, with a parade, bands, historical talks, softball and golf tournaments, midway rides, food, fun and fellowship. In other words, it's everything you'd expect from an annual small town affair. Of course, it's a good thing they hold it before the wild strawberries get ripe lest attendees might be tempted to take any historic re-enactment too far.

And Colonial Days is just one example. Why, I bet, chances are, if you take any random country road during a summer weekend, you'd eventually find a small town festival. This is true. This happened to me.

My wife grew up in Jamestown and we regularly take several summer sojourns there. Usually we take the Thruway as it allows us to pay homage to my childhood roots. Literally. My childhood home abuts the Thruway, as does my grandfather's house (our backyard bordered his backyard). In fact, just south of my grandfather's house lies an open field – still undisturbed by developers – where my mother, my brother and I would regularly walk into each June to pick Tupperware containers full of wild strawberries.

One July 4th weekend we decided to take the slow leisurely back roads through Livingston County, Wyoming County and Cattaraugus County before finally ending up in Chautauqua County. I like this route, especially on a nice sunny summer day. That's what it was like when we started. By the time we got to the Town of Ellicottville and its Village, dusk had descended and we noticed something strange. The quiet serenity of the country had given way to a frenzied mosh pit. A mass of humanity clogged the intersection of Jefferson Street and Route 219. I turned to my wife and said, "We're in the middle of a local festival."

It was the annual Ellicottville Summer Music Festival, featuring everything from rock to blue grass to classical. It even has a strawberry festival as part of it. Fortunately for us, the music wasn't playing when we passed. If it was, we'd no doubt still be stuck in traffic.

Oddly, we were heading to Jamestown this particular weekend to give our kids a chance to experience the July 4th Chautauqua Lake Ring of Fire event. At a given time, businesses and cottages surrounding the lake would light flares, creating a ring of bright strawberry red fire along the lake's shore. Such festivals capture the spirit of small town – or small lake – living. But you don't need a party to feel the days of yore. Sometimes, it involves a long standing tradition, service or activity – one that had its origins in a different century. That's our next hidden gem. And we don't have to travel far to get there. It's right down the lake.

CHAPTER 44: A CHAUTAUQUA BOAT RIDE

In the Clint Eastwood classic *The Outlaw Josey Wales*, we learn what a Missouri boat ride is when Josey Wales shoots the tow rope sending the simple river ferry for a wild trip down the stream's undulating current.

Our story in this chapter takes place not on a river in Missouri, but on a lake in New York. Western New York. Greater Western New York. They say the "Chautauqua" of Chautauqua County comes from an Indian word meaning "a bag tied in the middle." They say that because Chautauqua Lake looks like a bag tied in the middle. The narrowest point sits between Bemus Point in the Town of Ellery and Stow in the Town of North Harmony. At that point, it is 968 feet from one side of the shore to the other, short enough for many people to swim. My mother-in-law is one of those many.

In the spring of 1806, William Bemus arrived at his namesake point as its first white settler.[1] Earlier that same year, in January, his son Thomas became the first settler in what is now the Town of North Harmony on the opposite side of the narrows from Bemus Point.[2] Now, let's use a little common sense here. If you're the first two settlers in an otherwise uninhabited region, and you happen to be father and son, and you find yourself separated by a thousand feet of water, what do you do? You paddle, row, swim – whatever – from one side of the lake to the other.

After about five years, this form of ad hoc transportation probably got boring, or tiring, to Thomas Bemus. He decided to give things a more permanent fix. In 1811, he applied for and received a license to operate a flat bottom boat between Bemus Point and Stow.[3] What started as a simple log raft guided by a paddle, soon became an honest-to-goodness ferry, towrope and all.[4] It started to look and feel like the raft seen by Josey Wales. It even had the misfortune of having its rope snapped on occasion, although usually as the result of a steamboat paddle cutting the line rather than due to the expert marksmanship of a fugitive rebel.[5] Replacing the rope with steel didn't help, either, and the Lake Authority had to intervene, forcing boats to sound their horn when approaching the narrows.[6]

In 1906, the ferry transported its first automobile.[7] Even today, driving around the lake from Bemus Point to Stow takes a good while. The ferry, by saving loads of time, proved very popular to both locals and tourists. Indeed, no doubt the many visitors of Chautauqua Institution helped keep the ferry in business. One could easily imagine them seeking respite from the quiet religious sobriety (remember, alcohol was not allowed) of the Institution in the maelstrom of turpitude that was Bemus Point. Not that Bemus Point was a den of sin or anything, but by the late nineteenth century, it was a hoppin' place.

Why else would Pittsburgh steel magnate James Selden open The Casino there in May of 1930? Back in those days, despite the depression, the Casino did a thriving business, becoming famous for bringing in big bands and vaudeville acts. National headliners making their way to Bemus Point included The Tommy Dorsey Band (with a young Frank Sinatra), The Glen Miller Orchestra, Louis Armstrong, Ozzie and Harriet Nelson, Cab Calloway and Al Jolson. One of Lucille Ball's early performances included being part of a vaudeville act at the Casino.

The Casino has the honor of holding a spot in the Guinness Book of World Records. In 1985, it broke the record for the most chicken wings served in a 24-hour period. It was a close call. The deep fryers experienced a technical problem during the contest period. But, using that Greater Western New York grit we're all so used to, the Casino staff kept on course to earn their place in culinary history.

Having a ferry (or a bridge) where the bag is tied in the middle, i.e., the narrows of Chautauqua Lake, would benefit many a weary traveler. After nearly a century-and-a-half of private ownership, the ferry fell into the hands of the County, who operated it until the nearby Chautauqua County Veterans' Memorial Bridge was opened in 1982.[8] Since then, it's been operated by the Chautauqua Lake Historic Vessels Co.[9]

Chautauqua Lake, being rather placid most of the time, doesn't offer much of chance for a loose ferry to ever go on one of them thar Civil War Era "Missouri boat rides," whether that's a Hollywood term or a real term. Greater Western New York does, however, have an even stronger link to the south when it comes to the War Between the States. And it was kept secret from more than eighty years. We'll explain how it was finally revealed – and in Hollywood fashion – in the next chapter.

CHAPTER 45: DIXIE'S LAST STAND

One can forgive the tiny hamlet of Town Line for having a bit of an identity crisis. First off, it's a hamlet. The municipal code of New York State has room for counties, cities, towns and villages. It says nothing about hamlets. Hamlets don't exist. This presents a bit of a problem if you live or work – like I do – in a hamlet. (I work in the hamlet of Mendon.) With no formal identity, there are no formal borders. It's more of a feeling thing, as in "you'll know you're there when you're there."

But the legalese of civic law presents the least of Town Line's identity problems. Another sticky-wickets deals with its physical location. Town Line sits on the border of two towns, the Town of Alden and the Town of Lancaster. So which is it? Is Town Line in Alden or is it in Lancaster? It turns out, it's a little bit of both. Or neither. It depends who you ask. Town Line locals have the same spirit of independence and self-reliance you find among almost every community in Western New York.

At least they can all agree they're in Erie County. And in the Greater Western New York. And in New York State. And in the United States of America.

Wait. That last one isn't as obvious as you think. History shows Town Line has had a difficult time agreeing that it's part of the United States of America. For eighty-five years, it wasn't. This fact surprises many people. It surprised me when I discovered it at the 2011 Erie County Fair.

I was strolling through the Historical Society's Building when I came upon the display of the Alden Historical Society. The year 2011 marked the 150th anniversary of the secession of the hamlet of Town Line. That's right. In 1861, Town Line voted to secede and joined the Confederacy. Could this be true? There must have been a catch? Why didn't they teach us this in school? Intrigued, I started on the long road of research.

The first stop on the road was Karen Muchow, the head of the Alden Historical Society and the curator who designed the original display I saw at the Hamburg Fair. She was kind enough to give me copies of source material, a quick overview of the basic story and a bit of her own analysis. She also gave me an important lead. Next I visited Edward Mikula, Town of Lancaster Historian and his able assistant Marie Schu. Since Town Line has no official office or historical society, and since it's technically located in both towns, I needed to get the perspective from both towns. Mikula and Schu provided me with still more source documentation, including personal notes.

I saved the best for last. At Muchow's suggestion, I visited – unannounced – Lisa Blair. Her family runs Blair's Hardware Shop in Town Line. She has taken it upon herself to collect, archive and display as much as possible of the artifacts, relics and stories surrounding the Town Line secession story. Her husband's grandfather actually witnessed and participated in the event which culminates the story. She provided yet more source material (including contemporary newspaper accounts), filled in some of the missing blanks and added some personal touches only she could.

What follows reveals the combined reflections of these three sources, the material they provided and additional follow-up research.

In Walt Whitman's poem "Year of Meteors (1859-60)," published in his celebrated collection *Leaves of Grass*, the wordsmith writes of actual astronomical events that occurred in those years. Astronomers have identified the comet Whitman refers to as the Great Comet of 1860, which occurred in January. Many had speculated the poet alluded to the Great Fireball of 1859. Astronomers today cite the year 1859, in particular, as one to remember. On the morning of September 1, 1859, a gigantic sunspot exploded, spewing forth the greatest magnetic storm in recorded history. Known as the Carrington Event, this superstorm knocked out our infantile telegraph system for a while and spread brilliant aurorae throughout the northern hemisphere. If a similarly intense storm happened today – well – let's just say you would have wasted money on that surge protector. And don't even think about calling for a refund, since it might take days, weeks, months (but hopefully not years) for the grid to recover. These are things you learn when you study astronomy.

The people of Town Line witnessed these astronomical phenomena and, like most people of the time, felt they presaged bad events. And it seemed they were correct. One of the many suspicious fires that occurred that year consumed the tavern Thurston Carpenter's family established when they first arrive in Town Line in 1812.[1] Interviewed by Buffalo's Courier Express during the 1930s, George Huber, a long-time Justice for the Town of Lancaster and a lifelong Democrat,[2] called wheel-chair bound Carpenter "an argumentative invalid" and a "red-hot Republican."[3] He was also a known abolitionist, which might have had something to do with his tavern's burning.

On the opposite side sat banker George Bruce, who started Merchants Bank in Lancaster in 1850 and might have used that leverage to influence his clientele, mostly farmers dependent on bank loans.[4] Huber said Bruce "was the center of a group of rabid Southern sympathizers and avowed Democrats. He made no pretense of concealing his sympathy for the South."[5]

Although Town Line voted for Abraham Lincoln "by a small margin"[6] in the election of 1860, an article in the *Buffalo Courier Express* cites "an old Lancaster newspaper" (no date given) that ran an account of an "angry" meeting of "copperheads" shortly after the Civil War broke out in April of 1861.[7] Huber, despite his age, remembered the events well:

> When war was declared, Lancaster seethed with the news and many were the nights we stayed up as late as 12 o'clock to talk things out. The first war meeting was held on the evening of April 23rd at the American Hotel and was addressed by Dr. Hunt and Almon Clapp from Buffalo. I was twelve years old at the time, but I remember the stern faces of the elders and the storm of passionate and angry discussion. Soon the town split into two factions, it was a very tense situation... Bruce and Carpenter clashed daily. These men formed, as it were, two hostile camps, between which occasionally there would be a parley, but more often a bitter verbal war. As you went out of an evening for a walk after dinner--and everybody walked after dinner in those days--you could see the partisans of both groups dividing on the street as naturally as oil and water divide. And often the excitement ran so high that if a man in either group had made the slightest sign, neighbors would have been at each others throats and fists would have taken the place of words.[8]

Let's take a moment to leave Town Line and recall the thirty-thousand-foot view of the Civil War's first year. First, the terrorist work of John Brown and Kansas Red Legs notwithstanding, polite society considered the War Between the States as something between a gentleman's duel and a sibling squabble. Secession was viewed as the political "next-step" following the intensely partisan 1860 Presidential election. This election would mark the end of the generations-long dominance of the Democrats and the advent of a new national party – the Republicans.

In nine southern states, Lincoln received not a single vote, but the southern Democrats and the northern Democrats ran (and voted for) two different tickets. Lincoln (Republican) won 40% of the popular vote; Stephen Douglas (Northern Democrat) won 30% of the vote; John Breckinridge (Southern Democrat) won 20%; and, John Bell (for the dying Whig Party) won 10%. The nation was less split than we think today, and many felt the issue of state independence – and eventually slavery – could be resolved eventually but peacefully. Although the Southern Democrats threatened secession in the lead up to the election, most felt it was an election ploy.

The South seceded in January of 1861. Lincoln was inaugurated in March and the South first shoots on Fort Sumter in April. In the following months, West Virginia seceded from Virginia to become its own state and, while four slave states joined the Confederacy, another four states opted to stay in the Union. The inevitable ground battle finally occurred at Bull Run in July. Many expected the North to win decisively and quickly. Reporters covered the event like a prize fight and picnickers turned out like concert goers.

When the South sent the Union troops fleeing through the streets of Washington, the North lay dispirited and the South – and its cause – found encouragement. Sentiment began to change. The North realized it needed to muster and organize an army. Some even felt the longer the war lasted, the more likely the Confederacy would retain its independence.

Back to Town Line. The partisan split was one thing – it only impacted those involved. But with the Union loss at Manassas (a.k.a., First Bull Run) the threat of Federal intrusion became real. The already divisive Town Line met again, and this time the Copperheads came with papers of secession. We don't know the date for sure, but we know a meeting took place at the school and the "Articles of Secession" were voted on, passed by a count of 85 in favor, 40 against, and signed on the headmaster's desk.

"Why?" Clearly, it wasn't slavery. Town Line had at least two stops on the Underground Railroad. In addition, the immigrants who settled there came from countries that opposed slavery. Ah, the immigrants. Town Line had just witnessed an influx of skilled workers from Germany. For those of you not familiar with nineteenth century European history, this was the time of protracted civil war that eventually led to the unification of Germany in 1871. (Italy was going through a similar process.) It's likely these German immigrants were concerned they were leaving one civil war for another. They didn't want to see their sons drafted in Germany and they certainly didn't want to see them drafted in America. Strike one against the Union.

Rumors also included the threat of new taxes to fund the war effort. Even if you didn't have a son to send to Washington, many small businesses, like farmers, didn't want to see their hard-earned cash end up with the Federal Government. Strike two against the Union.

Finally, and most importantly, you had partisans like Bruce, who fervently opposed the Republicans, no matter what their policy. The existence of a strong Copperhead base ensured the issue would be brought to bear. And it was. Strike three against the Union.

"What were the implications of the vote?" Although there are stories Town Line sent five men to fight for the South, there's no documentation of this. Town Line did send men to fight for the Union. Also, since a hamlet has no legal authority, the resolution to pass the "Articles of Secession" had as much value as Monopoly money does at the bank. There's no recorded formal response. In fact, today, there's no formal anything – except for the headmaster's desk, (on display at the Alden Historical Society).

What happened to all the records? Huber noted "Lancaster was the center of a 'Copperhead' community, although it was loyal, but Town Line, just east of here, was a bit of Southern rebellion in the midst of what everybody thought was a united North. We people of the village were a bit embarrassed when Town Line seceded from the Union by a vote of its citizens."[9]

So the trail runs dry. Muchow takes stock in Huber's "embarrassment" theory. After all, once Union casualty lists included Town Line boys, the vote took on a more serious tone. It's thought the secessionists quieted as a result and eventually fled the town, possibly to Canada. Bruce closed his bank in 1862. In a short time, the hamlet of Town Line learned the practice of *omerta*, and no one spoke of, or admitted to, the vote – at least not officially. Blair told me a reporter came to Town Line in 1919 (or thereabouts) to ask questions. Town Line remained silent. And, despite a random newspaper article every now and then, silent it remained. Until 1945.

On July 4th, 1945, the assumed last bastions of the Confederacy – Vicksburg, Mississippi (which had not celebrated July 4th since 1863) and Dade County, Georgia – officially gave up the cause and voted to rejoin the Union. Stephen Feeley, a creative reporter for the *Courier Express*, decided the publicity surrounding the decision by Vicksburg and Dade County might be funneled to Greater Western New York. He resuscitated an old story his paper had been working on for decades – the story of Town Line's secession. This time Town Line agreed, albeit with some provisions. In Feeley's article, Alden Supervisor John H. Cooke, who otherwise supported Feeley's effort, was quick to emphasize "his ancestors had nothing to do with the break, his grandfather having fought for the Union."[10]

The following six months were a whirlwind for the otherwise quiet hamlet. The story of Town Line's proposed vote to rejoin the Union caught the nation's attention, from the White House to Hollywood. Even the Deep South got in the act. General T.W. Dowling of Valdosta Georgia, a 97 year-old Confederate veteran, advised Town Line, "We been rather pleased with the results since we rejoined the Union. Town Line ought to give the United States another try."[11] Alabama Senator John Sparkman wrote, "As one unreconstructed rebel to another, let me say that I find much comfort in the fact that you good people so far up in Yankee land have held out during the years. However, I suppose we grow soft as we grow older."[12]

The first vote failed 29-1, and Town Line officials, saying this was only a "test" vote, appealed to the White House for advice. President Truman played along, suggesting Town Line officials might be able to fashion a favorable result in the revote by using "roast veal" as an inducement. The

President wrote: "Why don't you run down the fattest calf in Erie County, barbecue it and serve it in the old blacksmith shop where the ruckus started? Who can tell? The dissidents might decide to resume citizenship."[13]

A new vote, complete with the Truman's trimmings, was set up. The school house that housed the original vote had been bought by Henry Urshel, who used it as a blacksmith shop. In October, the Hamlet decided to schedule an "official" vote in July 1946 at the Fireman's Parade.

Then Hollywood got involved. By coincidence, 20th Century had a movie called *Col. Effingham's Raid* set for release in early 1946. The comedy tells the story of an old Confederate veteran who, upon returning to his boyhood home town, must stop the establishment from renaming "Confederate Square" after a corrupt politician. The movie stars Charles Coburn and Joan Bennett. The studio decided the movie would premiere in Town Line the day of the vote. It arranged for Charles Coburn to broadcast an appeal from Georgia directly to Town Line and even sent movie stars Cesar Romero and Martha Stewart to personally read the results of the vote. [14] There was only one catch. The studio wanted Town Line to schedule the vote for January.

Schools were closed on January 24th, 1946 for the event. A special plastic coin was minted to commemorate the occasion. It had the motto "The Last Confederacy" stamped on it (Blair later bought the original plates on eBay). Perhaps to remind folks what Town Line's decision was NOT about, the coin was molded in the shape of a horseshoe. The horseshoe represents the secret symbol of the abolitionists' Underground Railroad, the route escaped slaves took for freedom. After the gala world premiere of *Col. Effingham's Raid* in the fire hall (the blacksmith shop wasn't big enough for the crowd), and after "Truman's Lunch" was had by all, the residents of Town Line voted. At exactly 3:21pm, Cesar Romero "raised his arm triumphantly, announcing 'a glorious victory for the Union.'"[15] The final vote: 90 for and 23 against.

And, like the first vote, this one melted into history. Except we've got a record of it. We've got newspaper articles. We've got pictures and home movies.[16] We even have MovieTone news, which filmed the parade down Route 20.[17] We still have the desk, but the former school house ultimately became a casualty of the widening of Route 20.

The mystery of the first vote remains, but the sense of embarrassment lends credence to the idea the initial vote was less seriously considered than it should have been. That doesn't mean the outcome would have been any different, but why else would the event have been buried, if not denied, for all these years? It shouldn't have been denied. As Colonel Effingham said, "A community's history is its family tree." Perhaps a subtle stigma sank in the soul of our region immediately after Town Line's secession. We'll next explore how our region more than paid its penance, before concluding with a true story of America's first rebel, how America is forever indebted to him and Greater Western New York's role in this story of early American History.

CHAPTER 46: A CIVIL WAR MEMORIAL

A merica's Civil War left nearly a million casualties and a national wound that would take generations to heal. Heal it did and the process began almost immediately. While a small hamlet in Greater Western New York was busy forgetting its recent past, another of our villages became the first to keep from forgetting. If we travel east of Town Line on Route 20, we pass through the heart of our region. Just past Geneva and before we reach Seneca Falls, we come to the not-so-small Village of Waterloo in Seneca County. Waterloo's a big village, reaching into three towns – Waterloo, Seneca and Fayette.

When the Union veterans began returning to Waterloo, a forty-five year old druggist took note. He noted how the residents greeted all those who returned with honors and celebrations. What bothered him, though, were the ones who didn't return. Who would honor their memories? Perhaps he was compelled by his own personal experience. He himself had only the memory of his three children, all of whom died in childhood.

Born in Glastonbury, Connecticut on May 13, 1821, Henry C. Welles (not to be confused with Henry Wells of Palmyra and Buffalo and co-founder of Wells-Fargo), came to Waterloo with his family sometime after 1825. A hard worker and proud of his community, he soon became a much respected druggist and elected official. When he saw how many soldiers didn't return, he had an idea. In the summer of 1865, he attended a social gathering with some friends. It was there he first proposed his idea of placing flowers on the graves of the war dead, but nothing came of it.[1]

In early 1866, he told General John B. Murray of his idea. Murray, originally from Vermont, was a lawyer and teacher from Seneca Falls. He joined the 148th Regiment of New York State Volunteers in 1862 and commanded them as a captain. He held the rank of brigadier general when he was discharged in 1866. He had just moved to Waterloo to assume office as newly elected County Clerk of Seneca County when he met Welles. He very much liked the idea of a "Decoration Day," (as Memorial Day was originally called).

Welles and Murray organized a committee of local citizens and, with Murray enlisting veterans' support, held the nation's first official Decoration Day on May 5, 1866. They adorned the Village of Waterloo with flags (all at half-mast) draped with evergreens and mourning black. They then collected a group of citizens, community organizations and veterans and, as the band played marching music, paraded to each of the Villages three cemeteries, where they held a short ceremony amidst the decorated graves of soldiers who gave their lives. This was repeated on the same day the following year, but moved permanently to May 30th in 1868 in harmony with the orders of Major General John A. Logan, who, as head of the Grand Army of the Republic, organized the first national Decoration Day and led services in Arlington Cemetery.

Just two months after experiencing the nationalization of his idea, Welles died. A year later, in 1869, Murray moved back to Seneca Falls. Between Welles' early death and Murray's natural speaking and leadership abilities, many assumed the idea for Decoration Day came from Murray. Indeed, given his skills as an orator and prominence as the co-organizer of the first Decoration Day, he quickly became a much sought-after speaker. Contemporary newspapers, however, did give Welles the credit he was due.[2]

It wasn't until after World War I that Memorial Day was expanded to honor fallen soldiers of all American wars. The name Memorial Day wouldn't officially replace Decoration Day until Congress passed legislation renaming the holiday in 1967.

At least 25 other communities, many from the south, claimed to have been the first to establish a Decoration Day, but Waterloo was the first to do so formally, as a community wide event and as a continuing annual memorial. To honor Waterloo, in 1966 as part of the Centennial Celebration of Memorial Day, Congress and President Lyndon Johnson officially declared Waterloo in Greater Western New York as the "birthplace" of Memorial Day. In 1971, the "official" Memorial Day shifted from May 30th each year to the last Monday in May.

Memorial Day would be but the first of the three patriot traditions established in the United States following the Civil War. In keeping with its role as the heart and soul of America, Greater Western New York would also have a hand in the other two.

CHAPTER 47: AMERICA'S PLEDGE

When many people think of Mount Morris, they think of the dam built by the U.S. Army Corps of Engineers. Completed in 1952, its purpose is to control the water flow in the lower Genesee River watershed. Post-Civil War records indicate from 1865 to 1950 the Genesee River valley experienced a major flood on average once every seven years.[1] Indeed, the dam at Mount Morris saved jobs, property and people by holding back the raging flood waters of Hurricane Agnes in 1972. But there's something Mount Morris produced that has had an even greater impact. In fact, schools, youth organizations and adult service clubs across the nation pay in a way homage to this peaceful town every day.

He was born on May 18, 1855, graduated from the University of Rochester in 1876 and, in 1892, he wrote perhaps the most famous anthem in American history. His name is Francis Bellamy.

Bellamy, though a native of Mount Morris in Livingston County, moved to Rome, New York when he was four and was raised there by his mother following the death of his father in 1864. At the University of Rochester he prepared for life as a Baptist minister. Following his graduation from the U. of R., he entered the Rochester Theological Seminary. Once he graduated from there, he left Greater Western New York for good.

But, just like any ex-pat of today, Greater Western New York did not leave him. The patriotic fervor of Memorial Day was just starting during his second stay in our region, and it's possible that remained a latent spark within him as he conducted his various ministries.

Upon the advice of his friend Daniel Ford, Bellamy took a position as a writer to work with Ford's nephew James Upham at Ford's magazine *The Youth's Companion*. A year later, in 1892, there was a national push to celebrate the 400th anniversary of Christopher Columbus' discovery of America.

Upham wanted to use the effort to advance his idea of a school flag movement. Bellamy agreed and would eventually find himself picked to chair a committee tasked with identifying a way to incorporate a national Columbian Public School Celebration into the 400th anniversary activities. It was through this effort that Bellamy would introduce his pledge to the flag concept.

Bellamy wrote the original *Pledge of Allegiance* in August 1892 and it was published in *The Youth's Companion* on September 8, 1892.[2] The original form read as follows:

> "I pledge allegiance to my Flag and the Republic for which it stands, one nation, indivisible, with liberty and justice for all."

In 1923, "my Flag and the Republic" was replaced with the words "the Flag of the United States of America and to the Republic." In 1954, under the urging of President Eisenhower, Congress added the words "under God." Bellamy's daughter objected to this.[3]

Bellamy originally included an open palm salute (known as the "Bellamy Salute") with his program. This was switched to the right hand over the heart salute we're familiar with today because the Bellamy Salute looked too similar in appearance to Hitler's Nazi salute.

The original intention was to have the school children recite the *Pledge of Allegiance* during the 400th Anniversary celebration. The ideal was to have them recite it each morning. This tradition quickly took hold and the use of opening other public and private gatherings with the *Pledge of Allegiance* spread like wildfire. Today, you can attend almost any school or civic meeting and find the very first item on the agenda is the recitation of the *Pledge of Allegiance*.

At the heart of it, Bellamy and Upham wanted to memorialize the spirit of America in the same way Welles wanted to memorialize the soldiers who gave their all for our Country. Coincident to the movement to adopt the Pledge of Allegiance was another national movement. As we'll see in the next chapter, it has "beef" written all over it.

CHAPTER 48: WISCONSIN WINS THIS ONE

I f you're so inclined to take a stroll through Forest Lawn Cemetery in Buffalo and you happen to find yourself by Mirror Lake, look around at the tombstones. If you're lucky (it ought to be easy to find, it's the only one with the huge flagpole), you'll find one that reads:

Sara M. Hinson
Dedicated Teacher
Who with Others
Gave Us Flag Day
1841 – 1926

On February 25, 1841, George Hinson's wife gave birth to a baby girl. The parents named her Sara. Sara Hinson would go through the Buffalo School System before being sent to finishing school. Upon completion of her education, she began teaching at Buffalo PS 13 before being moved to School #4. In 1864, as the Civil War was ending, Hinson was 23 and she transferred to School #31, where she taught the fourth grade for thirty years before spending the next twenty as principal.

Hinson is credited with being one of the first to advocate the celebration of Flag Day. Although most sources imply she independently determined to celebrate Flag Day on June 14th – the day the Continental Congress formally accepted Betsy Ross' design in 1777 – there are plenty of sources citing other teachers as picking the same date on or around the same year. Most websites – and I wasn't able to locate an original source – claim she taught children how to salute the Flag and repeat the Pledge of Allegiance at her first Flag Day in 1891. This can't be true since (or at least the date is wrong), as we learned in the previous chapter, the *Pledge of Allegiance* wasn't written and published until the late summer of 1892.

Based on a *Chicago Tribune* article, Bernard J. Cigrand is most often cited as being known as the "Father of Flag Day."[1] It's said he held his first "unofficial" observance when he was a school teacher in Waubeka, Wisconsin in 1885. (What is it about Wisconsin nosing in on our claims!)

How credible are these claims? Consider this: Cigrand was a prolific writer and did found the National Flag Day Organization, through which he "relentlessly campaigned and lectured all over the country to have Flag Day made a national holiday."[2] But as far back as 1885? All we can see is an unsubstantiated account that he assigned his eighth grade class an essay assignment to write about the flag.[3]

I'm not saying our claims are any more solid, but Cigrand might be Murray to Hinson's Welles. We'll never know for sure.

What we do know is, on June 14, 1916, President Woodrow Wilson agreed to set aside June 14th as a day of "national observance of Flag Day." It didn't become a "national holiday" until 1949, when President Harry Truman signed legislation declaring it so.

It's likely both Hinson and Cigrand, as well as numerous other teachers around the nation, heard of Francis Bellamy's ideas for promoting the Flag in schools and joined the effort. The coincidence of the timing of Bellamy's *Pledge of Allegiance* and the Flag Day promotion is just too remarkable to believe.

Being the charitable kind of guy that I am, and since I've already established the chronological primacy of our invention of the hamburger, I'd be apt to give Wisconsin Flag Day, with all due respect to Sara Hinson (her tombstone does, after all, admit she gave us Flag Day "with others"). Hopefully, Wisconsin doesn't have a beef with this.

Still, we'll grant Hinson as much for her patriotic efforts. I'd say it's in the water, but our next hidden gem proves he didn't need to drink our water to make a difference. What does it say that, once he gave up everything to save America, he came to Greater Western New York to live the rest of his years?

CHAPTER 49: WE'RE BAAACK!

Rain fell in dreary mists as we make our way south on a narrow country road in Livingston County. The boring gray skies overhead could not contain my excitement. We are heading to one of the last sites I need to visit in researching this book. I smile and look to my wife as we slow down to stop behind a line of cars. (A traffic jam? In the middle of nowhere?) Ignoring these obvious questions, she returns my gaze from the passenger seat of our car and smiles that special loving smile only she could smile.

That's when the guilt hits...

My father-in-law is a masterful genealogist. His command of detail and stick-to-itiveness proved the perfect combination for uncovering the often hidden trails that meandered back through the generations. Unfortunately for him, his parents came from Sweden and, after a generation or two, his inability to speak fluent Swedish and the physical separation between his home in Jamestown and his parent's homeland in the Nordic lands of Europe proved an insurmountable barrier.

Did he give up? Heck, no. He is, after all, a native Greater Western New Yorker. Tenacity isn't just a mere act of self-discipline, it's a part of our vital essence, a lifeblood flowing through our veins. How else does one explain our vicious inner pride when we hear Bruce Smith, despite knowing full well we're going into the game as odds-on underdogs, delightfully announce to the world before yet another Super Bowl, "We're baaack!" Face it. There's a bit of stubbornness in our spirit, dating back to at least the War of 1812, when the residents of the ashen village that was Buffalo insisted on rebuilding, notwithstanding the burning – and building – occurred during mid-winter.

Stopped on his own branch, my father-in-law shifted seamlessly to my mother-in-law's side. She's only half Swedish. The other half traces back through the Mayflower to the English monarchy and beyond. My father-in-law salivated at the prospect of rediscovering his children's past. My sister-in-law, eleven years older than my wife, was already married when the genealogy bug bit in earnest. It was my wife, then, who, as a young girl, found herself dragged across the innards of New York and Massachusetts. Along the way, she and her parents would stay in roadside motels and visit endless cemeteries.

She told me this story – repeatedly – early in our marriage as she accompanied me from small town to large city almost anywhere in the northeast seeking the remnants of railroads of yore. I was a budding industrial archeologist and my wife knew it. At many a stop I would hear her sigh, "At least it's not another cemetery." I assured her train artifacts aren't buried in cemeteries; they're strewn across the landscape from the disheveled wilds of overgrown fields to the well-ordered displays of curated museums. No, there would be no cemeteries for us. And I stayed true to my word...

Until now. For we are heading down West Swamp Road (NY Route 256) in the Town of Conesus. Our destination: Union Cemetery just north of the hamlet of Scottsburg. Worse, today is on the day of our anniversary.

The muddy road seemed to hardly merit the official route number New York State had assigned it. A "repaving" project had caused the traffic jam, and presumably most of the mud. The rain had stopped when we begin to climb the small slope that would lead us to Union Cemetery. Union Cemetery is closed to new burials now, but the grave I'm looking for is from 1825.

We pull into the gravel road that circles through the interior of the cemetery. I'm not sure where the grave is. My research indicates there's a marker. I'm thinking it marks the actual grave. I see a marker by the roadside at the edge of the cemetery. Turning into the graveyard, I assume that's where the grave is, but as I drive up the moist lane, I notice yet another sign – not a marker, but a real sign – indicating the grave I seek lies well within the burial grounds. I exit the car, with camera, and walk in the direction the sign designates.

I see the well-marked grave and position myself to the west of the headstone to snap a picture. The tombstone reads "Capt. Daniel Shay (sic) – Revolutionary War – 1747-1825." The heavy granite stone doesn't look vintage, at least compared to the contemporary gravestones that surround it. Planted next to it is an easily seen metal sign with "Captain Daniel Shays" printed in gold on a blue background.

Before I take a picture, I can't help but stand in awe of the scenic view before me. Union Cemetery sits at the crest of one of the many rolling hills that surround the swampy valley to the south of Conesus Lake. It's a perfect resting place for an American hero, the kind of storybook ending one might expect to find to cap the celebration of a character that, whether he knew it or not, has come to exemplify the persona of all that is Greater Western New York...

Daniel Ogden Shays was a Revolutionary War hero. The Massachusetts native worked as a lower class farm laborer when the War broke. He joined the militia and saw action at Bunker Hill, Ticonderoga, Saratoga and Stony Point. When Shays retired from service in 1780, the Marquis de Lafayette recognized his exemplary record by presenting him with a ceremonial sword.[1]

But that's not why he's famous.

Following his retirement, Shays led the quiet farm life in the western Massachusetts town of Pelham (now called Prescott). Things didn't stay quiet. Most Revolutionary War veterans found themselves paid in Continental Script. The economic recession that followed the Revolutionary War made this paper currency worthless. The government of Massachusetts, consisting mainly of the wealthy class, decided it would only accept hard money (gold and silver) to pay taxes. Making matters worse, the State's huge war debt led to an aggressive tax policy. The farmers of western Massachusetts couldn't get paid in hard currency and couldn't afford the higher taxes.

After the government rebuffed the farmers' pleas, tax assessors started obtaining foreclosures from the courts. Looking for a leader, the abused citizens turned to their local War hero Daniel Shays for leadership. Shays, at first reluctant, stepped into the role after Governor James Bowdoin publicly denounced the farmers' initial action to shut the courts. Shays then led a peaceful demonstration that again closed the courts. A second confrontation would prove disastrous for Shays' "Regulators."

By now, Massachusetts found itself in a virtual civil war, with the government's army manned mainly by elites from the eastern half of the state and Shays' men mostly poor farmers from the western half. In late January of 1787 (why does that year mean something?), Shays' army met the state forces at the Springfield armory, but did not fire. The government men-at-arms proved less accommodating and fired their canons into the crowd of protestors, killing four. From there, "Shays' Rebellion" ended and Governor Bowdoin charged Shays and his leadership with treason. Two were executed, but by then Shays had escaped. He would eventually settle in Scottsburg in what was then the Town of Sparta in Livingston County. Bowdoin lost the next election and the new governor – John Hancock – pardoned all the men.

Shays' contemporaries had mixed feeling about his actions. Some felt he was a traitor, fighting against the very democracy he fought for in the recent Revolutionary War. Others thought he was a true patriot, responding with consistency against one tyranny as he did against another. George Washington did not tolerate mutinous insubordination during the Revolutionary War (Pennsylvania Continentals Mutiny[2]) or during his Presidency (Whisky Rebellion[3]). Originally, General Washington, inspired by the Roman Cincinnatus, wished to stay retired on his Virginia farm. He repeatedly insisted we would not go to the proposed Constitutional Convention in Philadelphia. But Shays' Rebellion changed his mind, and may ultimately be the reason why George Washington became our first President. We know this because, in a letter to George Knox, Washington cites Shays' Rebellion as the reason he changed his mind about attending the Philadelphia Convention.[4] Both Abigail Adams and Samuel Adams sided with the eastern Massachusetts elites. Thomas Jefferson, on the other hand, in a January 30, 1787 letter to James Madison, wrote "I hold it that a little rebellion now and then is a good thing."[5]

Daniel Shays died in obscurity. A few months before Shays' death, Lafayette returned to America to celebrate the fiftieth anniversary of the start of the Revolutionary War. All surviving heroes were invited to see the elder French statesman. All except Daniel Shays.

Two centuries after the event, the positive impact of Shays' Rebellion in forging a new America is undisputed. To mark its 200th anniversary, President Ronald Reagan issued a proclamation declaring, among other things, "Shays' Rebellion did give impetus to the Federalists' call for the establishment of what George Washington termed 'a more efficient general government'" and "Shays' Rebellion was to have a profound and lasting effect on the framing of our Constitution and on our subsequent history."[6]

Like the fictional Colonel Effingham, Captain Daniel Shays took an unpopular stand to save a legacy he had a part in fighting for. Unlike the movie, though, Shays did not survive long enough to see a new generation take the reins from a sickly man to carry on the good fight. Colonel Effingham saw a community that did not surrender to an overbearing government made up of the self-serving rich. It was a storybook ending. For Shays, there would be no such conclusion to his life. Shays took the same risk, and died poor and unknown...

At his grave, lump forms in my throat. Remembering the disregard his contemporaries held for him, a tombstone with his misspelled name seems tragically ironic. But if the history of mankind tells us anything, it assures us Shays' fight continues and, given the nature of man, always will. Shays must see this from somewhere up wherever he is, and when he does, it's not hard to believe he's smiling and saying, "We're baaack!"

Perhaps some reader will have the mind to give a gift to the Scottsburg Union Cemetery. And speaking of gifts...

CHAPTER 50: IT'S A WONDERFUL GREATER WESTERN NEW YORK – OUR GREATEST HIDDEN GEM

For the umpteenth time I find myself watching Capra's It's a Wonderful Life. Yet, in all the years those reels have run through my retinal receptors, for the first time I really see the poignant – if unintended – metaphor.

We – Greater Western New York – are Bedford Falls.

I don't mean in the literal sense like Seneca Falls. I don't mean in the physical-proximity sense because the movie mentions Buffalo and Rochester. And I don't mean in the meteorological sense because those are definitely lake-effect snowflakes in the film. Rather, I speak of a much more mysterious philosophical aura that borders on the eerie similarities of tragic prognostication laced with a fringe of hope.

We are the dying unexciting old Bedford Falls.

We have watched our factories move. We wave good-bye to our sons and daughters as we send them off to college hoping they'll come back to relieve us. They rarely do. Our dream is to travel to some tropical isle, but we're lucky if we can get the time off from work (although many of us are happy just to have a job). We are small businesses producing a modest living for us and increasingly providing the lifeblood to our community. At the same time, we lurch constantly on the brink as big corporations and even bigger governments try their best to keep us small.

Yes, the same despair of Bedford Falls, a fictional town from which youth escape by going to Buffalo, Rochester, Elmira and Binghamton, has now visited those very real cities and, in particular, Greater Western New York.

We are the dutiful, honest-to-a-fault Bedford Falls.

We don't pretend to represent perfection and, as if to prove it, quickly complain of our plight when offered the opportunity. But our modesty does not prevent us from stepping up when a void needs filling, even if it's not in our own best interests. Our economic muscle and youthful vigor might slowly seep to warmer climes, but our loyalty to any obligation stays with us, as strong and vibrant as ever.

Yes, we remain reliable, even as some merely call us "reliable dupes." Not taken in on some wild scheme – we're much too steadfast for that – but dupes in the way any Tom Sawyer can get us to paint his fence. In other words, we're not afraid to give of ourselves to brighten the community.

Still, we are also the rock solid resilient Bedford Falls.

Chris Berman knows a thing or two about our community when he says "nobody circles the wagons like the Buffalo Bills." No matter what ills befall us – man-made or natural – we vow to keep the home fires burning, the factories open and the streets plowed. We readily maintain all that is – if not all that was – so we can welcome home, for however as brief a time, our itinerant family and friends. They still – and always will – consider Greater Western New York their home. And they should. And we hope they come back.

And some do.

So we are all George Bailey. We try our best to improve our community. We strive to convince others to stay, to lure still others to relocate. We fight the good fight against the behemoths that seek only to extract and keep us down. We may lose, but we believe we'll win.

Why?

Because deep in the heart of Greater Western New York we know we'll always have Clarence.

And that makes us as rich as anyone can ever be.

But wait. There's more to this story. As you've traveled through these 50 chapters of hidden gems, you've no doubt noticed the number of amazing gifts we've given to our community, our nation and even the world. Is there something in our spirit of living that has made Greater Western New York such a fountain of helpful, practical and invigorating ideas? What makes our character so creative yet so generous? As I'm writing this particular passage, we are within ten days of Christmas. I can't help but think how our regional personality resembles Santa Claus.

And then I discover this.

Not only do we have the same jolly, giving, never-give-up disposition of Santa Claus, but we also have Santa himself! Yes, you heard it here, folks. Santa Claus was born right here in Greater Western New York. Orleans County, to be exact. Albion, to be precise.

On June 15, 1896, the good Lord blessed William Asa and Martha Howard with a baby boy whom they named Charles W. Howard. In fourth grade, he was picked to play Santa Claus in a school play. There was no turning back. He soon found himself playing the part for church plays, then at stores in Rochester, Buffalo and Albion. A reporter, noting he was getting too many gigs to fill personally, suggested he start a Santa Claus School to train potential stand-ins. In 1937, Charlie did, and his Santa Claus School in Albion would become world famous (so much that it continues to train Santas today, some 45 years after Charlie passed away). His correspondence school once boasted Jimmy Cagney and Orson Wells as pupils.

But his big break would come in 1946, when Twentieth Century Fox would hire him as a technical advisor for their classic movie *Miracle on 34th Street*. From there he would go on to serve as the Macy's Thanksgiving Day Parade Santa Claus for 17 years from 1948 through 1965. That exposure led him to television appearances on *What's My Line*, *To Tell the Truth* and *The Tonight Show*.

A man of many talents and interests, Charlie was a serial entrepreneur. In 1919, at the age of 23, he started his own toy company, the Medina Toy Company and marketed his products under the brand "Sturdy Toys." A big fan of ice cream, he once developed his own recipe and started "Howard's Ice Cream."

Charlie, though, was first and foremost, the ultimate community minded citizen. He lived in the same house in Albion all his life. He traveled the nation and could have set up shop anywhere, but he brought his business – and customers – back to his home town. When local farmers needed help with publicity, Charlie made the world's largest apple pie and once built a scale replica of Niagara Falls with apple juice. He made the rounds at all the local fairs and even got involved in community theatre, where he wrote, directed and acted in many plays across the region.

In the end, Charlie Howard – the world's greatest Santa Claus – embodied the ideal of the Greater Western New York character and continues to serve as a role model for all of us. He loved his work and made it his play, but he never let his work change him. Ironically, as someone famous for playing Santa Claus, he never grew a beard. Perhaps, unlike Albion native Grace Bedell's letter to Abraham Lincoln, he never received a letter from an Albion girl suggesting he grow one. (Grace actually sent the letter from Westfield in Chautauqua County, where her family briefly lived.)

Charlie did understand how to integrate his work in his life and his life in his work. He's famous for espousing a Santa-centric philosophy of optimism and benevolence. He once said:

> "To say there is no Santa Claus is the most erroneous statement in the world. Santa Claus is a thought that is passed from generation to generation. After time this thought takes on a human form. Maybe if all children and adults understand the symbolism of this thought we can actually attain Peace on Earth and good will to men everywhere."

And maybe that's the perfect way to end. May I close by saying to all, no matter what time of year and what time of day, "Merry Christmas to all, and to all a good night!"

APPENDIX I: ANSWERS TO FUN TRIVIA GAME: GUESS THE COMPANY

1.   The largest mailbox manufacturer in North America.
f.   Gibraltar Industries, Inc. – Located in Hamburg, Erie County, the origins of this company date back to 1972, when Dr. Ken Lipke bought Gibraltar Steel Corp, a single facility steel processing business with $9 million in annual sales. Following an aggressive acquisition strategy, in the last two decades alone the company has grown from nine facilities mainly in the Great Lakes region to a firm that today operates coast-to-coast with 41 facilities in 20 states, Canada, England, and Germany, bringing in $767 million in annual sales, according to its 2011 Annual Report. Adopting a model similar to Jack Welch's GE, Gibraltar seeks to establish a leadership position in all of its product lines. As of 2012, it's North America's leading manufacturer of ventilation products, mail storage (solutions including mailboxes and package delivery products), rain dispersion products and accessories, bar grating, expanded metal, metal lath, and expansion joints and structural bearings. You know all those mail boxes you see in Lowes and Home Depot? They're probably made by Gibraltar Industries. For those of you with a connection to Bethlehem Steel, this is about as close as you'll get to it. Although it lists its headquarters as "3556 Lake Shore Rd., Buffalo, New York," those of us who know better know it's located in Woodlawn across from the 179 interchange in the former Bethlehem Steel headquarters. In fact, if you walk into Gibraltar's lobby, you'll be greeted by a huge panoramic of real steel plant pictures. This leads to an interesting story. For years, Wall Street would draw the ire of Chairman Brian Lipke. Whenever steel manufacturers had a bad inning, analysts would punish the entire industry by bidding down stock prices. Gibraltar – a processing company, not a manufacturing company – actually benefited from lower steel prices. Nonetheless, because the official name of the company was "Gibraltar Steel," lazy analysts would assume it was a steel manufacturer and bid down Gibraltar's stock price along with all the others. Of course, smart analysts knew this was exactly the time you'd want to be buying the company. Gibraltar finally solved this misconception by changing its name from Gibraltar Steel to Gibraltar Industries. One more thing of note about Gibraltar – do you know it may be the only Greater Western New York company to have its product find itself on the planet Mars? That's right, Gibraltar supplied the circular aluminum grating for the Mars Lander/Rover.

2.   The company with a large stable of products, including the one with the most Facebook likes in its industry.

e.   Constellation Brands, Inc. – Located in Canandaigua, Ontario County, this company was formed in 1945 and, according to its 2012 About Us page on its web-site (http://www.cbrands.com/about-us), it's the leading premium wine producer in the world, the leading premium wine company in the U.S., the leading wine company in Canada, a leading supplier in New Zealand and leading beer importer and marketer in the U.S. through our Crown Imports joint venture with Mexico's Grupo Modelo. More interesting, however, is it's leading edge use of Facebook to engage its customers. According to Patty Yahn-Urlaub, VP, Investor Relations, Constellation's Arbor Mist product has more than a half million fans on its Facebook page, making it the most popular wine cooler fan page. But that's not all. Yahn-Urlaub says, "It is such an important vehicle for us that all our digital advertising efforts drive fans to Facebook. So instead of a homepage or landing page like companies did in the past, we now send all traffic directly to Facebook. We post daily, and have detailed strategies around content/tone/messaging which we review regularly. We also use Facebook to respond to consumer praise or complaints. The goal for us is engagement, and our engagement is quite strong! Yes we have used Facebook in the past to help us figure out which flavors to launch, which we will continue to do in the future. We also poll fans on occasion to see if they are trying new flavors, and if the Facebook site has driven new purchase or loyalty (which it has!)" Not only does the company regularly engage its fans to improve the product, its level of engagement is impressive. For example, in June 2012, interaction with Arbor Mist fans matched that of the largest beverage brands in the nation, despite having but a fraction of their total fan counts. Specifically, Arbor Mist received nearly three times as many likes vs. Gatorade, even though Gatorade has 9-10 times more fans. It saw twice as many comments as Pepsi, even though the popular soft drink has 13-14 times more fans. Finally, Arbor Mist generated just as many shares as Dr. Pepper, even though Dr. Pepper has 20 times more fans. It just goes to show, when it comes to maximizing social media engagement, some of the most creative minds are right here in Greater Western New York.

3.   The #1 manufacturer of hoists in North America, selling more units than all its competitors combined.

h.   Columbus McKinnon Corporation – Located in Amherst, Erie County, if you lift it, move it, position it or secure it, chances are this 135-year old company manufactures one of the leading components necessary to do the job. In particular, it owns the North American hoist market. What's a hoist? You know what a crane is, right? Well, as Tim Tevens, president of Columbus McKinnon Corporation, told me when I asked him to explain it in terms a middle-schooler would understand, "a hoist is a mechanical device that is the lifting engine component of the crane." But don't give me one of those ho-hum yawns thinking hoists means only "boring" industrial usage. In fact, you probably don't know this, but hoists are an important element to almost everything we do. For example, in the summer of 2012, Bruce Springsteen and the E Street Band took their "Wrecking Ball Tour" across North America and Europe. That's not all they brought. Per the Columbus McKinnon July 12, 2012 press release, among its "truckloads of equipment and tons of gear, including heavy-duty rigging hoists that are also born in the USA -- nine 2-ton and twenty-five 1-ton Lodestar hoists, manufactured by Columbus McKinnon." Greater Western New York has a proud manufacturing tradition. It's sometimes a little surprising to discover just how good it is and how much it can influence the everyday lives of all Americans (and even some Europeans).

4. The only manufacturer of standard size 9-volt batteries designed to last 10 years when used in ionization-type smoke alarms.
i. **UltraLife Corp.** – Located in Newark, Wayne County, this company originally formed in December 1990. Three months later, in March 1991, Ultralife Corp. purchased the 9-volt lithium-manganese dioxide non-rechargable battery business from Eastman Kodak Company. Ultralife went public in 1992 and is currently listed on the NASDAQ trading under the ticker symbol ULBI. It has since grown via both acquisition and organic sales. It has revenues of about $140 million in 2011. The above comes from page 7 of Ultralife's 2011 Annual Report. See, there's a reason to read those things.

5. One of the few companies whose product was featured in a classic Top 40 radio hit.
c. **Eastman Kodak, Inc.** – Located in Rochester, Monroe County, at the time of writing this venerable 120 year-old company finds itself in the throes of a bankruptcy from which it might never escape. Ironically done in by a product it invented – the digital camera – years of complacency, much like the peregrine falcons that nest on its 16-story headquarters building, appear to have come home to roost. But the news was not always this dire. In fact, the term "Kodak Moment" has become forever etched in the memories of every American. At the height of this Bill Cosby led advertising campaigns in the 1970's, Paul Simon created the now classic top 40 hit "Kodachrome." The song hit #2 on Billboard in 1973, staying there for two weeks on July 7 and 14, 1973 (in both cases behind Billy Preston's "Will It Go Round In Circles." Simon told Katherine Lanpher in an September 25, 2008 interview for Barnes & Noble he initially used the working title "Goin' Home" but he thought it too conventional. He decided he liked the word "Kodachrome" much better even though he didn't know what it was. Kodachrome is a film produced by Kodak from 1935 until officially retiring it on June 22, 2009. The last roll of

Kodachrome was processed at Dwayne's Photo in Parsons, Kansas on December 30, 2010 ("End of an era: Last roll of Kodachrome film developed as digital revolution brings 75 years of camera history to a close," Daily Mail, December 31, 2010). Kodachrome was known for its warm vibrant colors, which fit perfectly with the lyrics Simon wrote. When Kodak discovered Simon wrote this song, its lawyers decided to require Simon to include verbiage on the album cover to indicate Kodachrome was a registered trademark of Kodak. Interestingly, the song was banned in England because it was considered a product endorsement.

6.   The ~~second~~ largest operator of short line and regional freight railroads in North America.
j.   Genesee & Wyoming, Inc. – Although actually headquartered in Greenwich, Connecticut, its administrative headquarters is in Rochester, Monroe County. Indeed, its historic origins are in Greater Western New York, specifically the village of Retsof in the Town of York, Livingston County. It started in 1894 as a 14 mile short-line from the salt mine in Retsof (interchanging with the Delaware, Lackawanna and Western Railroad and the Pennsylvania Railroad) to P&L Junction in Caledonia (interchanging with the Erie Railroad, New York Central, Lehigh Valley and Buffalo, Rochester & Pittsburgh Railroad). The Retsof Salt Mine had been the largest salt mine in North America until, on March 12, 1994, a ceiling collapsed, causing ground water to enter the previously dry mine. The event registered 3.6 on the Richter scale. This mine was closed but four years later a new mine was built in Hampton Corners near Mt. Morris. Incidentally, a fellow by the name of William Foster helped launch the original Retsof Mining Company. Foster didn't want the community to name the village after him, so they named it "Retsof," which is Foster spelled backwards. For years the railroad remained this humble, but effective, 14-mile shortline. Then, in 1980, the Staggers Act deregulated railroads, and the company began an aggressive acquisition strategy that continues through today. In fact, in 2012 Genesee & Wyoming Inc. acquired RailAmerica, Inc., to become the largest operator of short line and regional freight railroads in North America. Pretty good for starting only with 14 miles and a few bags of salt!

7.   A company whose product is on nearly every jet fighter in the Western Hemisphere.
a.   Astronics, Corp. – Located in East Aurora, Erie County, this company is a leader in advanced, high-performance lighting, electrical power and automated test systems for the global aerospace and defense industries. It's also a sentimental favorite, as it represented one of the first holdings in the Bullfinch Fund Greater Western New York Series and the *Buffalo News* chose their location to get a picture of us for their article on the launch of the new

fund. The company, originally formed in 1968, now deals with nearly all things related to lighting and power on commercial and defense aircraft. You know those emergency lights you see on the aisle? That's Astronics. You know that cockpit lighting you see when you peak in to check out the pilots? That's Astronics. You know those TVs you watch when riding in those big jumbo jetliners? That's Astronics. You know those lights on the outside of the aircraft? That's Astronics. Heck, they're even getting into runway lighting. I'd tell you more about what they do on the military side of things, but I'd need to see your security clearance first. Just rest assured, every Boeing Dreamliner being produced today contains Astronics engineering running through its arteries.

8.   A grocery store on the "must see" list of nearly every visiting celebrity.
g.   Wegmans Food Markets, Inc. – Headquartered in Chili, Monroe County, Wegmans Food Markets, Inc. is an 80-store supermarket chain with stores in New York, Pennsylvania, New Jersey, Virginia, Maryland, and Massachusetts. The family-owned company, founded in 1916, is recognized as an industry leader and innovator. Wegmans has been named one of the '100 Best Companies to Work For' by FORTUNE magazine for fifteen consecutive years. In 2012, Wegmans ranked #4 on the list. Wall Street industry analyst Neil Stern, quoted in a 1994 front-page story about Wegmans in the Wall Street Journal, said, "We consider them the best chain in the country, maybe in the world." Perhaps he wished they were publicly traded. Wegmans has also been the sponsor and great supporter of the annual LPGA tournament in Rochester. This event brings professional woman golfers from all over the world to Greater Western New York to play in one of the tour's premier events. Perhaps its most famous customer is Alec Baldwin's mom, whom he claims refuses to move because she'd miss shopping at Wegmans. When Cher performed in Rochester, one of the first questions she asked upon arriving was "Where's Wegmans?"

9.   The company everyone turns to whenever there's a major earthquake.
d.   Taylor Devices, Inc. – Located in North Tonawanda, Erie County, this company makes huge shock absorbers. How big are they? They can be used in large skyscrapers to help absorb the shaking caused by earthquakes. Indeed, it's not unusual to see this company's name in the news whenever a sizeable earthquake strikes anywhere in the world. The applications for these things are just amazing. For example, eight Taylor dampers were installed in Seattle's new major league ballpark. Each rated at more than 1 million pounds of force, they're used to help the roof withstand an earthquake of up to a magnitude of 8.5 on the Richter scale. But Taylor is not all about big. The

military places their custom recoil buffers at the bottom of the mortar tube on light armored vehicles so firing the weapon doesn't rattle the folks inside too much. And Taylor doesn't just provide its product to American customers. The Greater Western New York company manufactured eight giant shock absorbers and shipped them to China for the 4.7 mile Sutong Bridge, which spans the Yangtze River just north of Shanghai. At the time of its completion in 2008 it was the largest cable-stayed bridge in the world. These giant shock absorbers will protect the bridge both from earthquakes and typhoons. The 57 year-old company is recognized around the world as a leader in shock absorption, rate control and energy storage devices.

10. A manufacturer that not once, but twice and separated by 50 years, rode a major technology wave to spectacular growth.
b.   Corning, Inc. – located in Corning, Stueben County, this company began as the Brooklyn Flint Glass Works. In 1868, they loaded the whole kit and caboodle onto canal boats and sent them up the Hudson River, onto the Erie Canal, through the Seneca Canal, onto Seneca Lake, to the Chemung Canal until finally polling upstream on the Fedeer Canal. Corning's 160 year history contains some of the most dramatic moments in glass making history, including the famous 200 inch lens for Mt. Palomar Observatory. Much of this history is captured in the Corning Glass Museum also (you guessed it) in Corning. One pair of breakthroughs, though, show how history can repeat itself. In the 1950's, famed investor Philip Fisher, when, on the cusp of the TV age, was asked which television manufacturer to invest in, he reportedly said to invest not in the manufacturers, but the main supplier of picture tubes – Corning Glass Works (the company's official name from 1875 to 1989). Corning made the picture tubes for the TV manufacturers and Fisher was right, of all the companies involved with making TVs, Corning did the best. Fast forward to the end of the 1990's and the advent of flat panel screens. With all the TV and computer screen manufacturers, it was the maker of flat panel glass that did the best. Who was it? Corning. And the story doesn't end there. It turns out a Corning invention from the 1960s – Gorilla Glass – is just what the doctor ordered for the burgeoning mobile device market. This is what happens when you continually invent, innovate and invest in a future you cannot yet even predict. Very few companies can do this – ever – or as consistently as Corning.

APPENDIX II: FOOTNOTES

Chapter 1: Little Red House
[1] Red House, New York, *Wikipedia*,
http://en.wikipedia.org/wiki/Red_House,_New_York
[2] Red House, New York, *Enchanted Mountains of Cattaraugus County*, Cattaraugus County Tourism, http://enchantedmountains.com/community/red-house
[3] "Allegany State Park named an 'Amazing Spot'," Cattaraugus County Web-site, February 26, 2008, http://www.cattco.org/news/200873-allegany-state-park-named-amazing-spot
[4] Gibson, Campbell, "Population of the 100 Largest Cities and Other Urban Places in the United States: 1790 to 1990," U.S. Census Bureau, June 1998, Table 13, http://www.census.gov/population/www/documentation/twps0027/twps0027.html
[5] "2011 Census Estimates for Largest Cities Released," *Metro Jacksonville*, July 10, 2012, http://www.metrojacksonville.com/article/2012-jul-2011-census-estimates-for-largest-cities-released
[6] Everts, L.H., Franklin Ellis, Editor, Mary Anne Lee, Transcriber, , *History of Cattaraugus County, New York*, Philadelphia, 1879, p.502, http://www.rootsweb.ancestry.com/~nycattar/1879history/redhouse.htm
[7] Ibid., p.502

Chapter 3: The Night They Burned Old Buffalo Down
[1] *The Buffalo Express – Extra Number*, Sept. 1888, p.6
[2] Ibid, p.6
[3] Ibid, p.6
[4] Ibid, p.6
[5] Ibid, p.6
[6] Ibid, p.6
[7] Larned, Josephus Nelson. *A History of Buffalo: Delineating the Evolution of the City*, (New York: The Progress of the Empire State Company, 1911), p. 23
[8] Larned, Josephus Nelson. *A History of Buffalo: Delineating the Evolution of the City*, (New York: The Progress of the Empire State Company, 1911), p. 24
[9] *The Buffalo Express – Extra Number*, Sept. 1888, p.11
[10] Smith, H. Perry, ed., *History of the City of Buffalo and Erie County, Volume 1: History of Erie County*, (Syracuse: D. Mason & Co., 1884), p. 157
[11] *The Buffalo Express – Extra Number*, Sept. 1888, p.11
[12] Ibid p. 11
[13] Ibid p. 11
[14] Smith, H. Perry, ed., p. 159

Chapter 6: Such is Fame: The Real Enduring Legacy of Niagara Falls
[1] "America's 'Magnificent Seven,'" *U.S. News and World Report* 78 (April 21, 1975), pp 56-57

2 Pierson, George W., *Tocqueville and Beaumont in America*, Oxford University Press, NY, 1938, excerpt from Beaumont letter written August 21, 1831, http://www.tocqueville.org/ny4.htm#0819
3 Runte, Alfred, *National Parks: The American Experience (Third Edition)*, University of Nebraska Press, 1997, p.5-6
4 Ibid., p.6
5 Ibid., p.6
6 Sax, Joseph L., "America's National Parks: Their Principles, Purposes, and Prospects," Natural History, October 1976, http://www.naturalhistorymag.com/htmlsite/master.html?http://www.naturalhistor ymag.com/htmlsite/editors_pick/1976_10_pick.html
7 Olmsted, Frederick Law, Yosemite and the Mariposa Grove: A Preliminary Report, 1865 http://www.yosemite.ca.us/library/olmsted/report.html
8 Ibid.
9 Runte, p.59
10 Ibid., p.45
11 Ibid., p.45
12 Ibid., p.45
13 "Sam Patch, the 'Jersey Jumper,'" *Weird N.J.*, http://weirdnj.com/weird-news/sam-patch/
14 Rosenberg-Naperstek, Ruth, "The Real Simon Pure Sam Patch," *Rochester History*, Vol. LII, No. 3, Summer 1991, http://www.libraryweb.org/~rochhist/v53_1991/v53i3.pdf

Chapter 7: The Absolutely True Story Behind the Real Birth of Greater Western New York

1 The Paleontology Portal, "the Devonian – 417 to 354 Million Years Ago" http://www.paleoportal.org/index.php?globalnav=time_space&sectionnav=period& period_id=13
2 "Devonian Stratigraphy and Fossil Assemblages of WNY," Dr. Jörg Maletz, Stratigraphy and Paleontology http://www.geology.buffalo.edu/contrib/people/faculty/gly216trip.htm
3 The Paleontological Research Institution and The Museum of the Earth, *The Teacher-Friendly Guide to the Geology of the Northeastern U.S.*, "Mountain Building Part III: *the Acadian Mountains*," http://geology.teacherfriendlyguide.org/index.php?option=com_content&view=arti cle&id=62&Itemid=82
4 "Geology of Chautauqua County, New York: Part I – Stratigraphy and Paleontology (Upper Devonian)," Irving H. Tesmer, *New York State Museum and Science Service, Bulletin Number 391*, The University of the State of New York, The State Education Department, Albany, N.Y., September, 1963, page 45, http://nysl.nysed.gov/Archimages/77617.PDF
5 "Understanding Late Devonian and Permian-Triassic Biotic and Climatic Events: Towards an Integrated Approach, edited by D.J. Over, J.R. Morrow and P.B. Wignall, 2005 Elsevier B.V. page 96 http://www.ohio.edu/people/stigall/PDFs/StigallRode_GARP_06_noappendix.pdf

[6] The Devonian Coast, *Nature's Blog*, April 29, 2007,
http://naturesblog.blogspot.com/2007/04/devonian-coast.html
[7] "Why does salt melt ice," *General Chemistry Online!*
http://antoine.frostburg.edu/chem/senese/101/solutions/faq/why-salt-melts-ice.shtml

Chapter 8: The Lost Tribe of Western New York

[1] *Dictionary of Canadian Biography Online*, (University of Toronto, 2000), 1000-1700
(Volume I), http://www.biographi.ca/009004-119.01-e.php?&id_nbr=109
[2] Mansfield, J.B., ed., *History of the Great Lakes (Volume I)*, Chicago: J. H. Beers & Co.,
1899, Chapter 3,
http://www.maritimehistoryofthegreatlakes.ca/documents/hgl/default.asp?ID=c007
[3] Larned, Josephus Nelson. *A History of Buffalo: Delineating the Evolution of the City*, (New
York: The Progress of the Empire State Company, 1911), p. 4
[4] Erie History, http://www.dickshovel.com/erie.html
[5] Larned, Josephus Nelson. *A History of Buffalo: Delineating the Evolution of the City*, (New
York: The Progress of the Empire State Company, 1911), p. 4
[6] Ibid, p.4
[7] *Handbook of Indians of Canada*, James White, ed., Published as an Appendix to the
Tenth Report of the Geographic Board of Canada, Ottawa, 1913, 632p., pp. 72-73,
http://faculty.marianopolis.edu/c.belanger/quebechistory/encyclopedia/Erieindians.htm
[8] Erie History
[9] *Handbook of Indians of Canada*
[10] Ibid.
[11] Ibid.
[12] Erie History
[13] *The Lost Erie Tribe*, unclesamshistory, October 16, 2011,
http://unclesamshistory.wordpress.com/2011/10/16/the-lost-erie-tribe/
[14] Erie History
[15] Axtell, Fred (Dancing Owl) and Victoria Taylor-True, *Erie Indian History*, Erie
Indian Moundbuilders, 2005-2009,
http://www.eriemoundbuilders.com/erie_indian_history/
[16] Erie History
[17] *Handbook of Indians of Canada*
[18] Axtell, Fred
[19] *Handbook of Indians of Canada*
[20] Ibid
[21] Ibid
[21] Ibid
[22] Ibid
[23] Ibid
[24] Ibid
[25] Smith, H. Perry, ed., *History of the City of Buffalo and Erie County*, (D. Mason & Co.,
Publishers, Syracuse, NY, 1884), Volume 1, p. 25,26
http://64.30.240.5/buffhist/erie1.html
[26] Ibid
[27] Ibid
[28] Ibid
[29] Ibid

[30] Smith, H. Perry, p. 27
[31] Axtell, Fred

Chapter 9: We Preempt Westward Expansion for…
[1] Hilbert, Alfred G., "The Pre-Emption Line – Part I," *The Crooked Lake Review*, 1990, http://www.crookedlakereview.com/articles/1_33/31oct1990/31hilbert.html
[2] Buchanan, Jr., E. Everett, "A Brief History of 'The Preemption Line' and 'The Preemption Road'," Chemung County Historical Society, 1957, http://www.joycetice.com/articles/preempti.htm
[3] Hilbert, Part I
[4] Buchanan
[5] Hilbert, Part I
[6] Ibid.
[7] "Settlement Of Western New York," Office of the County Historian, Wayne County, http://www.co.wayne.ny.us/departments/historian/mfsettlement.htm
[8] Hilbert, Alfred G., "The Pre-Emption Line – Part III," *The Crooked Lake Review*, 1990, http://www.crookedlakereview.com/articles/1_33/33dec1990/33hilbert.html
[9] Emmons, E. Thayles, "Col. Maxwell Notes Silent on Pre-Emption 'Mistake'," The Geneva Times, January 22, 1965, p. 14

Chapter 10: Whole Greater than the Sum of Its Parts
[1] Source: U.S. Census Bureau, Population Division, Table 1. Annual Estimates of the Resident Population for Counties of New York: April 1, 2010 to July 1, 2011 (CO-EST2011-01-36), Release Date: April 2012, http://quickfacts.census.gov/qfd/states/36000lk.html
[2] Executive Office of the President, Office of Management and Budget, Washington, D.C., December 1, 2009 http://www.whitehouse.gov/sites/default/files/omb/assets/bulletins/b10-02.pdf
[3] Guide to State and Local Geography – Selected Data from the 2010 Census, U.S. Census Bureau Geography Division, Created: September 6, 2011, Last Revised: October 20, 2011, http://www.census.gov/geo/www/guidestloc/select_data.html
[4] Ibid.
[5] Vermont's Declaration of Independence , January 15, 1777, Source: Second Vermont Republic, http://vermontrepublic.org/vermonts-declaration-of-independence-1777
[6] "Syracuse, NY: A Great Test Market," *The Research Bunker*, February 3, 2011, http://rmsbunkerblog.wordpress.com/2011/02/03/syracuse-ny-a-great-test-market-market-research/

Chapter 11: It's Not What You Say, It's How You Say It
[1] "Talking the Tawk," *The New Yorker*, November 14, 2005, http://www.newyorker.com/archive/2005/11/14/051114ta_talk_seabrook
[2] "American Accent Undergoing Great Vowel Shift," *All Things Considered*, NPR News, February 16, 2006, http://www.npr.org/templates/story/story.php?storyId=5220090
[3] "Do You Speak Bostonian?" *U.S. News and World Report*, January 25, 1999, p. 56, http://www.ling.upenn.edu/phono_atlas/usnews/usnews1.jpg

4 Ibid., p.57, http://www.ling.upenn.edu/phono_atlas/usnews/usnews2.jpg
5 http://www.gotoquiz.com/what_american_accent_do_you_have
6 "SNL skit mocks Buffalo broadcast news stations," *Buffalo.com*, September 26, 2011, http://www.buffalo.com/entertainment/blog/snl-skit-mocks-buffalo-news-station-broadcasters/

Chapter 12: Greater Western New York's Split Personality Explained

1 McKelvey, Blake, "Historic Aspects of the Phelps and Gorham Treaty of July 4-8, 1788," *Rochester History*, Vol. 1 No. 1, (January 1939), p.4, http://www.rochester.lib.ny.us/~rochhist/v1_1939/v1i1.pdf
2 Ibid., p.6
3 Ibid., p.7
4 Ibid., pp.8-9
5 Hilbert, Alfred G., "The Pre-Emption Line – Part II," *The Crooked Lake Review*, November 1990
http://www.crookedlakereview.com/articles/1_33/32nov1990/32hilbert.html
6 Hilbert, Alfred G., "The Pre-Emption Line – Part I," *The Crooked Lake Review*, October 1990
http://www.crookedlakereview.com/articles/1_33/31oct1990/31hilbert.html
7 Ibid.
8 Milliken, Charles F., *A History of Ontario County, New York and Its People, Volume 1*, Lewis Historical Publishing Co., New York, 1911, p.333, http://books.google.com/books?id=wGIEAAAAYAAJ&pg=PA351#v=onepage&q=pulteney&f=false
9 McIntosh, Jr, John and Franciska Safran, "Surveying the Holland Purchase, Part 1," *Professional Surveyor Magazine*, May/June 1998, https://www.profsurv.com/magazine/article.aspx?i=285
10 Weissend, Patrick R., *The Life and Times of Joseph Ellicott*, Holland Land Purchase Historical Society, Batavia, New York, 2002, p.3
11 Hilbert, "The Pre-Emption Line – Part II"
12 Weissend, p.6
13 Ibid., p.12
14 Kauffman, Bill, *The History of the Holland Land Office Museum, Batavia and Genesee County New York*, Holland Purchase Historical Society, Batavia, NY, pp.5-6
15 Ibid., pp. 6-7
16 Ibid, p.7
17 Ibid, p.9
18 Ibid, p.9

Chapter 13: Back at the Old Pizza Stand

1 Taussig, Ellen, *Reflections of AMERICA'S County Fair, 1841-2000*, Erie County Agricultural Society, 2001, Forward
2 Ibid., Forward
3 Ibid., Forward
4 Ibid., Forward
5 Ibid., p.1
6 Ibid., Forward

7 Ibid., p.2
8 Ibid., Forward
9 Ibid., Forward
10 Ibid.,p.12
11 Ibid.,p.31
12 Leary, Thomas E. and Elizabeth C. Sholes, *Buffalo's Pan-American Exposition*, Arcadia Publishing, Charleston, South Carolina, 1998, p. 13
13 The Erie County Fair web-site, http://www.ecfair.org/about-the-fair/
14 Taussig, p.31-32

Chapter 15: The Wild West Rides Again

1 Wolcott, Bill, "Buffalo Bill: Lockport woman completing restoration on 1878 billboard," *Lockport Union-Sun & Journal*, July 22, 2007, http://lockportjournal.com/local/x212269553/BUFFALO-BILL-Lockport-woman-completing-restoration-on-1878-billboard
2 Schell, Laura, "Saving Buffalo Bill: Discovery of the Jamestown Buffalo Bill Billboard," Western New York Heritage, Winter 2011, p.34
3 "First Poster Piece Shown; Reg Lenna Gets Funds," *Genealogical and Historical Review of the International Cody Family Association*, Volume 38, No. 1, June 2005, http://www.cody-family.org/review/reviewv38n1.pdf
4 Thompson, Carolyn, "Buffalo Bill billboard restored," *The Seattle Times*, June 3, 2007, http://seattletimes.com/html/nationworld/2003732686_buffalo03.html
5 Foster, Margaret, "Restored Buffalo Bill Billboard on Display," *Preservation Magazine*, August 7, 2007, http://www.preservationnation.org/magazine/2007/todays-news-2007/restored-buffalo-bill.html
6 Schell, p.42
7 Downs, John P., Editor-in-Charge and Fenwick Y. Hedley, Editor-in-Chief, *History of Chautauqua County, New York and its people*, American Historical Society, Inc., 1921, p.187, http://archive.org/stream/historyofchautau02downs#page/n263/mode/2up/search/gerry
8 Gerry Rodeo website, History page, http://www.gerryrodeo.org/history.html

Chapter 16: The Best Little Hole House in Greater Western New York

1 "French Invaded Its Shores, Indians Whooped War Cries," IrondequoitBay.com, http://www.irondequoitbay.com/french/french.htm
2 Ibid.
3 Map of Seabreeze, Plat book of Monroe County, New York, 1902, http://www.rworr.net/stations/seabreeze.html
4 Russell, Harold, History of the R.W. & O., http://www.rworr.net/history/russell-history.html
5 Park History page, Seabreeze Amusement Park Website, http://www.seabreeze.com/gallery.asp?action=view&cat=6
6 "Serving Seabreeze for 125 Years," See the Lights.com web-site, http://seathelights.com/ilt/ilt7.html
7 Ibid.
8 "Top roller-coasters in North America, scariest to coolest," CBS News, August 18, 2012, http://www.cbsnews.com/8301-33816_162-57495910/top-roller-coasters-in-north-america-scariest-to-coolest/

[9] Ibid.

[10] Haeber, Jonathan, "History of Miniature Golf," Bearing, October 6, 2010, http://www.terrastories.com/bearings/miniature-golf

[11] Ibid.

[12] Ibid.

[13] Ibid.

[14] Ibid.

[15] Ibid.

[16] Ibid

[17] National Register of Historic Places Registration Form, http://pwa.parks.ny.gov/hpimaging/hp_view.asp?GroupView=11127

[18] Iqbal, Zain, Fore! Tee Off At America's Classic Miniature Golf Venues," *NileGuide Travel Blog*, June 14, 2010, http://www.nileguide.com/blog/2010/06/14/fore-tee-off-at-americas-classic-miniature-golf-venues/

[19] Whirty, Ryan, "Whispering Pines mini golf course a throwback," ESPN, May 14, 2011, http://espn.go.com/espn/page2/index?id=6546701

Chapter 17: "Low Bridge, Everybody Down"

[1] The Erie Canal Song website, http://www.eriecanalsong.com/

[2] Ibid.

[3] Ibid.

[4] Ibid.

[5] Niagara Escarpment page, Lake Ontario Waterkeeper website, http://www.waterkeeper.ca/2010/12/03/niagara-escarpment/

[6] "Escarpment Geology," Hamilton Naturalists Club, http://www.hamiltonnature.org/habitats/escarpment/escarpment_geology.htm

[7] Ibid.

[8] History 1816-1840 page," eLockport.com, http://elockport.com/history-lockport-ny.php

[9] Erie Canal Discovery page, Niagara County Historical Society website, http://niagarahistory.org/discovery-center/

[10] Dunn, Edward T., A History of Railroads in Western New York, Second Edition, Canisius College Press, 2000, p.11-12

[11] History 1816-1840 page

[12] Home page, Lockport Cave and Underground Boat Ride website, http://lockportcave.com/

[13] Ibid.

[14] Glaser, Susan,"In Lockport, M.Y., cruise the Erie Canal and take a cave tour," *Cleveland Plain Dealer*, June 13, 2010, http://www.cleveland.com/travel/index.ssf/2010/06/in_lockport_ny_cruise_the_erie.html

Chapter 18: Postcard Perfect, No Matter What the Season

[1] Early American Railroads, U.S. History website, page 25b, http://www.ushistory.org/us/25b.asp

[2] The Mohawk and Hudson Railroad page, American-Rails.com, http://www.american-rails.com/mohawk-and-hudson-railroad.html

[3] Ibid.

[4] Early American Railroad, page 25b

[5] Dunn, Edward T., A History of Railroads in Western New York, Second Edition, Canisius College Press, 2000, p.15

[6] Ibid., p.24

[7] Springirth, Kenneth C., *Arcade and Attica Railroad*, Arcadia Publishing, 2009

[8] Our History page, Arcade and Attica Railroad website, http://www.arcadeandatticarr.com/our_history.php3

[9] Ibid.

[10] Ibid

Chapter 19: A Bridge Too Quiet

[1] Bunnell, A. O., *Dansville; Historical, biographical, descriptive*, Instructor Pub. Co., Dansville, NY, 1902, http://archive.org/stream/cu31924028823791/cu31924028823791_djvu.txt

[2] Squire, Roger L., *Erie County Railroads, 1836-1972, Origin and Development*, Buffalo and Erie County Historical Society, Volume XX, 1972, p.15

[3] "Empire State Express NO. 999, Historian's Note," *Genesee County History Department website*, History Stories page, http://www.co.genesee.ny.us/departments/history/empire_state_express_no_999.html

[4] Ibid.

[5] Ibid.

[6] Burt, William D., "Erie's River Line Part 2: Leap for the Brass Ring," *The Diamond*, Volume 5, Number 2, Erie Lackawanna Historical Society, 1990, p.8

[7] Pomeroy, Jim, "Caneadea Here and There," *Town of Caneadea website*, History page, http://townofcaneadea.org/content/History

[8] "Erie Lackawanna RR," *Allegany County Historical Society* website., http://www.alleganyhistory.org/places/towns-and-villages/a-e/caneadea/related-articles/2205-erie-lackawanna-rr

[9] Burt, William D., "Erie's River Line Part 3: Long Summer on the Cutoff," *The Diamond*, Volume 6, Number 1, Erie Lackawanna Historical Society, 1991, p.11

[10] Bunnell

[11] "Erie Lackawanna RR"

[12] "Erie Lackawanna RR"

Chapter 20: Seeds of a New Movement

[1] Baxter, Henry H., *Buffalo's Grain Elevators*, Buffalo and Erie County Historical Society, Volume XXVI, Buffalo, NY, 1980, p.1

[2] "Bankwatch – Views of the Erie Canal," *Erie Canal – 175th Anniversary* website, Union College, 2003, http://www.eriecanal.org/UnionCollege/Bankwatch.html

[3] Ibid

[4] "Table 6. Population of the 90 Urban Places: 1830," *U.S. Bureau of the Census*, Internet Release Date: June 15, 1998, http://www.census.gov/population/www/documentation/twps0027/tab06.txt

[5] "Table 8. Population of the 100 Largest Urban Places: 1850," *U.S. Bureau of the Census*, Internet Release Date: June 15, 1998, http://www.census.gov/population/www/documentation/twps0027/tab08.txt

[6] "Table 9. Population of the 100 Largest Urban Places: 1850," *U.S. Bureau of the Census*, Internet Release Date: June 15, 1998, http://www.census.gov/population/www/documentation/twps0027/tab09.txt

[7] Tielman, Timothy, ed.,"Elevators: Monolith Monsters," *Buffalo's Waterfront, A Guidebook*, The Preservation Coalition of Erie County, Buffalo, NY, 1990, p.56
[8] Ibid, p.56
[9] "Grain Elevators – A History," *Buffalo History Works*, web-site, 1981, http://www.buffalohistoryworks.com/grain/history/history.htm
[10] Hitchcock, Henry-Russell, "Buffalo Architecture in 1940," *Buffalo Architecture: A Guide*, The MIT Press, Cambridge, Mass, 1981, p.29
[11] "Dart Street in Buffalo; So Who was Dart," *The Buffalo History Gazette*, May 17, 2011, http://www.buffalohistorygazette.com/2011/05/dart-street-in-buffalo-so-who-was-dart.html
[12] Ibid
[13] Baxter, p.2
[14] "Grain Elevators – A History"
[15] Baxter, p.2
[16] Welch, Samuel M., *Home History: Recollections of Buffalo During the Decade from 1830 to 1840, or Fifty Years Since*, Peter Paul & Bro., 1891, http://babel.hathitrust.org/cgi/pt?u=1&num=24&seq=7&view=image&size=100&id=yale.39002008407018
[17] Leary, Thomas E. and Elizabeth C. Sholes, *Buffalo's Waterfront*, Arcadia Publishing, 1997
[18] Baxter, p.5
[19] "Wollenberg Grain Elevator, 1912-2006," *FixBuffalo* blog, October 1, 2006, http://fixbuffalo.blogspot.com/2006/10/wollenberg-grain-elevator-1912-2006.html
[20] Tielman, p.21
[21] Tielman, p.41
[22] Tielman, p.42
[23] Jager, Ivonne, "The Grand Ladies of the Lake," *Reconsidering Concrete Atlantis: Buffalo Grain Elevators*, The Urban Design Project, School of Architecture and Planning, University of Buffalo, State University of New York, The Landmark Society of the Niagara Frontier, Buffalo, New York, 2006, p.48, http://128.205.118.147/pub/pdf/concrete_atlantis.pdf
[24] National Register of Historic Places, http://www.nationalregisterofhistoricplaces.com/ny/erie/state.html
[25] Steiner, Hadas, "Silo Dreams," *Reconsidering Concrete Atlantis: Buffalo Grain Elevators*, p.107
[26] Ibid, p.107
[27] Tielman, p 60
[28] Steiner, p.107
[29] Tielman, p.58
[30] Steiner, p.111
[31] Tielmen, p.60
[32] Ibid, p.18
[33] Ibid, p.34

Chapter 21: Like a Bridge Over Roman Waters

[1] Sadowski, Jr. Frank, E., *Erie Canal* home page, Dragon Design Associates, 2000-2012, http://www.eriecanal.org/

2 Ibid
3 "Glacial Geology," *The Natural History of Perinton*, Town of Perinton, 2012, http://www.perinton.org/Departments/hist/nathist/
4 "Rochester's Man-Made Wonder: The Erie Canal," *visitRochester.com*, http://www.visitrochester.com/includes/media/docs/Rochester_s_Marvel_The_Erie_Canal.pdf
5 Fairchild, H. L., "Kame Areas in Western New York South of Irondequoit and Sodus Bays," *The Journal of Geology*, Vol. 4, No. 2, Feb. – Mar., 1896, p.133. http://www.jstor.org/stable/pdfplus/30054321.pdf?acceptTC=true
6 Farley, Doug, "Canal Discovery: The Irondequoit Embankment," Lockport Union-Sun & Journal, February 20, 2010, http://lockportjournal.com/canaldiscovery/x1720288134/CANAL-DISCOVERY-The-Irondequoit-Embankment
7 Ibid
8 Ibid
9 Ibid
10 "History," *Richardson's Canal House* web-page, http://richardsonscanalhouse.net/History/tabid/55/Default.aspx
11 Ibid
12 "Richardson's Tavern – Bushnell's Basin, NY," *Waymarking* website, Groundspeak, 2012, http://www.waymarking.com/waymarks/WMDC3J_Richardsons_Tavern_Bushnells_Basin_NY
13 "New York – Monroe County," National Register of Historic Places website, http://www.nationalregisterofhistoricplaces.com/ny/Monroe/state3.html
14 Shilling, Donovan A., "The Great Water Bridges: The Story of the Magnificent Genesee River Aqueducts," *The Crooked Lake Review*, June 1994, http://www.crookedlakereview.com/articles/67_100/75june1994/75shilling.html
15 Ibid
16 Ibid
17 "Site History," *Historic Erie Canal Aqueduct and Broad Street Corridor Master Plan*, City of Rochester, 2008, http://www.broadstreetcorridor.com/history.html
18 "Old Rochester Aqueduct, Genesee River, Rochester, NY" *The Travels of Tug 44*, http://www.tug44.org/canal.history/rochester-aqueduct/
19 "Site History"

Chapter 22: While Strolling Through the Parks One Day…

1 "A Short Biography," FrederickLawOlmsted.com, http://www.fredericklawolmsted.com/bioframe.htm
2 "Niagara Falls State Park," New York State Office of Parks, Recreation & Historic Preservation website, http://nysparks.com/parks/46/details.aspx
3 "Genesee Valley Park,", FlowerCityChallenge.com, Fleet Feet Sports, 2012, http://www.flowercitychallenge.com/genesee-valley-park
4 "Arboretum," University of Rochester Facilities and Services Home Page, University of Rochester, 2010, http://www.facilities.rochester.edu/arboretum/hort.php
5 "Buffalo, New York," FrederickLawOlmsted.com, 2011, http://www.fredericklawolmsted.com/buffalo.html

[6] Ibid

[7] "Cazenovia Park," Olmsted in Buffalo, http://www.olmstedinbuffalo.com/olmsted-parks-in-buffalo-new-york/cazenovia-park/

[8] "The Olmsted City – The Buffalo Olmsted Park System: Plan for the 21st Century," The Olmsted Parks Conservancy, January 2008, http://bfloparks.org/images/uploads/masterplan.pdf

[9] "History," Buffalo Olmsted Park Conservancy website, http://bfloparks.org/index.php/conservancy/History

[10] "History," The Electric Tower website, Iskalo Development Corp., http://www.electrictower.com/history/

[11] "Chestnut Ridge," ClassicBuffalo.com, http://www.classicbuffalo.com/WNYOutdoors/ChestnutRidge.htm

[12] "Eternal Flame Falls – Chestnut Ridge Park, Orchard Park, NY.," WNY Trails Forum, December 20, 2010, http://www.wnytrails.com/?p=243

[13] "History of the Gardens," BuffaloGardens.com, http://www.buffalogardens.com/pages/history

[14] "South Park," Olmsted in Buffalo, http://www.olmstedinbuffalo.com/olmsted-parks-in-buffalo-new-york/south-park/

Chapter 23: The Miracle of Limestone Hill

[1] Villarrubia, Eleonore, "The Servant of God, Father Nelson Baker," Saint Benedict Center, January 31, 2006, http://catholicism.org/nelson-baker-sog.html

[2] Rovnak, Tamie, "Father Baker's – AKA The Limestone Institutions," *Buffalo Orphanage Studies*, http://buffalo-orphanage-studies.com/FatherBakerBegin.html

[3] Ibid.

[4] "A Time of Need – 1882-1891," Father Nelson Baker, Our Lady of Victory Institutions, 2002, http://www.ourladyofvictory.org/FatherBaker/need.htm

[5] Ibid.

[6] Ibid.

[7] Ibid.

[8] "Twilight – 1921-1936," Father Nelson Baker, Our Lady of Victory Institutions, 2002, http://www.ourladyofvictory.org/FatherBaker/twilight.htm

[9] Senner, Madis, "The Fountain of Compassion and Giving Our Lady of Victory Basilica Buffalo, NY," http://www.jubileeinitiative.org/sacredbasilica.html

[10] "Our Lady of Victory Basilica and National Shrine," Buffalo Architecture and History, http://www.buffaloah.com/a/LACK/ridge/767/ext/source/2.html

[11] Kowsky, Francis R., et. al., "Our Lady of Victory Basilica," *Buffalo Architecture: A Guide*, The MIT Press, Cambridge, Mass, 1981, p.290

[12] "On-Line Tour of the Our Lady of Victory Basilica & National Shrine – Exterior," Our Lady of Victory Institutions, http://www.ourladyofvictory.org/Basilica/tourex.html

[13] "Twilight – 1921-1936"

[14] Levin, Scott, "Father Baker Boys Reminisce About Life At The Orphanage," *WGRZ Channel 2*, Buffalo, Multimedia Entertainment, Inc., May 24, 2012, http://www.wgrz.com/rss/article/169249/13/Father-Baker-Boys-Reminisce-About-Life-At-The-Orphanage

[15] Burgess, Ryan, "Father Baker Closer to Canonization," *YNN*, Buffalo, Time Warner, Inc., January 14, 2011,

http://buffalo.ynn.com/content/all_news/530142/father-baker-closer-to-canonization/

[16] "Prudential (Guaranty) Building," National Historic Landmark Program, National Park Service, http://tps.cr.nps.gov/nhl/detail.cfm?ResourceId=1351&ResourceType=Building

[17] Kowsky, p.68

[18] Ibid., p.68

[19] Ibid., p.81

[20] Brooks, Dana, "Daniel H. Burham, Joseph Ellicott and The Ellicott Square Building, Buffalo Architecture and History, 2005, http://www.buffaloah.com/a/main/295/brooks.html

[21] "Ellicott Square Building," Ellicott Development website, Ellicott Development, http://www.ellicottdevelopment.com/portfolio/commercial/office/ellicott-square-building-295-main-st-buffalo/

[22] "Ellicott Square Beehive," *Buffalo Evening News*, February 1, 1897, http://www.buffaloah.com/a/main/295/hist/source/13.html

[23] Cauchon, Dennis, "For many on Sept. 11, survival was no accident," *USA Today*, December 20, 2001, http://usatoday30.usatoday.com/news/attack/2001/12/19/usatcov-wtcsurvival.htm

Chapter 24: The Greatest Invention in the History of the World

[1] Blumenthal, Heston, *Further Adventures in Search of Perfection: Reinventing Kitchen Classic*, Bloomsbury UK, April 1, 2009, http://books.google.com/books?id=4goQ9DzRITUC&pg=PA21&lpg=PA21&dq=%22hamburg+fair%22+ny&source=bl&ots=PdQS6JSc0H&sig=ixVpo97KzW1kv4e3WH1wOfHd0Z8&hl=en&sa=X&ei=dgd6UNbyIKaV0QHhwoEQ&ved=0CE4Q6AEwBQ#v=onepage&q=%22hamburg%20fair%22%20ny&f=false

[2] Lousi' Lunch, A Local Legacy., *America's Story from America's Library*, The Library of Congress, http://www.americaslibrary.gov/es/ct/es_ct_burger_1.html

[3] Louis' Lunch home page, http://www.louislunch.com/

[4] Pohlen, Jerome, "Oddball Ohio: A Guide to Some Really Strange Places," Chicago Review Press, 2004, http://books.google.com/books?id=bQdDmKyZu6IC&pg=PA230&lpg=PA230&dq=%22Erie+County+fair%22+1885&source=bl&ots=q9CN1BvRe8&sig=rDKknq4OTvystX4JM_czTpElcJk&hl=en&sa=X&ei=VhJ6UNjEIIeB0QHDnoCwAw&ved=0CDAQ6AEwAA#v=onepage&q=%22Erie%20County%20fair%22%201885&f=false

[5] Tolbert, Frank X., *Tolbert's Texas*, Doubleday, 1983, p.133, http://athenstx.org/press/history-of-the-hamburger

[6] Ozersky, Josh, *The Hamburger: A History*, Yale University Press, 2008, p.17, http://books.google.com/books?id=MjP0Jf2DGkEC&pg=PA99&lpg=PA99&dq=the+invention+of+the+hamburger&source=bl&ots=q2P7lllugm&sig=mGQi9wQwBqCKXwVSiy2rVDJxcBI&hl=en&sa=X&ei=xzFNUI-bLOPv0gHEsICgDw&ved=0CE4Q6AEwBjgK#v=onepage&q=menches&f=false

[7] Barenblat, Rachel et al, *Wisconsin: The Badger State*, Gareth Stevens Publishing, 2001, p.32, http://books.google.com/books?id=NSJZyig3DfkC&pg=PA32&lpg=PA32&dq=history+of+%22outagamie+county+fair%22&source=bl&ots=Ur8vYxVFBO&sig=6-mkacI8mXcClfAFWrju-

iKh3WM&hl=en&sa=X&ei=8TRNUIS3GMrq0gHjyYCoBA&ved=0CC8Q6AEwA
A#v=onepage&q=hamburger&f=false

[8] "Seymour's First Annual Fair an Unprecedented Triumph," *Appleton Post*, Appleton Wisconsin, October 15, 1855, http://www.homeofthehamburger.org/history.html

[9] Stradley, Linda, "Hamburgers – History and Legend," *What's Cooking America*, 2004, http://whatscookingamerica.net/History/HamburgerHistory.htm

[10] Kunzog, John C. Tanbark and Tinsel: A Galaxy of Glittering Gems from the Dazzling Diadem of Circus History. Jamestown, New York: author, 1970

[11] Wright, Darcie, "John Christian Kunzog," Find A Grave website, October 10, 2007, http://www.findagrave.com/cgi-bin/fg.cgi?page=gr&GRid=22079759

[12] Teter, Seth, "the best things since sliced bread," ourohio.org, Ohio Farm Bureau Federation, Inc., 2008-2012, http://ourohio.org/index.php?page=the-best-things-since-sliced-bread-2

[13] "Hamburg celebrates namesake," *The Daily Record*, Ellensburg, Washington, July 26, 1985, http://news.google.com/newspapers?nid=860&dat=19850726&id=VZhUAAAAIB AJ&sjid=-o4DAAAAIBAJ&pg=6754,2798900

[14] Taussig, Ellen, *Reflections of AMERICA'S County Fair, 1841-2000*, Erie County Agricultural Society, 2001, p.26

[15] Ibid, p.24

[16] "USA Today's "51 Greatest Burger Joints'," *USA Today*, October 1, 2010, http://aht.seriouseats.com/archives/2010/10/usa-todays-51-great-burger-joints.html

[17] Appell, Howard W., "Tom Wahl's picked for state's best burger," The Daily News, Batavia, New York, October 16, 2010, http://thedailynewsonline.com/lifestyles/article_9b31cef0-d873-11df-9135-001cc4c002e0.html

[18] "Wahlberg brothers pay for NY co.'s 'burger' name," *New York Post*, August 25, 2011, http://www.nypost.com/p/news/national/wahlberg_brothers_pay_for_ny_co_97C NechNKixOg3NnWmqKCK

[19] "Welcome to Wahlburgers," *Wall Street Journal*, August 26, 2011, http://blogs.wsj.com/speakeasy/2011/08/26/welcome-to-wahlburgers-justin-biebers-christmas-album/?KEYWORDS=wahlberg+brothers+tom+wahl%27s

[20] Mannino, Brynn, "8 Best Boardwalk Foods in the U.S.," Woman's Day. August 10, 2010, http://shine.yahoo.com/shine-food/8-best-boardwalk-foods-in-the-u-s-2279098.html

Chapter 25: Our Just Desserts

[1] "The M&Ms Candy Cow Promotion," Behind the Scenes Marketing, http://www.behindthescenesmarketing.com/events-tshws-props/01_cow.html

[2] Wyman, Carol, Jell-O: A Biography, Harcourt, Inc., 2001, p.3,4

[3] Ibid., p.5

[4] Ibid., p.5

[5] Ibid., p.14

[6] Ibid., p.7

[7] Lowe, Judy, "The history and mystery of Jell-O," The Christian Science Monitor, November 21, 2001, http://www.csmonitor.com/2001/1121/p17s2-lifo.html

[8] The JELL-O Gallery website, http://www.jellogallery.org/Index.html

9 Wyman, p.85

10 Turner, Orsamus, George E., "Index to History of the Pioneer Settlement of Phelps & Gorham's Purchase, and Morris' Reserve, Including Supplement of Monroe County in First Edition and Supplement for Counties of Wayne, Ontario, Yates, Livingston and Allegany in Second Edition of 1852," Wayne County Historical Society, 1973, http://www.websterbookstore.com/?page=shop/flypage&product_id=1490900

Chapter 26: The Greatest Business Tradition

1 Raphael, Ray, "Debunking Boston Tea Party Myths," *American History Magazine*, April 1, 2010, http://www.historynet.com/debunking-boston-tea-party-myths.htm

2 "Coffee Break History," The Coffee News Channel, December 2, 2010, http://coffeenewschannel.com/the-dramatic-history-of-coffee/coffee-break-history/

3 Stamberg, Susan, "The Coffee Break," *Present At the Creation*, National Public Radio, December 2, 2002, http://www.npr.org/programs/morning/features/patc/coffeebreak/index.html

4 "The Coffee Break: New Industry Turns Problem into Profits," *Time Magazine*, February 27, 1956, http://www.time.com/time/subscriber/article/0,33009,866822,00.html (subscription only)

5 "Autos: Year of the Coffee Break," *Time Magazine*, June 26, 1964, http://www.time.com/time/subscriber/article/0,33009,898199,00.html (subscription only)

6 "Coffee Break History," Stoughton, Wisconsin website, August 13, 2011, http://stoughtonwi.com/coffeebreak/history.asp

Chapter 28: A Model of Christian Spirit

1 Bernard Bailyn, *The Ideological Origins of the American Revolution*, (1992) pp. 249,273-4, 299-300

2 Scott, Donald, "Evangelicalism, Revivalism, and the Second Great Awakening," National Humanities Center, October, 2000, http://nationalhumanitiescenter.org/tserve/nineteen/nkeyinfo/nevanrev.htm

3 Hambrick-Stowe, *Charles E., Charles G. Finney and the Spirit of American Evangelicalism*, William B. Eerdmans Publishing Company, 1996, p.101, http://books.google.com/books?id=oRNQamJnDuUC&pg=PA159&dq=Albert+Baldwin+Dod+#v=snippet&q=erie%20canal&f=false

4 Ibid., p.116

5 Ibid., p.104

6 Hansen, Colin and John D. Woodbridge, *A God-Sized Vision: Revival Stories That Stretch and Stir*, Zondervan, 2010, p.60, http://books.google.com/books?id=479ru8ULVskC&pg=PA60&dq=Charles+Finney+autobiography+%22Burned-Over+District%22&hl=en&sa=X&ei=oPa2UK6JD6m20QHCmoDADA&ved=0CEsQ6AEwCQ#v=onepage&q=Charles%20Finney%20autobiography%20%22Burned-Over%20District%22&f=false

7 Macdonald, Pastor Marty, "The Second Great Awakening," *United States History*, http://www.u-s-history.com/pages/h1091.html

[8] "Sacred Grove, Manchester (near Palmyra)," *Joseph Smith Historic Sites*, Intellectual Reserve, Inc., 2010, http://www.josephsmith.net/josephsmith/v/index.jsp?vgnextoid=ac6968f0374f1010VgnVCM1000001f5e340aRCRD

[9] "Smith Family Log Home, Palmyra," *Joseph Smith Historic Sites*, Intellectual Reserve, Inc., 2010, http://www.josephsmith.net/josephsmith/v/index.jsp?vgnextoid=889968f0374f1010VgnVCM1000001f5e340aRCRD

[10] "Hill Cumorah, Manchester (near Palmyra)," *Joseph Smith Historic Sites*, Intellectual Reserve, Inc., 2010, http://www.josephsmith.net/josephsmith/v/index.jsp?vgnextoid=014968f0374f1010VgnVCM1000001f5e340aRCRD

[11] Applebome, Peter, "A Mormon Spectacle, Way Off Broadway," *The New York Times*, July 13, 2011, http://www.nytimes.com/2011/07/14/nyregion/hill-cumorah-pageant-offers-mormon-spectacle-way-off-broadway.html?pagewanted=all&_r=0

[12] Ibid.

[13] "Donny Osmond Sheds Dreamcoat To Star in Mormon Pageant July 11-19," *Playbill.com*, Playbill, Inc., July 12, 1997, http://www.playbill.com/news/article/34552-Donny-Osmond-Sheds-Dreamcoat-To-Star-in-Mormon-Pageant-July-11-19

[14] Higgins, Sue, "Donny Osmond sightings reported around Palmyra," *Wayne Post*, Gatehouse Media, Inc., July 21, 2010, http://www.waynepost.com/feature/x700420060/Donny-Osmond-sightings-reported-around-Palmyra

[15] Stuart, Nancy Rubin, "The Fox Sisters: Spiritualism's Unlikely Founders," *American History Magazine*, August, 2005, http://www.historynet.com/the-fox-sisters-spiritualisms-unlikely-founders.htm

[16] Ibid.

[17] Ibid.

[18] Ibid.

[19] "Bones in 'Old Spook House'," *The Boston Journal*, November 23, 1904, http://www.geohanover.com/images/spook.jpg

[20] Nickell, Joe, "A Skeleton's Tale: The Origins of Modern Spiritualism," Skeptical Inquirer, Volume 32.4, July/August 2008, http://www.csicop.org/si/show/skeletons_tale_the_origins_of_modern_spiritualism/

[21] Gilbert, Bil, "In Good Spirits," *Smithsonian Magazine*, June 1, 2001, http://www.smithsonianmag.com/history-archaeology/interest_jun01.html

[22] Ibid.

[23] Nagy, Ron, "History of Lily Dale – 1st Handout," *Ron Nagy's Blog*, February 1, 2010, http://ronnagy.net/ronsblog/2010/02/history-of-lily-dale-1st-handout/

[24] "Fox Sisters," Gale Encyclopedia of Occultism & Parapsychology, http://www.answers.com/topic/the-fox-sisters

Chapter 29: The Shining City on the Lake

[1] "Lewis Miller," Hall of Fame/inventor profile, National Inventors Hall of Fame, 2006, http://www.invent.org/hall_of_fame/290.html

[2] Kilde, Jeanne Halgren, *When Church Became Theatre: The Transformation of Evangelical Architecture and Worship in the Nineteenth-Century*, Oxford University Press., 2002, p.177, http://books.google.com/books?id=eYNjS56yx-0C&pg=PA269&dq=John+Fletcher+Hurst+-#v=onepage&q=lewis%20miller&f=false

[3] Vincent, Leon H., *John Heyl Vincent: A Biographical Sketch*, The Macmillan Company, New York, p.82, http://archive.org/stream/johnheylvincenta013525mbp#page/n7/mode/2up

[4] Ibid., p.85

[5] Ibid., pp.86,87

[6] Ibid., pp.107, 108

[7] Ibid., p.118

[8] "Chautauqua Lake," *Town of Busti – History*, Town of Busti, http://www.townofbusti.com/chaut_lake.html

[9] Vincent, Leon H., p.119

[10] "Chautauqua Lake"

[11] Vincent, John H., *The Chautauqua Movement*, Chautauqua Press, Boston, 1885, pp.16-17, https://play.google.com/books/reader?id=lqsMAAAAYAAJ&printsec=frontcover&output=reader&authuser=0&hl=en&pg=GBS.PR2

[12] Ibid., p.17

[13] Young, Andrew W., History of Chautauqua County, Matthews and Warren, Buffalo, NY, 1875, p.664, http://books.google.com/books?id=4xItpINmJmgC&q=fair+point#v=snippet&q=fair%20point&f=false

[14] Vincent, John H., p.40

[15] Maxwell, Jeffrey Scott, "A Guide to What 'Chautauqua' Means in America," *The Complete Chautauquan*, 2000, http://www.crackerjackcollectors.com/Jeffrey_Maxwell/alphachautauquan/what.html

[16] Vincent, John H., p.270

[17] Vincent, John H., p.22

[18] Vincent, John H., p. v

[19] Vincent, John H., p. vi

[20] "Canandaigua Lake"

[21] "The Chautauqua Charter of 1902," Chautauqua Property Owners Association, http://www.cpoa.ws/webhelp/cpoa.htm

[22] "Founding and History," *Chautauqua: An American Narrative*,Western New York Public Broadcasting Association, 2012, http://www.pbs.org/wned/chautauqua-american-narrative/founding-history.php

[23] Chautauqua Institution Visitors Guide, Chautauqua Institution, 2012

[24] Chautauqua Property Association Board Meeting, June 28, 2006, http://www.google.com/url?sa=t&rct=j&q=&esrc=s&source=web&cd=1&ved=0CDMQFjAA&url=http%3A%2F%2Fwww.cpoa.ws%2Fwebhelp%2FCPOA_Brd_Mtg_Minutes_6-28-06.doc&ei=z4zDULHJM_Ox0AHf04DYCg&usg=AFQjCNHQ6AzX352F9DuNBFSEXPhzxkFtnA&sig2=W6a1s1JWs_Orj_rTtE1Dxw

[25] Odland, Steve, "The Magic of Chautauqua," Forbes, July 7, 2012, http://www.forbes.com/sites/steveodland/2012/07/09/the-magic-of-chautauqua/

Chapter 30: I'll Have One for the Road and Two for the Sea

1 "Biography of James Fenimore Cooper (1789-1851)," *James Fenimore Cooper: A Literary Pioneer*, University of Virginia, http://xroads.virginia.edu/~ug02/cooper/cooperbiography.html

2 Phillips, Mary Elizabeth , *James Fenimore Cooper*, John Lane Company, New York, London. p.56, https://play.google.com/books/reader?id=so4DAAAAYAAJ&printsec=frontcover&output=reader&authuser=0&hl=en&pg=GBS.PA56

3 Lounsbury, Thomas R., "James Fenimore Cooper," *American Men of Letters*, Houghton, Mifflin and Company, Boston, 1886, p.28, http://www.mohicanpress.com/mo08002.html

4 Ibid., p.17

5 (uncredited), "The Spy," *Old and Sold*, ca. 1900s, http://www.oldandsold.com/articles25/cooper-2.shtml

5 "Autos: Year of the Coffee Break," *Time Magazine*, June 26, 1964, http://www.time.com/time/subscriber/article/0,33009,898199,00.html (subscription only)

6 "History of Lewiston," *Historic Lewiston, New York* website, Historical Association of Lewiston, Inc., much of the content being attributed to: *Lewiston: A Self-Guided Tour*, by Barbara I. Hill, Janet M. Domzella, Kenneth Tracey; published by Friends of the Lewiston Library, Inc. 1986 http://www.historiclewiston.org/history.html

7 Ibid.

8 Ibid.

9 Ibid.

10 Ibid.

11 "Artpark Dedication – A Transfigured Night," BPO Archive website, Buffalo Philharmonic Orchestra, July 25, 1974, http://www.music.buffalo.edu/bpo/art-ded.htm

12 "Images and Pictures of Lewiston, NY," *Historic Lewiston, New York* website, Historical Association of Lewiston, Inc., http://www.historiclewiston.org/pictures.html

13 "Installation," *Owen Morrell* website, Owen Morrell, http://owenmorrel.com/installationsandstatment/

14 Phillips, p.84

15 Lounsbury, p.28

16 Farley, Douglas, "The First Cocktail," *Niagara County Bicentennial Celebration* website, Niagara County Bicentennial Committee, 2008, http://www.niagara2008.com/history99.html

17 Lewis, Clarence O., "Wife Served with '76 Soldier," Niagara Falls Gazette, Wednesday, December 17, 1958, p.28, http://fultonhistory.com/newspaper%208/Niagara%20Falls%20NY%20Gazette/Niagara%20Falls%20NY%20Gazette%201958%20Dec%20Grayscale/Niagara%20Falls%20NY%20Gazette%201958%20Dec%20Grayscale%20-%200672.pdf

18 Cooper, James Fenimore, The Spy, a Tale of the Neutral Ground, pp.180-181, https://play.google.com/books/reader?id=TXE4AAAAMAAJ&printsec=frontcover&output=reader&authuser=0&hl=en&pg=GBS.PA181

[19] Robson, Margeret, *Under the Mountain*, H. Stewart, Buffalo ,1958, http://openlibrary.org/works/OL7527545W/Under_the_mountain
[20] "History of Lewiston"
[21] "The Origin of the Cocktail," The Museum of the American Cocktail website, Museum of the American Cocktail, http://www.museumoftheamericancocktail.org/museum/thebalance.html
[22] Lewis
[23] Ibid.

Chapter 31: Putting the "West" in Greater Western New York
[1] "Robert F. Rockwell, Jr.," *The Leader*, Corning, NY, April 20, 2009, http://www.the-leader.com/obituaries/x1092976094/Robert-F-Rockwell-Jr
[2] "Robert F. Rockwell, Jr. Biography," *Rockwell Museum of Western Art*, http://www.rockwellmuseum.org/Robert-F-Rockwell-Jr-Biography.html
[3] Ibid.
[4] Miran, Pat, "Rockwell Museum of Western Art, Corning NY," *2 Talk Horses*, January 17, 2012, http://gs90.inmotionhosting.com/~ntalkh5/?p=2665
[5] "Robert F. Rockwell, Jr. Biography"
[6] Ibid.
[7] Ibid.
[8] Miran, Pat
[9] "About the Museum," *Rockwell Museum of Western Art*, http://www.rockwellmuseum.org/About-the-Museum.html
[10] "Miran, Pat
[9] "Smith Family Log Home, Palmyra," *Joseph Smith Historic Sites*, Intellectual Reserve, Inc., 2010, http://www.josephsmith.net/josephsmith/v/index.jsp?vgnextoid=889968f0374f1010VgnVCM1000001f5e340aRCRD
[10] "Hill Cumorah, Manchester (near Palmyra)," *Joseph Smith Historic Sites*, Intellectual Reserve, Inc., 2010, http://www.josephsmith.net/josephsmith/v/index.jsp?vgnextoid=014968f0374f1010VgnVCM1000001f5e340aRCRD
[11] "Robert F. Rockwell, Jr. Biography"
[12] "Linsly-Chittenden Hall – 1907," *Preserving the Past, Building the Future*, Yale University website, http://buildings.yale.edu/property.aspx?id=35
[13] Conniff, Richard, "A Tale of Two Windows," *Yale Alumni Magazine*, January/February 2010, http://www.yalealumnimagazine.com/issues/2010_01/tiffany4449.html
[14] "White House Timelines: Decorative Arts," *White House Historical Association* website, http://www.whitehousehistory.org/whha_timelines/timelines_decorative-arts-02.html

Chapter 32: Dinner and a Movie
[1] *Baker Church History*, http://bakerchurch.org/media/Baker_Church_History0001.pdf
[2] Ibid.

[3] "The History of Baker Memorial United Methodist Church," Baker Memorial United Methodist Church website, http://bakerchurch.org/Baker_History.wss

[4] Ibid.

5 Ibid.

[6] "Baker Memorial United Methodist Church," *Buffalo as an Architectural Museum* website, http://www.buffaloah.com/a/EastAur/baker/tc.html

[7] "St. Luke's Episcopal Church," National Register of Historic Places, http://nrhp.focus.nps.gov/natregsearchresult.do?fullresult=true&recordid=132

[8] A Brief History In Celebration of 150th Anniversary of the Church Building, 1855-2005, St. Luke's Episcopal Church, Brockport, New York, p.4, http://stlukesbrockport.org/images/history/1855-2005/slides/04-1855-2005.html

[9] Gable, Walter, "A History of Trinity Episcopal Church," May 2010, p.3, http://www.co.seneca.ny.us/history/Trinity%20Episcopal%20Church%20in%20Seneca%20Falls.pdf

[10] Ibid.,p.4

[11] Kahn, Eve M., "A Celestial Show From a Tiffany Winder," *New York Times*, October 11, 2012, http://www.nytimes.com/2012/10/12/arts/design/louis-c-tiffany-and-the-art-of-devotion-at-biblical-art.html

[12] Wemett, Laurel C., "Take a Walking Tour of a Model Village," *Life in the Finger Lakes*, Fahy-Williams Publishing Inc, Geneva, NY, Summer 2009, http://www.lifeinthefingerlakes.com/articles.php?view=article&id=500

[13] "Historical Fact Sheet," *Village of Clifton Springs* website, http://www.cliftonspringsny.org/history.htm |

[14] "About Clifton Springs Hospital," Clifton Springs Hospital and Clinic website, http://www.cshosp.com/Our-Commitment/About-CS-Hospital-Redesign.html

[15] "History of the Festival," *Sulphur Springs Festival* website, Sulphur Springs Festival, http://www.sulphurspringsfestival.com/history.htm

[16] Conover, George S., editor, *History of Ontario County New York*, D. Mason & Co., Syracuse, NY 1893, http://history.rays-place.com/ny/manchester-ny.htm

[17] Kahn

[18] "St. Paul's Episcopal Church," Chris and Luke Explore the Burned Over District, June 18, 2012, http://exploringtheburnedoverdistrict.wordpress.com/2012/06/18/st-pauls-episcopal-church/

[19] Ibid.

[20] "History of George Eastman House," Eastman House International Museum of Photography and Film website, http://www.eastmanhouse.org/museum/history.php

[21] "The Motion Picture Collection," Eastman House International Museum of Photography and Film website, http://www.eastmanhouse.org/collections/motion-picture.php

[22] Ibid.

Chapter 33: The Hollywood Ideal?

[1] Grimes, Karolyn, "Was Seneca Falls the inspiration for Bedford Falls?" *Essays Thoughts & Stories from Karolyn*, http://www.zuzu.net/essays/bedford_falls.html |

Chapter 34: Our Hit Parade

[1] Marren, Joe, *Buffalo's Brush with the Arts: From Huck Finn to Murphy Brown*, Western New York Wares, Inc., 1998, p.9

[2] Ibid., p.9

[3] Ibid., p.37

[4] Ibid., p.26

[5] Ibid., p.20

[6] Ibid., p.21

[7] Ibid., p.23

[8] Ibid., p.36

[9] Mallory, Michael, "The Mother of American Mystery: Anna Katharine Green," Mystery Scene Magazine, #94, Spring 2006, http://www.mysteryscenemag.com/index.php?option=com_content&view=article&id=1867:the-mother-of-american-mystery-anna-katharine-green&catid=20:articles&Itemid=191

[10] Ibid.

[11] Ibid.

[12] McClelland, P.C., "Lily Dale; Spiritualist Community in Up-state New York," Yahoo! Voices, Yahoo! Inc., July 19, 2010, http://voices.yahoo.com/lily-dale-spiritualist-community-state-york-6380730.html

[13] "Milestones," Time Magazine, April 22, 1935, http://www.time.com/time/subscriber/article/0,33009,762267,00.html

[14] Mallory

[15] Ibid., p.17

[16] JF, "Books: The Season's Leviathan – A Study of the Passion for Things Present and Things to Come," Time Magazine, May 12, 1923, http://www.time.com/time/subscriber/article/0,33009,846014-3,00.html

[17] Severo, Richard, "Buffalo Bob Smith, 'Howdy Doody' Creator, is Dead at 80," *The New York Times*, July 31, 1998, http://www.nytimes.com/1998/07/31/arts/buffalo-bob-smith-howdy-doody-creator-is-dead-at-80.html?pagewanted=all&src=pm

[18] "The Buffalo Broadcasters History of WGR-55," *Buffalo Broadcasters Association* website, The Buffalo Broadcasters, 2009, http://www.buffalobroadcasters.com/hist_wgr.asp

[19] Marc, David, "Buffalo Bob Smith," *American National Biography Online*, May 2008, http://www.anb.org/articles/18/18-03788.html

[20] Ibid.

[21] Barovick, Harriet, et al, "Milestones Aug. 10, 1998," Time Magazine, August 10, 1998, http://www.time.com/time/subscriber/article/0,33009,988892,00.html

[22] Ibid.

[23] Severo, Richard, "Mitch Miller, Maestro of the Singalong, Dies at 99," *The New York Times*, August 2, 2010, http://www.nytimes.com/2010/08/03/arts/music/03miller.html?pagewanted=all

[24] Ibid.

[25] "Biography – The Early Years," *The Official Harold Arlen* website, http://www.haroldarlen.com/bio-2.html

[26] Ibid.

[27] Ibid.

[28] Marren, p.83

[29] Ibid., p.75

[30] Ibid., p.75

[31]From the Roger Tory Peterson Institution of Natural History Mission State, adopted March 15, 2012) ,
http://www.rtpi.org/index.php?option=com_content&view=article&id=2&Itemid=3

Chapter 35: America's First Supermodel

[1] White, Justin D., "Rediscovering Audrey," *Queen of the Artists' Studio – The Story of Audrey Munson*, 2007, p.53,
http://www.andreageyer.info/projects/audrey_munson/munson_book/MunsonPages/PDF/JustinWhite.pdf

[2] Ibid., p.53

[3] Ibid., p.53

[4] "Ibid., p.54

[5] Geyer, Andrea, *Queen of the Artists' Studio – The Story of Audrey Munson*, Art in General, 2007, p.2,
http://www.andreageyer.info/projects/audrey_munson/munson_book/MunsonPages/02.html

[6] Geyer, Andrea, "A text Upon a Text Upon a Text," *Queen of the Artists' Studio – The Story of Audrey Munson*, 2007, p.21,
http://www.andreageyer.info/projects/audrey_munson/munson_book/MunsonPages/PDF/AndreaGeyer.pdf

[7] Ibid., p.21

[8] White, p.54

[9] Ibid., p.54

[10] "Audrey Munson," *New York City Statues* website,
http://newyorkcitystatues.com/audrey-munson/

[11] Librizzi, Jane, "Audrey Munson: Her Brilliant Career," The Blue Lantern website, April 16, 2009, http://thebluelantern.blogspot.com/2009/04/audrey-munson-her-brilliant-career.html

[12] Popik, Barry, "Audrey Munson (New York's 'Civic Fame' and 'Miss Manhattan,' San Francisco's 'World's Fair Girl')," The Big *Apple*, July 5, 2004,
http://www.barrypopik.com/index.php/new_york_city/entry/audrey_munson_new_yorks_civic_fame_and_miss_manhattan_san_franciscos_worlds/

[13] Lot 4421, "1915-S $50 Panama-Pacific 50 Dollar Octagonal MS63 NGC....," *Heritage Auctions* website,
http://coins.ha.com/c/item.zx?saleNo=1157&lotIdNo=125083

[14] Sanders, Steve, "Audrey Munson, the 'Exposition Girl'," Remnants of a Dream,
http://home.comcast.net/~sgsanders/pages/appendix_5.html

[15] Janet, "Women in Film," *Supermuse*, January 30, 2008,
http://my.opera.com/SuperMuse/blog/2008/01/30/women-in-film

[16] Ibid.

[17] Janet

[18] Inspiration playbill, http://www.silentfilmstillarchive.com/inspiration.htm

[19] Geyer, p.21

[20] White, p.56

[21] Geyer, p.23

[22] "Audrey Munson is Out of Danger," New York Times, May 29, 1922, http://query.nytimes.com/mem/archive-free/pdf?res=9D0DE3DE1231EF33A2575AC2A9639C946395D6CF
[23] Ibid.

Chapter 36: Watch Out for that Hole!
[1] Brown, Pamela A. and Heather J. Schneider, *Remembering Panama – Glimpse of the Past*, History Press, Charlestown, South Carolina, 2011, p. 65
[2] "Geology and History," *Panama Rocks Scenic Park* website, http://www.panamarocks.com/history-and-geology-1
[3] Downs, John P., Editor-in-Charge, *History of Chautauqua County and Its People*, American Historical Society, Inc, 1921, p.5, http://www.archive.org/stream/historyofchautau02downs#page/n4/mode/1up
[4] Young, Andrew W., *History of Chautauqua County, New York, From its First Settlement to the Present Time*, Matthews & Warren, Buffalo, NY, 1875, p.438, http://www.gooboogeni.com/index.php?option=com_content&view=article&id=2012:history-of-chautauqua-county-new-york-1875&catid=128:state-and-local-histories&Itemid=113
[5] Downs, p.199
[6] Brown et al, p.64
[7] Ibid., p.20 (probably originally from Fowler, George, *History of the Town of Harmony*, Ovid, NY: Morrison & Co., 1976
[8] "'The Mystery Medallion' of Panama Rocks," *Panama Rocks* website, http://panamarocks.com/medal.htm

Chapter 37: Gold. Black Gold. Cuba Tea.
[1] Wayman, Dorothy G., translation of Fr. Joseph de La Roche Daillon's letter of July 18th, 1627, St. Bonaventure Library archives, July 16, 1959, http://web.sbu.edu/friedsam/archives/herscher/images/DelaRochetrans.pdf
[2] "Spörer Minimum," Encyclopedia Britannica, http://www.britannica.com/EBchecked/topic/1773016/Sporer-minimum
3 Jouve, O., "Joseph de La Roche Daillon," *The Catholic Encyclopedia*, New York, Robert Appleton Company, 1910, http://www.newadvent.org/cathen/09004c.htm
[4] "Petun Trube," Sessional Papers, Fourth Session of Eleventh Legislature of the Province of Ontario, Volume XL, Part VIII, L.K. Cameron, Toronto, 1908, p.241, p.290, http://books.google.com/books?id=9GI0AQAAMAAJ&pg=PA290&lpg=PA290&dq=Father+Joseph+de+la+Roche+d%27Aillon&source=bl&ots=UEFjrwR2tH&sig=TMqVXrE39iZvsEHHUaAlJ0y08hY&hl=en&sa=X&ei=GGvGUIGIHsm60AGh4CwBA&ved=0CEYQ6AEwBA#v=onepage&q=tobacco&f=false
[5] Wayman
[6] Ibid.
[7] Ferguson, W.A., *History of Allegany County*, Sun Publishing Association, Alfred NY, 1896, p.813, http://www.archive.org/stream/alleganycountyit00mina/alleganycountyit00mina_djvu.txt
[8] Ibid., p.40
[9] Ibid., p.41

[10] "Tour Stop 11. Seneca Oil Spring," *Friedsam Memorial Library* archives, St. Bonaventure University,
http://web.sbu.edu/friedsam/archives/history/driving_tour/driving_tour11.htm
[11] "American Petroleum Industry to Celebrate End of First Century," *Cuba Patriot and Free Press*, Volume XCVI, No. 34. August 26, 1959, p.3,
http://fultonhistory.com/Newspaper%2018/Cuba%20NY%20Patriot/Cuba%20NY%20Patriot%201958-1959/Cuba%20NY%20Patriot%201958-1959%20-%200547.pdf
[12] Robinson, David D., "More on the Bluff Point Ruins," *The Crooked Lake Review*, Chautauqua Press, Boston, May 1996,
http://www.crookedlakereview.com/articles/67_100/98may1996/98robinson.html
[13] "Eastern Regional Office," *The Archaeological Conservancy* website,
http://www.americanarchaeology.com/eastern.html
[14] Gibbon, Guy E. and Kenneth M. Ames, *Archeology of Prehistoric Native America: An Encyclopedia*, Guy Gibbon, 1998, p.442,
http://books.google.com/books?id=_0u2v_SVnmoC&pg=PA442&lpg=PA442&dq=prehistoric+lamoka+archaeological+site+new+york&source=bl&ots=ORs6TA-P9G&sig=qm_N6pfyJFdeEFWPphfFjtAsHhs&hl=en&sa=X&ei=f_3IUNCgMofy0gGg3oGwBA&ved=0CEEQ6AEwAg#v=onepage&q=lamoka&f=false
[15] Stout, Andy, "The First Archaic Site," *American Archeology*, Vol. 10, No. 2, Summer 2006, p.48,
http://www.americanarchaeology.com/images/Magazine%20files%20for%20index/10.2%20Sum%2006%20%20singles%20LR.pdf

Chapter 38: Commander Tom to Ground Control
[1] Myers v. The State of New York, #2003-009-27, Claim No. 101708, Motion Nos. M-66346, CM-66412, June 30, 2003,
http://vertumnus.courts.state.ny.us/claims/html/2003-009-27.html
[2] "Karl Lyle Myers (b. September 27, 1972, d. April 05, 1999)," *Ancestry.com*,
http://familytreemaker.genealogy.com/users/m/a/p/Katherine-Mapstone/WEBSITE-0001/UHP-0020.html

Chapter 39: Shangri-La or Death Valley?
[1] "Zoar Valley Multiple Use Area, *Department of Environment al Conservation* website, New York State, http://www.dec.ny.gov/lands/36931.html
[2] Castner, Brian, "Get Outside/Zoar Valley," *Buffalo Spree*, September 2011,
http://www.buffalospree.com/Buffalo-Spree/September-2011/Get-Outside-Zoar-Valley/
[3] Miller, Rick, "Zoar Valley is Gorge-ous Example of Tallest Trees," *Olean Times Herald*, The Times Herald, Olean, NY, September 24, 2001,
http://epicroadtrips.us/2003/autumn/Jtown_October/Jtown/olt/index.html

Chapter 40: A More Civilized Nature
[1] Pevsner, Donald, L., "The Bridge Over Letchworth Gorge Must Be Saved," *Livingston County News*, December 6, 2011, http://thelcn.com/2011/12/06/bridge-over-letchworth-gorge-must-be-saved/

[2] "Burning of a Bridge," *The New York Times*, May 7, 1875,
http://query.nytimes.com/mem/archive-
free/pdf?res=F70C15FB355D1A7493C5A9178ED85F418784F9
[3] Cook, Tom, "The Portage Bridge," *Letchworth Park History* website,
http://www.letchworthparkhistory.com/bridge.html
[4] Letchworth, William P., "Portage Bridge, Its Destruction as Described by an Eye-
Witness," *Buffalo Courier*, Buffalo NY, May 8, 1875,
http://www.letchworthparkhistory.com/burningbridge.html
[5] Pevsner
[6] Ibid.
[7] Ande, Howard, "Railroads Aim to Replace or Revamp Aging Bridges," *Progressive
Railroading*, Trade Press Media Group, October 2011,
http://www.progressiverailroading.com/mow/article/Railroads-aim-to-replace-or-
revamp-aging-bridges--28321
[8] Ibid.
[9] "To Bridge the Gorge – Letchworth Park to be Made More Accessible," Wyoming
County Times, March 13, 1913,
http://fultonhistory.com/Newspaper%2013/Warsaw%20NY%20Wyoming%20Cou
nty%20Times/Warsaw%20NY%20Wyoming%20County%20Times%201913/Warsa
w%20NY%20Wyoming%20County%20Times%201913%20-%200059.pdf
[10] Cook, Tom, "Letchworth Park's Prisoner of War Camp," *Letchworth Park History*
website, http://www.letchworthparkhistory.com/powglimpse.html
[11] Head, Justin, "Buffalo Teen Dies After 300 ft. Letchworth Fall," *Hornell Evening
Tribune*, GateHouse Media, Inc., July 4, 2010,
http://www.eveningtribune.com/news/x1143346527/Buffalo-teen-dies-after-300-ft-
Letchworth-fall
[12] Wray, Charles F., "Rivers and Lakes of Rochester," *Rochester Academy of Science*
website, http://www.rasny.org/geostory/riv-lake.htm
[13] Ibid.
[14] Wishart, James S., "Glacial Geology," *Rochester Academy of Science* website,
http://www.rasny.org/geostory/glacigeo.htm
[15] Fairchild, H.L., "Glacial Lakes of Western New York," *Bulletin of the Geological Society
of America*, Volume 6, Geological Society of America, Rochester, 1895, p.358,
http://books.google.com/books?id=vCFYAAAAYAAJ&pg=PA358&lpg=PA358&dq=delaw
are+lackawanna+railroad+dansville+cut&source=bl&ots=O0cFsV_og8&sig=FKWd5aOsoBz
n7iP4vZuoZCQB4wo&hl=en&sa=X&ei=uDeXUPDdIq-
N0QGIw4DwBQ&ved=0CFcQ6AEwCA#v=onepage&q=genesee%20river&f=false
[16] Wray
[17] Grabau, Amadeus William, A Textbook of Geology: General Geology, D.C. Heath
& Co., 1920, p.779,
http://books.google.com/books?id=GxxaAAAAYAAJ&pg=PA834&lpg=PA834&d
q=dansville+ny+glacier+valley&source=bl&ots=ZQRCjyYT9-&sig=ZXS-
mKb6F1cNQ_rWdAZKJJz4p5s&hl=en&sa=X&ei=cC2XUIGTIfG50QHBxYDIC
w&ved=0CDIQ6AEwBDgU#v=onepage&q=genesee%20river&f=false

Chapter 41: Life is a (Small Town) Carnival

[1] *Frontier Herald*, Vol. 39, No. 13, July 14, 2012,
http://fultonhistory.com/Newspaper%2011/Blasdell%20NY%20Frontier%20Heral

d/Blasdell%20NY%20Frontier%20Herald%201959-
1961/Blasdell%20NY%20Frontier%20Herald%201959-1961%20-%200400.pdf
2 "Big Tree VFC – Parade," *Big Tree Volunteer Fire Company* website,
http://www.bigtreevfc.com/parade.php3
3 Ibid.

Chapter 42: The Best Small Town in America

1 "The Story of Painted Post," *The New York Times*, August 13, 1893,
http://query.nytimes.com/mem/archive-
free/pdf?_r=1&res=9A04E2D7143EEF33A25750C1A96E9C94629ED7CF
2 Erwin, Charles H., *Early History of Painted Post and the Town of Erwin*, The Automated
Press., 1917, p.7,
http://books.google.com/books?id=jW5HAAAAYAAJ&pg=PA61&lpg=PA61&dq
=roland+montour+cornplanter&source=bl&ots=WllXBBhZu5&sig=yir-
wGp2RVnFwygpldlInITzbxU&hl=en&sa=X&ei=uefLUIaVAu-
n0AHah4HwBA&ved=0CDsQ6AEwAQ#v=onepage&q=roland%20montour%20c
ornplanter&f=false
3 Ibid., p.8

Chapter 43: Festiv-al-us for the Rest of Us

1 "The Story of Painted Post," *The New York Times*, August 13, 1893,
http://query.nytimes.com/mem/archive-
free/pdf?_r=1&res=9A04E2D7143EEF33A25750C1A96E9C94629ED7CF
2 Erwin, Charles H., *Early History of Painted Post and the Town of Erwin*, The Automated
Press., 1917, p.7,
http://books.google.com/books?id=jW5HAAAAYAAJ&pg=PA61&lpg=PA61&dq
=roland+montour+cornplanter&source=bl&ots=WllXBBhZu5&sig=yir-
wGp2RVnFwygpldlInITzbxU&hl=en&sa=X&ei=uefLUIaVAu-
n0AHah4HwBA&ved=0CDsQ6AEwAQ#v=onepage&q=roland%20montour%20c
ornplanter&f=false
3 Ibid., p.8

Chapter 44: A Chautauqua Boat Ride

1 Downs, John P., Editor-in-Charge, *History of Chautauqua County and its People*,
American Historical Society, 1921, p.155,
http://archive.org/stream/historyofchautau02downs#page/154/mode/2up/search/Bemus
2 Ibid., p. 197,
http://archive.org/stream/historyofchautau02downs#page/196/mode/2up/search/Bemus
3 "Bemus-Stow Ferry Brings Passengers, Cars, Nostalgia Across Chautauqua Lake,"
Star News Daily, National Public Radio, July 20, 2009,
http://www.starnewsdaily.com/viewby/contributor/starnewsdailycom/story/-
Bemus-Stow-Ferry-Brings-Passengers-Cars-Nostalgia-Across-Chautauqua-Lake
4 Ibid.
5 Ibid.
6 Ibid.
7 Ibid.
8 Ibid.

9 "A Brief History of the Bemus Point-Stow Ferry," Sea Lion Project website, http://www.sealionprojectltd.com/ferry.htm

Chapter 45: Dixie's Last Stand
1 Maryniak, Benedict, "Town Line, N.Y. – The Last Legal Confederate Community, *Civil War Round Table of Buffalo Newsletter*, Buffalo & Erie Historical Society, July/August 1985, p.2
2 "George Huber," *Find a Grave* website, http://www.findagrave.com/cgi-bin/fg.cgi?page=gr&GRid=68078116
3 "Hamlet of Town Line 'Heads South' in 1861," *Buffalo Courier Express*, Buffalo NY, September 3, 1933 and February 21, 1937, http://www.buffalohistorygazette.com/2011/01/hamlet-of-town-line-heads-south-in-1861.html
4 Maryniak
5 Ibid.
6 Needell, Thomas, "Wish You Were in Dixie? Visit Town Line," *Buffalo Courier Express*, Buffalo NY, December 11, 1933
7 "Hamlet of Town Line 'Heads South' in 1861"
8 Ibid.
9 Ibid.
10 Feeley, Stephen V., "Secession Still Stands in Hamlet of Town Line," *Buffalo Courier Express*, Buffalo NY, July 1, 1945
11 "Georgians Advise Town Line to Give U.S. Another Try," *Buffalo Evening News*, October 2, 1945
12 Needell
13 Fess, Leroy E., "Truman Takes Hand To Bring Town Line Back Into U.S. Fold," *Buffalo Courier Express*, October 7, 1945
14 "Movie Premier Will Escort Town Line Back," *Buffalo Evening News*, January 23, 1946
15 "The Rebels Last Stand," *Buffalo Courier Express*, Buffalo NY, January 25, 1946
16 "Town Line Rejoins The Union," *youtube.com*, https://www.youtube.com/watch?v=EGW3HI9DpZI
17 Maryniak

Chapter 46: A Civil War Memorial
1 "The History and Origin of Memorial Day in Waterloo, New York," *Waterloo New York* website, http://www.waterloony.com/memday.html
2 "Henry C. Welles, 1821-1868," *Ancestry.com*, http://www.rootsweb.ancestry.com/~nyseneca/welles.htm

Chapter 47: America's Pledge
1 "History of the Dam," *US Army Corps of Engineering Mount Morris Dam* website, http://www.lrb.usace.army.mil/Missions/Recreation/MountMorrisDam/ProjectHistory.aspx
2 "The Pledge of Allegiance," *Historic Documents*, USHistory.org, http://www.ushistory.org/documents/pledge.htm
3 Ibid.

Chapter 48: Wisconsin Wins This One

[1] "History of Flag Day," *United States Flag Store* website, http://www.united-states-flag.com/flag-day-history.html
[2] Hillinger, Charles, "Stamp Slight Still Miffs Villagers: Flag Day Is Biggest Day at Holiday's Birthplace," *Los Angeles Times*, June 15, 1987, http://articles.latimes.com/1987-06-15/news/mn-4222_1_waubeka
[3] Ibid.

Chapter 49: We're Baaack!

[1] "Daniel Ogden Shays," *Find a Grave* website, http://www.findagrave.com/cgi-bin/fg.cgi?page=gr&GRid=946 |
[2] "The American Revolution," *The George Washington Papers at the Library of Congress*, http://memory.loc.gov/ammem/gwhtml/1781.html |
[3] Hoover, Michael, "The Whiskey Rebellion," *Alcohol and Tobacco Tax and Trade Bureau*, U.S. Department of Treasury, http://www.ttb.gov/public_info/whisky_rebellion.shtml |
[4] "George Washington discusses Shays' Rebellion and the upcoming Consitutional Convention, 1787, The Gilder Lehrman Institution of American History, http://www.gilderlehrman.org/history-by-era/creating-new-government/resources/george-washington-discusses-shays%E2%80%99-rebellion-and-up |
[5] "Thomas Jefferson," Springfield Technical Community College website, http://shaysrebellion.stcc.edu/shaysapp/person.do?shortName=thomas_jefferson |
[6] Reagan, Ronald, "Proclamation 5598 – Shays' Rebellion Week and Day, 1987," Office of the Federal Register, January 14, 1987, http://www.reagan.utexas.edu/archives/speeches/1987/011387b.htm |

INDEX

ABOUT THE AUTHOR

By day, you might know Christopher Carosa as the oft-quoted President of the Bullfinch Fund and its investment adviser Carosa Stanton Asset Management, LLC. When he's not helping his exclusive group of clients achieve their lifetime dreams, he writes. The author of two books on investing, a stage play and more than 400 articles on everything from Modern Portfolio Theory to white cream donuts, Mr. Carosa has been a popular and entertaining speaker from coast to coast. Besides the local media, he has been interviewed and quoted in *The New York Times*, *Barron's*, CNN and Fox Business News. But what he enjoys most, though, is sharing the spell-binding stories of Greater Western New York's hidden gems with area clubs, societies and organizations. Now, for the first time, he shares some of those same stories with fans, friends and followers of our region. Those willing to join him on his crusade to promote all things Greater Western New York are invited to visit GreaterWesternNewYork.com to learn more.

Mr. Carosa has also written *401 Fiduciary Solutions – Expert Guidance for 401(k) Plan Sponsors on How to Effectively and Safely Manage Plan Compliance and Investments by Sharing the Fiduciary Burden with Experienced Professionals* (Pandamensional Solutions, Inc., 2012); *The Macaroni Kid* (a stage play first produced before sold out audiences in 2008); A Life Full of Wonder (an unpublished novel written in 2005); and, *Due Diligence: The Individual Trustees Guide to Selecting and Monitoring a Professional Investment Adviser* (ARDMAN Regional, Ltd., 1999). In addition to other publications, he has written more than 300 articles for *FiduciaryNews.com*.

If you'd like to read more by Mr. Carosa, feel free to browse his author's site, ChrisCarosa.com; his site to another book he's working on, LifetimeDreamGuide.com; his site devoted to his first love, AstronomyTop100.com and a site where both he and his daughter offer reviews to classic Hollywood movies, MightyMovieMoments.com.

Mr. Carosa lives in Mendon, NY with his wife, Betsy, three children, Cesidia, Catarina and Peter, and their beagle, Wally.

Made in the USA
Middletown, DE
21 December 2021